ACTION
LEARNING

SECOND EDITION

A guide for professional, management
and educational development

Ian McGill and Liz Beaty

KOGAN
PAGE

London • Philadelphia

First published in 1992
Reprinted 1993
This second edition published in 1995
Reprinted 1996

Kogan Page Limited
120 Pentonville Road
London N1 9JN

British Library Cataloguing in Publication Data

A CIP record for this book is available from the British Library.

ISBN 0 7494 1534 7

Typeset by DP Photosetting, Aylesbury,
Printed and bound in Great Britain by Clays Ltd, St Ives plc

Contents

CONTENTS

Acknowledgements

We would like to thank once again all those who helped us through the pleasure and toil of the first edition, along with those who supported us in writing this second edition.

There are many whose help we wish to acknowledge, many more than we can name. In particular we wish to thank all those who have been set members in sets that we have facilitated over the period of the writing. We originally wanted to name them with their agreement. The number of people would have been extensive. To omit others would have been invidious. To all set members with whom we have worked we can only express our thanks for what we have learned through your contributions, struggles and development using action learning.

Our thanks to those who made action learning happen for staff and management development purposes in some of the organizations in which we have had the opportunity to engage as set advisers 'over the period. In particular we would like to thank Judi Clements, Mike Elbro, Judith Drury, Stella Jackson, Chloe Stallibrass.

Much of our work owes its origins and continuation to the creative and supportive culture at the University of Brighton Business School where we have done much of our formative work with independent sets, self-facilitated sets and the integration of action learning into mainstream courses. Tom Bourner, Mary Britton and Paul Frost were with us in those developments and are still treading new ground. Jon Bareham as Dean helped to ensure with other staff the conditions for action learning to take root.

We wish to thank those who have taken the time to contribute ideas and to read critically our drafts. Once again we would like to thank Anne Brockbank of the University of North London for her reading of our skills chapters and ideas about learning and development. To Mike Sharples of the University of Sussex for his continued insights. Thanks to Bob Sang of the University of Brighton and the King's Fund for his reflections on the management development chapters and the final chapter. Our thanks to Russ Vince and Linda Martin for their clarity in giving concept to the emotional and political aspects of learning and development which helped us to draw together some of the ideas we were struggling with in the first edition. Nichola Haistead of the Institute of Personnel and Development kindly gave valuable comment on our chapter on continuing professional development. Tom Bourner put in substantial time on reading much of the material, particularly Parts I and II and the chapter on higher education. Susan Weil of the Office of Public Management took on the task of reading the whole final first edition draft prior to publication. Our appreciation to Susan and those who gave us their support and encouragement. We take full responsibility for the outcomes.

Thanks to Helen Carley, Robert Jones, Clare Andrews and Liz Roberts at Kogan Page for working with our time schedules and having patience with our idiosyncrasies.

As authors we have enjoyed working together and developing our ideas as we wrote; we hope our enthusiasm comes over to readers.

Finally we would like to add a comment made recently by Jon Bareham:

> When I first came across the concept of action learning I had a degree of cynicism and hesitation. As both a participant in action learning sets and as an observer of the value of the process to others, I now believe the concentration on and support for the learning of the individual results in a speed and depth of learning and often 'cognitive leaps' which other processes do not engender.

Ian McGill, Liz Beaty
London and Brighton
April 1995

Chapter 1

Using the Guide

Action learning is a process of learning and reflection that happens with the support of a group or 'set' of colleagues working with real problems with the intention of getting things done. The participants in the group or 'set' each take forward an important issue with the support of the other members of the set. The process helps people to take an active stance toward life and helps overcome the tendency to be passive toward the pressures of life and work.

The guide is for users to practise action learning – the *how* and *doing* of action learning. There is much written at theoretical and descriptive levels and many examples of the practice of action learning sets. Our endeavour is to detail how action learning can be made accessible so that users can create and run action learning sets themselves with growing confidence. We set out the key procedures and skills that participants need to gain effectively from action learning. We review the potential of action learning for continuing professional development, management development and show how it can be a significant vehicle for learning in higher education.

Users of the guide

The guide is intended for people who want to use action learning. It is for those who wish to introduce the idea to their colleagues and for those who wish to take part in action learning for effective personal learning and develop-ment. The guide can be used to introduce the concepts and processes involved to new practitioners and as a manual for those who facilitate action learning.

The guide is a practical contribution for individuals to engage in their personal development. By 'personal development' we mean how a person can reflect on their work and life (we prefer not to make a separation between work and the rest of our lives) with a view to making things happen or change.

At a task level it may be tackling a problem like making better use of time or working through a project. At a more reflective level it may be whether to change the direction of a career or how to find the 'right' balance in life between competing interests.

We use the term 'manager' frequently in the text. We use a very broad definition of managers as people who *take* responsibility for their lives and work. In this sense 'everyone a manager' enables all to think and act managerially (Boydell *et al*, 1991). This also means that within organizations all staff can be considered in terms of their developmental needs.

Action learning in companies and the public and voluntary sectors

For organizations wanting to develop their staff, action learning sets provide a means of enabling that development to happen. The process combines a person's direct work experience with their learning as opposed to the traditional separation of direct work experience from learning associated with education. Being in-house, about real issues and continuous, a person's learning tends to be cumulative and relevant as opposed to off-site workshops and residentials that may not be geared to the individual's needs and where the fall-off in learning is known to be significant. Moreover, the action learning process develops and enhances skills and qualities that are required by organizations for their effective operation, contributing to the development of the organization as well as the individuals employed.

Our guide is addressed to those in industrial and service organizations (private, public and voluntary) who can influence and determine staff and management development policy and its implementation. The guide is for staff to use as a resource in securing their own development needs and enhancing their skills through participation in action learning sets.

Continuing professional development

As professionals, once qualified and trained, we can no longer rest on the laurels of the letters after our name. Given the obsolescence of knowledge and practice it is inevitable that development is part of professional life as opposed to something gained and boxed neatly in the past. Many professions are meeting the need by introducing programmes of continuing professional development as a requirement to maintain individual quality of work and in the process maintain the integrity and credibility of their profession.

Continuing professional development is significantly based in the practitioner's experience, centred on relevant problem-based learning, self-directed and structured to encourage reflective learning. We endorse the practice that centres on the learner professional. We are also aware of the effort, potential pain and struggle associated with 'keeping-up' as well as the pleasure and affirmation associated with maintaining professional credence. Learning and development can be very hard work, however well integrated into professional life.

Professional development is rightly self-directed. Implicit here is the tendency to believe that the learner professional is on their own because the learning is managed by the individual learner. Part of our reason for advocating action learning is that we believe learning is also very much a social process. We learn with and from each other in dialogue. The guide is designed to enable professionals to work together on their continuing development with the structured support and challenge of others using action learning.

Action learning in higher education

Higher education has traditionally been characterized by a clear separation from industry and service organizations. Characteristically, students get taught/learn in colleges and then go on to work following completion of the course with little linkage between the two worlds. Moreover, students of higher education have traditionally been taught didactically, 'one subject/discipline' in lecture-receiving mode. The trend toward student-centred learning, transferable skills and closer links with industry and services has required higher education institutions to look to ways of linking with the 'outside' world and introducing more effective methods of student learning. Action learning provides a method of enabling that learning as well as acquiring and enhancing a significant range of transferable skills.

In higher education at undergraduate and postgraduate levels the guide is useful to teaching staff, including course organizers, who wish to move toward alternative teaching and learning methods. Course designers and teaching staff can adopt the method, develop the skills, and use action learning sets as a primary mode of learning or as a supplement to other methods. Student learners can use the guide to enhance their practice in action learning sets.

Independent action learning sets

One of the liberating features of action learning for us has been the ability to create our own sets which were independent of the organizations in which we happened to be employed. Indeed our experience of independent sets has been one of the motives in compiling this guide. Independent sets can be self-facilitated by the members; alternatively the set can be facilitated by a set adviser who has the skills to get the set up and running. Once the set members have acquired the skills the set adviser withdraws.

We found that the support and challenge of a set met many of our needs for our own personal development. We could share the struggle of learning and grappling with change which otherwise we do in isolation from others and without the feedback of others. Realizing that we need not be on our own in whatever our struggle gave us a strong commitment to action learning.

Colleagues, friends and students can therefore use the guide to set up their own action learning sets.

Action learning for trainers and developers

Trainers, consultants and developers may also find our guide useful to extend their repertoire as professional practitioners and advocates of effective development using action learning as the method of development.

How the guide is organized

We seek to enable people to benefit from *using* the guide to *do* action learning as opposed to simply reading about action learning. The organization of the chapters reflects that purpose.

Part I, Doing Action Learning (Chapters 2 to 6), conveys detailed descriptions of the practice of action learning for those who wish to be effective set members and for those who facilitate action learning. These chapters are intended for readers to become familiar with the method and feel confident about *doing* action learning.

Chapter 2 sets out what action learning is. The aim is to de-mystify the term, encourage the use of action learning and to explain how to organize and run sets. Chapter 3 defines how a set works once the set has formed. Set meetings are put into the context of the action which a set member takes between set meetings. We describe the basic procedures of the set – what to do and when – and examine in more detail the processes of set meetings – the *how* of action learning set meetings. It is important that the set reflects on its processes: how the set is working, what is happening below the surface. An examination of the process, as opposed to what is being discussed (a set member's issues or content) deals with how individual set members are feeling and how the whole set is working. Chapter 4 examines how to be an effective set member from three perspectives: as a set member receiving support; as a set member giving support to another member who is addressing her/his issue; and finally as part of the whole set. Facilitators, when to use them, their role and qualities forms the basis of Chapter 5. Here we examine how the skills and qualities needed by facilitators are acquired and enhanced. This chapter is useful for set members as it may help them 'model' their own set practice on the facilitator for, in a sense, all members of the set are facilitators. Further, facilitators should, in our view, be aiming to make themselves redundant as the set becomes self-facilitating and independent of the facilitator. Chapter 6 introduces different types of action learning, how it can be used as a training and development vehicle in organizations, in higher education, and outside organizations amongst friends and colleagues. Sets may start as self-facilitated sets. This chapter will help those who wish to initiate self-facilitating sets by explaining out the *how* of self-facilitation.

Part II, Developing Action Learning Skills, Chapters 7 to 9, introduces the skills used for effective action learning. Given support for the idea of action learning, how is it introduced to potential users? To obtain a real sense of what action learning will be like it is insufficient merely to describe it in words. Chapter 7 shows how action learning can be introduced to potential users by doing it. The chapter provides a workshop format for the person introducing it and shows how to design and run the workshop. The workshop conveys to participants an understanding of what it would feel like to be in a set. Once participants agree to become part of a set they enter the formation stage which is usually the first meeting. This is the stage when participants really decide to continue. Membership of the set must be voluntary to ensure real commitment.

There are a number of basic (but sophisticated) skills that we bring to all interpersonal situations. An action learning set places significant emphasis on some of these. Examples include our skills of listening, reflecting back, disclosure, empathy, giving and receiving feedback, questioning and specifying actions. The aim of Chapters 8 and 9 is to make the skills required for effective set membership more explicit and to enable potential set members to reflect on and enhance their own skills.

In Part III, The Uses of Action Learning, we consider the relationship of action learning to learning and development. Applications include its use for continuing professional development, management development, the contribution to learning in higher education, and the features in the guide that we consider take action learning forward. In Chapter 10 we examine the potential richness of action learning for real learning and development alongside some forms of traditional learning. In addition we relate action learning to some theories of learning.

In Chapter 11 we examine the contribution that action learning can make to add qualitatively to the experience of continuing professional development by enhancing the structured support to learning. In Chapter 12 we consider how action learning can contribute to management development in organizations in terms of relevance and the development of the whole person. This fits with the trend of ensuring that employees can be adaptive in their own interests as well as that of the employer. We go further in these chapters to show how action learning can contribute to the systems for management development, organizational learning and the emerging notion of the learning company (Pedler *et al*, 1991).

In Chapter 13 we examine how action learning can be used in higher education: as an effective means of enabling and enhancing transferable skills and learning to learn into course development and delivery; to provide more flexible teaching/learning methods; as a basis for greater interaction with industry and the service sector.

Finally, in Chapter 14 we examine the features of the guide that we consider take action learning forward, particularly with this second edition, and extend its use in contributing to individual, organizational and social change.

Routes through the guide

People will have different purposes in using the guide. We do not intend that the guide be taken in at one reading from page one onwards. We have included a glossary for users unfamiliar with action learning. We suggest some routes, depending upon the intention, role and background of the user, as:

- a potential set member intending to join an action learning set – Chapters 2, 3, 4 and later 8 and 9
- an existing set member wishing to reflect upon and enhance their experience of sets – 4, 5, 6, 8, 9 and Part II, 10, 11 and 12 and/or 13, 14
- set members with some experience of action learning on wanting to work in self-facilitated and possibly independent sets – 5, 6, 8, 9 and 14
- facilitators of sets – 5, 8, 9 and 7

- professionals engaging in continuing professional development with:
  - some knowledge and experience of action learning - 6, 11, 14
  - little knowledge and experience of action learning - 2, 3, 4, 6, 11, 14
- management developers, human resource development specialists and managers with responsibility for action learning with:
  - some knowledge and experience of action learning - 6, 12, 14 and 7
  - little knowledge and experience of action learning - 2, 3, 4, 6, 12 and 14
- course organizers, developers in higher education with:
  - some knowledge and experience of action learning - 5, 6, 13, 14, 7, 8, 9 and 10
  - little knowledge and experience of action learning - 2, 3, 4, 13, 6, 7, 8, 9 and 10

Where we are coming from

We are writing this guide as enthusiastic practitioners of action learning. We work as facilitators of sets or as set members, and our development has benefited from both. We work in the public and private sector and in higher education using action learning as a major vehicle for development and change in individuals and organizations. In contributing to making action learning more accessible we also wish to encourage more experimentation with its use, both in terms of ways of enabling people to develop and learn and to serve a range of purposes in and outside organizations.

We work with women and men. The text reflects this with examples that are gender-specific rather than attempting a neutral and genderless language.

Our collaboration in writing this guide comes from our shared belief and experience in the methods and benefits of action learning sets which can be dramatic, leading to lasting, effective and productive learning. Finally, we cannot omit the contribution of Reg Revans (1980; 1983) to the initial creation of the idea of action learning and its long advocacy over years in conditions where few people could understand its potential. The conditions for its use now appear to be more fruitful due, in part, to his tenacity.

PART I
DOING ACTION LEARNING

Chapter 2

What is Action Learning?

Action learning is a continuous process of learning and reflection, supported by colleagues, with an intention of getting things done. Through action learning individuals learn with and from each other by working on real problems and reflecting on their own experiences. The process helps us to take an active stance towards life and helps to overcome the tendency to think, feel and be passive towards the pressures of life.

Action learning is based on the relationship between reflection and action. We all learn through experience by thinking through past events, seeking ideas that make sense of the event and help us to find new ways of behaving in similar situations in the future. This thinking through or reflection is the essential link between past action and more effective future action. In our everyday lives, however, we do not always find time for reflection. It is easy just to let things happen and respond to the demands of our lives without much thought of our own part in it. In times of crisis or radical change reflection becomes more important and also more difficult: it is at these times that we make powerful decisions about our future. Action learning builds on this normal human process of learning, making the links more clearly in order to make them effective. We believe that reflection is a necessary precursor to effective action and that learning from experience can be enhanced through deliberate attention to this relationship.

Action learning involves a group of people (called a set) working together for a concentrated period of time. We know that making powerful decisions is greatly enhanced by working with others. The focus, however, is essentially on the individual. It is the individual who comes to the set to learn from experience and to move on to more effective action. The set enables this process to take place through concentrated group effort focused on the issues of each individual.

When I join a set other people help me to understand my situation; to explore issues and pressures around me and help me to form a sound judgement about my future action. It remains for me to decide how to act or to decide not to act as a result of this work in the set. With action learning I can be more powerful by bringing to conscious awareness feelings and reflections on my past and current situation which can usefully inform my next action. The members of my set will help me to do this by supporting my reflections and challenging my assumptions. The action that I decide as a result of this will be clearer, better informed and more likely to be undertaken.

Why use the term 'action learning'?

The term 'action learning' says it all: learning through action. 'Action' because the group is more than a simple support group; each member takes action on their own issue after reflection with the group. 'Learning' because the opportunity to reflect on experience with the support of others followed by action means that set members engage in learning from experience in order to change rather than simply repeating previous patterns. The essential point is that action learning is an intentional strategy based on normal, but unusual, effective practice. If, for example, I really am stuck and don't know what to do, I will seek out a trusted friend or colleague to discuss what I could do. The people who help me most will usually not attempt to tell me what I should do but rather listen attentively and help me to find my own way towards a next step. This is what I need in order to act decisively and in a way which will take me forward. Sometimes I feel that to ask for this quality of attention is an imposition even though I will be able to reciprocate at another time. The joy of action learning in sets is the feeling of helping as much as receiving help – in the same session. It also allows me to explore this way of learning from experience for less crucial events, making it part of my normal approach to life rather than kept only for times of crisis. It also legitimates something rare in normal interaction – a situation where a group of people focus all their attention on supporting one person. The times I have asked for help from a trusted friend have been one-to-one interactions or a series of one-to-one interactions. A set is an efficient way of accelerating this kind of support.

Often in describing the basic process to colleagues they say, 'Ah yes! We do that all the time'. It is useful to talk through ideas and reflect with other people – why use jargon? On closer examination the difference is usually in the intentional nature of the set. Set members have joined together expressly to work on a project, issue or problem which they intend to undertake, progress or solve. Furthermore the set members intend to learn from this process in order to develop personally and/or professionally. People will often reflect on past actions and next steps with friends or colleagues and can learn from doing so. With action learning it is the learning through action and reflection that is the reason for meeting. It is the legitimacy and formalization of these events over an extended period of time with a consistent group membership that makes it special. The intention to act and to learn from experience as a result of the learning is the rationale for the group discussion rather than a by-product of it. The action learning set meetings end with each individual having clear and specific action points which they have committed themselves to as a result of the meeting.

What is an action learning project?

Action learning is based on individuals learning from experience through reflection and action. The action side of the equation is called a project. An action learning project can be anything that a set member wishes to work on with the aid of the set process. Projects can be specific issues or problems; they can be clearly specified or complex and messy. The important thing is that the project is not one where the end point and the stages in between are clearly mapped out in advance – in this case the set would be of little help to the presenter of the project unless time and motivation were to be the issues brought to the set. Other projects that would benefit little from action learning are ones that are really only puzzles which have a right or wrong answer and all the set member needs is the answer. Joining a set is unlikely to be the most efficient way of getting the answer.

Projects do not have to start when the set begins and finish as the set ends: there might be a one-to-one correspondence between a project and the life of a set but this is rare. We have found that usually the project which a set member brings to the set has pre-dated the action learning set and often continues after the set has completed its cycle. Sometimes a member's project ends before the negotiated end-point of a set and here the set member might choose to bring another project to the set in order to maintain the membership until the agreed ending.

Projects have to be real and alive. That is, they should not be manufactured simply for the set – action learning is for enabling people to undertake action to further real issues or resolve real problems; it is not an artificial game to produce learning outside of experience. Set members also need to have some motivation in relation to the project, ie, they must want to do something about the issue or problem; they must be prepared to act – the set process is intended to empower. If a set member has no intention to further the project then the action learning process will be sterile.

In this book we use the term 'presenter' when we are referring to the set member as they bring their project to the set. The presenter does not 'do' the project in the set meeting, nor do they (necessarily) involve the other set members in any project-related task. The set meeting is the vehicle for reflection on actions in relation to the project and learning from the experience of that action. It is also the opportunity for deciding on the next actions to take.

Action learning and the individual

Action learning is a process which is effective in supporting projects but it is primarily an aid to learning. In undertaking to learn through a repeated cycle of reflection and action with the support of a set, individuals open up a powerful opportunity for personal development. The cycle of learning can be captured in four stages. First, there is experience: the delineating of a particular sub-set of past actions in order to learn from reflection on a past experience. Then there is an exploratory, diagnostic phase where there is learning through identifying patterns in experience. Third, there is formulation of plans for improvement and fourth a final action phase where the plan is tested in new experience (see Chapter 10 on learning and reflection).

As individuals we may not usually go through each of these phases in learning from our experience. As a self-confident risk taker, I may tend towards experimentation where trial and error are my teachers. I may find little time for reflection and even less time for considering theoretical ideas to support my actions. In this strategy I am missing a great deal of potential learning, my actions will be ill-informed and my development slow. I may on the other hand have a tendency towards introspection, I enjoy thinking through problems and issues but in the process I am slow to act on my thoughts. The world passes me by as I watch and ponder, but I will never quite know whether my ideas would have worked if I had tried them. Again my development is restricted, this time by the lack of an action phase. Action learning is a process which aids the individual to use both action and reflection in order to learn from the iteration between these phases. It externalizes the process of learning from experience in a constructive way. Individuals learn to use effectively a wider repertoire of processes in order to learn.

How is an action learning set different from other types of group?

The essence of an action learning set is its focus on the individual and their future action. The set has a basic design which is the 'one at a time' rule which produces a very different experience from working in many other types of group.

It is not like a seminar where a presentation is made on the basis of well-prepared material for a discussion by the group as a whole. Seminar papers are concerned with the world 'out there' but action learning sets are interested in the world out there as it is related to the individual set member and their particular context. Another difference is the lack of spontaneity in a seminar and the rules of discussion which are rarely focused on helping the individual who gave the seminar paper and still less based on action as a result of the discussion.

A set is not a team because a team has a well-defined group task whereas a set works on the action of individuals. A team must work for the benefit of the task they have to complete; they may care for each other but their rationale for being together is in order to work on a task. The rationale for a set to be together is to work on the future action and support the learning of each individual set member. If the set members shared a project they could work as a team as well as a set. Here the set structure would not be appropriate for every meeting of the team. The team would need to meet to undertake some of the actions that had been decided at the set meeting that involved the whole or part of the team working together. The main function of the set in a group project would remain, however, enabling each individual to progress with the project for him or herself.

Sets are not like formal meetings; they do not have a role for a chair or an agenda. Sets do not have free-flowing discussion or debate aimed at involving everyone in decision-making and they certainly do not have votes to decide on future action. The flow of set discussion is based around the presenter's issue and their need for support and challenge. The set may mirror formal meetings in having tight time constraints and in producing minutes, but the minutes of set meetings are simply the action points agreed and do not contain a record of the discussion.

A set is more than a support group because although set members are there to support each individual in moving forward with their issue they are also there to challenge and can take a more assertive role. The focus is on the learning from the actions taken with the aim of strengthening the individual as well as in getting things done. The supporting that is done leaves responsibility firmly with the presenter.

A set is not a counselling group. A set member presenting their issue to the set can expect to be listened to and to have questions and comments aimed at helping them but they should not expect counselling, and this is not what is on offer. Set members can find action learning a conducive environment to explore personal problems and discover underlying personal issues but they are unlikely to find, in the set, the therapy they might need to deal with psychological problems.

A set is also distinct from a self-development group in its concern with, and attention to, action. The set is concerned less with self-discovery and more with acting on the learning gained from reflection on experiences. The focus is on making a difference in the outer world, although the inner world is inevitably involved in the process of reflection.

Who can be set members?

The obvious but trite answer here is 'anyone and everyone', but this is less helpful than attempting to delimit the service that action learning affords. The best way to explore the limits of action learning is through examples. We have used action learning work-based sets for management development. Sets have been introduced as part of academic programmes of study for part-time students who have a professional role and for full-time students to support their project work. We have used it in training teachers. We have also used action learning sets in supporting change within organizations. We have ourselves been members of sets which are voluntary groups working within an organization but for the primary benefit of the staff rather than organization. The uses are many and divergent and therefore membership is likewise varied. These examples are illustrated and described more fully in Chapters 11, 12 and 13.

Another way to describe who can be a member of a set is to say, 'anyone who can benefit from the experience'. This might be anticipated by someone reading through the values underpinning the process and asking themselves if they would like to take part. People who started off sceptical have become ardent followers of the process but also some who try it have found that the process is not what they required at the time. The best way to find out about action learning is to do it.

Who is the set for?

The set is for the people within it. The focus of the action learning process is on individually based learning from action, which leads to development for the individual, and for their organization, through the project. Having made this point, however, we want now to qualify it. Working through action learning sets can have influence beyond the people immediately involved. The people who work closely with the set members will surely notice the difference in their demeanour and their ability to get things done. Over time they are likely to witness an individual with increased confidence and ability to respond and work through change. Depending on the focus of the project, they may witness a surge of energy and thoughtful activity that transforms the working context. If many people within the organization take part in the action learning sets, the organization itself may change. Not only do working arrangements and interpersonal relationships benefit from the projects and the increased empathy of the people but the people who make up the organization learn to manage the organization in a new way. They learn about the process of action learning which is transferable out of the set and into life in general. In short, where action learning becomes a feature of the organization itself, the organization takes on some of the features of a 'Learning Company' (Pedler *et al*, 1991).

An organization investing in its people through the provision of action learning programmes will find that it gains more than projects – as interest on its investment it will receive developed individuals and development of the organization itself. There must, however, be a personal pay-off for individuals. If the organization wishes to keep a tight control over the content of work within sets, the set may become impotent; set members will feel constrained to explore only the obvious and visible aspects of problems and issues rather than their bases. If this kind of control is required, other processes such as quality circles might be more appropriate. It is important that the set members have the support of their organization where they have clients for their projects. Negotiation of the original brief for the sets and for each individual project is essential. One company that has made use of action learning for its staff through a programme of study had this to say about its results:

> The action learning programme has been a cornerstone of our management development. The company has gained a trained management workforce but the time away from work has been justified as much for the work done for the company during that time as for the resulting development of its people. The projects have had real effects although they were originally designed primarily to be vehicles for learning. (Comment from a client/sponsor of a student on an action learning programme.)

One department in local government included the following statements from participants in its review of the process:

> It gave me peace of mind knowing that there is a date in my diary when I can raise matters with my colleagues.

> Where problems threatened to undermine my confidence often the set helped to empower me again.

> In the past twelve months I have made more progress than in the previous three years in the job and much has to do with my participation in the set.

> Learning to work better in a group has carried over in other group situations in my work and having greater confidence to speak, but also to listen. (Extracts from review document.)

What problems/issues can members bring to a set?

One answer to this question is 'anything'; however, there are some projects and some issues that would be helped very little by work through a set. Very trivial questions are unworthy of set time and problems that are outside my own authority to act upon are rather pointless projects for action learning. However my feelings about my lack of authority to act, and what to do about it, may be an excellent project. It is worth remembering when choosing a subject that I will be likely to learn more if the issue or project is important to me. Another likelihood is that the shape of the project or the way I describe it at the beginning of the set process is unlikely to be the way I describe it by the end. Most people find that the project transforms under the scrutiny of the set:

> What I thought was my problem turned out to be something else entirely – the set helped me to uncover layers upon layers until I hit upon the real issue – I would not have been able to describe this to anyone at the beginning.

The set process is different for different people. Some people spend a great deal of set time reflecting on their experience while others concentrate more on planning the next action. The balance can change from one set meeting to another so that on some occasions I may not have very much time at all to decide on my action plan while on others I spend the whole session in formulating it.

People also differ in their focus, some being very keen to explore the environment around them, the context they are in and the effects of different types of action, while other people are more at home describing the inner world of their feelings and thoughts in trying to understand themselves. Whichever is the main focus, the role of the other set members is to facilitate this so that the reflection can be effective in generating an action plan. Set members may also wish at times to challenge the focus being taken by the presenter. Thus if the presenter has spent all their time discussing the project in relation to the objective world 'out there', it would be of service to ask a question focusing on the inner world of feelings and vice versa. The focus on task and process is a continuum that can be usefully distinguished and explored separately in set meetings.

Life span of a set

Sets need some time to work properly. Because of the cycle of action and reflection, sets feed on the work that goes on in between the set meetings. The life of the set depends a great deal on the nature of the projects that individual set members bring and the frequency of set meetings. The set's life is complete when the individuals have gained all they can from the set with regard to the project they brought to it. This is complicated somewhat by the fact that projects are unlikely to end all at the same time. We have found that although sets vary in their life span, from six months to three years, there is usually a need for a clear initial commitment for a certain number of meetings and that reviewing after these has extended the set's life by general agreement or signalled the end of the set. In our experience there is generally an easy consensus on this issue. Where a minority of set members want a set for longer than others there is often the possibility of joining another existing set or forming a new one. The key word here is flexibility. The set works for as long as the members feel that it is helping them to progress. At some point the members will have completed the projects that they brought to the set and will either decide to remain in the set and bring another issue or to draw the set process to a close.

It is possible to get hooked on action learning. Both of us have rarely been without a set (as members not facilitators) since we first began working in this way and this is not rare. Many people who have been in sets we have facilitated have gone on to work in other sets or have started up new sets of their own. We believe that this cascade is a testimony to the effectiveness of the action learning process.

Underpinning action learning

Experiential learning cycle

The most important aspect of action learning is the relationship between action and learning. We can learn about the world and about ourselves through reflection on past action. We can construct our future action from our reflections on our learning. Kolb (1984) described this as a cycle of experiential learning, as shown in Figure 2.1.

Belief in the power of the experiential learning cycle is at the heart of our investment in action learning as a method for professional and personal

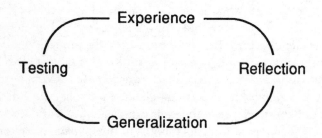

Figure 2.1 *The Kolb learning cycle*

development. The stages of reflection and generalization are undertaken with the help of the set. The presenter also designs their next action at the end of their time and then undertakes this action in the testing stage and experiences the results in order to bring this to further reflection and generalization in the next set meeting. The cycle continues until the issue is resolved and the learning complete for the time being. A corresponding stage view of this process has been captured by Pedler *et al* (1986) (see Figure 2.2).

Observing, reflecting on experience, leads to making sense of that experience in a new way, leading to understanding. Understanding can lead to insights which allow for new plans, new strategies for action and new modes

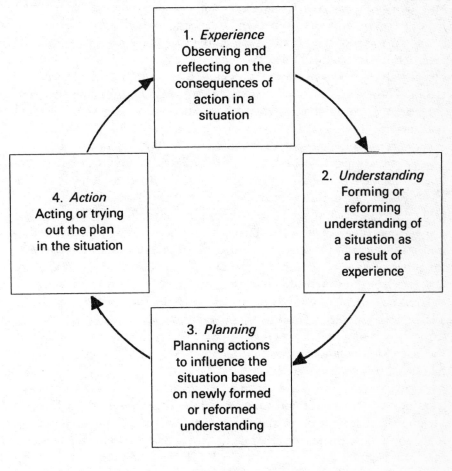

Figure 2.2 *The learning process* (Pedler *et al*, 1986)

of behaviour. These plans lead to new actions which have an effect in the context which lead to experience which can be as expected or have consequences quite different from those expected. This leads on through another evaluative cycle with reflection and learning occurring at each stage.

Action learning and action research

Here we want to make a distinction between action learning as a process of learning through action, and action research, which is a research method.

Both action learning and action research are based on the same learning cycle. They share the focus on learning from experience and they both have an action and a reflective phase. The traditions, however, are different and the concerns in terms of learning tend to diverge. Action research is one of a set of new methods that seek to question the traditional research paradigms copied from the natural sciences. Action researchers reject experimental design with its control groups and the external impartial scientific observer in favour of bringing research and the application of findings from research into one process. The action researcher is committed to learning from investigation, making decisions about necessary change, applying these and then evaluating the consequences (Carr and Kemmis, 1986; Zuber-Skerrit, 1992). This is done within the complexity of the world as it is and the researcher is usually an active participant within the application as well as in the investigative and evaluation phases. Action learning as a process is more general an approach to learning. Research is not the primary aim and the project may not involve any formal research at all. The individual is undertaking learning through the process of reflection in the set and therefore the process is essentially a group process. In action research the researcher may be a lone individual, although there will inevitably be others involved in the project. In action learning those involved in the project will tend not to be part of the learning set. So while action learning may involve some research in the action phase, it is not essentially a research-oriented venture and indeed the research undertaken may use techniques quite different from those advocated by action research.

An action researcher could use an action learning set to help him or her to learn from the action research project but does not necessarily do so. So there are many action researchers who do not have action learning sets and there are many action learning sets that do not use action research. Having made the distinction it is true to say that as well as sharing the same trusty learning cycle, action learning and action research share many of the same values.

Values underpinning action learning

The voluntary nature of set membership

Action learning is a voluntary endeavour. Being a member of a set cannot be compulsory. Membership cannot be imposed. The value of voluntary membership of sets underpins our book. We commend action learning as a form of management and personal development as well as a vehicle for organizational learning and development. However, we take as a given that to be effective for individuals and organizations action learning needs to be based on the fundamental value that joining in, starting, being in and if necessary leaving a set is a decision for the person who wishes to be a set member. Similarly, a person who takes on the role of set adviser cannot be required or obliged to take on the role.

A willing set member who wishes to get the most out of the time devoted to the set meeting will be *with* the set in an attentive way for her own benefit and that of the other members of the set. Involuntary membership will act as a block on the set member's willingness to engage in the working of the set. If a set member attends because she has been told to do so, then she is likely to display feelings of resentment or perhaps attempt to hide such feelings which would be conveyed in other ways. This can only be destructive of the group and its work.

We devote Chapter 7 to getting started with action learning. One of our intentions in writing that chapter is to enable those who are introducing action learning to give potential action learners an idea and feel of what it is like to do it. We also trust this book will help to make action learning accessible and easy to use.

Potential set members may come to action learning with some scepticism. That is different from hostility arising from imposition. A sceptical potential set member may have some of the same thoughts, feelings and questions. The solution is to provide the means for thoughts, feelings and questions to be addressed. *Describing* how action learning works may allay some of the concerns. *Doing* introductory sessions which defer commitment to the set is probably more helpful as this conveys a much fuller picture.

Commitment follows from the voluntary value. Set members once voluntarily wishing to be in the set develop a commitment to it. This means displaying in behaviour and actions a willingness to give some priority to set meetings and to be prepared to offer to other set members that degree of attention required to make the process work. In return for this commitment the set member will receive that quality of attention from other members when discussing her issue.

Action learning and a positive approach to life

Action learning is the antithesis of believing that we can do nothing about our situation. Whatever the context, people who use action learning believe that there is always something, however small, that can be done or positively not done. Believing that something can be done is not the same as saying that everything is under our control and still less that all problems are our fault. It does mean, however, that it is our responsibility first of all to review the situation and the context and to identify our own position and ability to manoeuvre within the situation. Very often our tendency is to blame others for things we don't like about our situation and therefore to stop thinking about our responsibility for our own problems. In using action learning I ask myself fundamental questions – what do I want to happen? What can I do to move towards this as an outcome? What can I do to cope with the situation in the meantime? Somewhat surprisingly, there is always something that I can do and in thinking through the issues involved I become clearer about my own contribution to the situation as presently constructed. Identifying what action it is possible to take also means that I may decide to take no action. This is an important point. The cycle of reflection on past action and present situation may reveal to me that the best thing to do next is *nothing*. In action learning there are usually three stages to go through: identification of the problem, identification of possible actions, identification of the specific action I want to take. I can at least make one person's worth of difference to the world.

Reflection is a key to learning from experience

Action learning is a process which adds structure to our experience by allocating particular time to reflection. The action learning set's two main functions are: to support individuals in reflecting on their past action in order to learn from experience; and to explore their current issue, concern or problem in order to help in the construction of the next actions. In both of these functions the quality of the reflection is the key to success. Reflection on past actions makes the difference between having 20 years of experience and having one year of experience 20 times.

With action learning, reflection in sets allows for a much greater level of awareness of the complexity of the internal and external world and their interrelationships through the support, challenge and empathy of the members of the set. The fact that I belong to a set which meets once a month means that I will spend time on reflection both at the set meetings and in preparation of them. The regularity of the set puts my issues higher on my list of priorities and means that I make an implicit (and sometimes formally written) contract to work on the issue, ie to take action in relation to it. Just the time allocation itself helps but the spur of peer pressure within the process of the set meeting is also an important motivator (cf voluntary nature). The structure of the set meeting with its focus on individuals gives a focus to my issue that I can't duck and the action points which I decide on at the end of my time adds an imperative to act on my reflections. Action learning is an effective way of making the cycle of action and reflection work.

No one is more expert than the presenter on her issue

The underlying principle in action learning sets is that the individual is and remains responsible for his or her own problem, issue or concern. In joining the set she or he can expect to find help in dealing with these things but cannot expect that anyone else will tell her what to do or solve his problem for him. In fact to be successful the set need not be made up of people who know each other, nor do they need to understand the context within which the others work. This knowledge is often irrelevant. The main function of set members is not to offer advice (although this has its place at times) but rather to help each individual to understand their situation better by exploration through reflection and to challenge assumptions underlying these reflections in order to decide the best course of future action. The information the individual has about his issue made up from his own view of the situation, his feelings about it and his knowledge of its context is fuller and more complex than any other individual could possibly have.

In an important sense the individual with the problem is the only person who really has access to the information needed to answer the fundamental questions: Why is this issue important to me? What do I feel about the situation? What happened the last time I acted in relation to it? What did that feel like? What do I believe could happen next? and so on . . . . This information is the data that the set works with to help the individual explore their issue, to learn from their experience and to formulate and plan new actions. The individual is truly the world expert in their own issue.

Support and challenge

We believe that support and challenge lie at the heart of the set member's role. Our development takes courage and in order to develop we need the support of others. Support can be offered in many different ways and the support offered by set members does not consist of taking over the doing of the project. No set member will volunteer to do my work for me but they will listen as I talk through what I want to do and the difficulties facing me. They will offer support through asking me questions that help me to explore the issues involved and through making suggestions about other angles I could explore. Support alone, however, may not be enough. It may produce a rather cosy atmosphere where I will not be spurred into action. The other aspect of the set member role is to challenge – to challenge my assumptions and my perspective – even to play devil's advocate and ask the uncomfortable 'what if' type of question. This challenging is not aggressive but rather supports my resolution into action and makes sure that the actions I choose have been reflected on as much as the problems that generated the need.

Sometimes the most supporting and the most challenging thing to say is nothing!

Empathy

At the centre of the set process is empathy. By empathy we mean the understanding of the position, context and emotional state of other set members. In order to know how best to enable the presenter to move forward with his project/problem or issue, I need to know what it feels like to be him right now. The more deep and full is my understanding, the more easily I can find the right words to enable him to progress. Empathy is not something that comes easily to most people and yet it is so useful in so many situations. Learning how to use empathy within a set can be one of the most important developmental experiences from the action learning process itself while guaranteeing a productive experience for the set as a whole. Empathy is described and discussed in some depth in Chapter 9.

Empowerment

Action learning is or should be easily accessible to most people. It is not a mysterious process which requires years of training. It has a clear structure and exists to serve a clear philosophy of learning – that which states that learning from experience requires reflection and action. We believe that action learning is of use far beyond its present boundaries and that it offers a democratic, liberating experience of learning to those who would try it. We also believe that it has great potential for developing organizations through harnessing the commitment of the people within the organization. By working in depth with individuals on organizational issues, the organization and the individual develop concurrently. The individual is empowered through being responsible for their own project while being supported throughout by the other set members. Action learning is empowering because it starts and ends with the individual and their project, making a necessary and direct link between thought and behaviour, theory and practice, reflection and action.

Quality of attention

Being a member of an action learning set takes a certain degree of commitment. Each member can gain a great deal for themselves from the work of the set but in return they commit to the set their attendance and good quality attention. In ordinary meetings we may attend selectively by focusing on issues of importance to us, relaxing our attention at other times when we are less concerned with the issue under discussion. In sets we attempt to give our whole attention to the presenter although the issue may be nothing whatsoever to do with us or to our advantage. This makes set working very different from our usual mode of operation and takes effort. The rewards are, however, very appealing. Having five people put all their attention at my disposal can be an overwhelmingly powerful event. The quality of my set time as presenter will be directly responsive to the quality of attention I am given by the other set members. If a spirit of giving is engendered in the set all the members gain.

Trust and confidentiality

For a set to work well there needs to be a feeling of security for all the participants. Friends and colleagues learn to trust each other over time and in a set this will also be the case. However, confidentiality is a ground rule at the basis of an effectively working set. Only when there is complete confidence in this can a member truly explore their feelings and possible future actions. An action learning set holds the potential for real development for an individual and this will be enhanced through an open environment where an individual feels that what they say will not be held against them in the future. For the time of a set meeting other relationships are put aside and the set helps the individual in their own terms, keeping their own agendas in relation to the topic firmly to one side. This is not to ignore the consequences; a presenter could be usefully challenged by the perspective of someone who might be directly or indirectly affected by a future action. The set members, however, undertake to keep the set discussions and action points confidential to the set.

Development takes time

What is at stake in action learning is not simply more effective action. The more important and longer-lasting outcome is development for the individuals. Development does not happen overnight nor is it necessarily painless but it is worth striving for. Action learning is a form of accelerated learning where reflection is aided by others who focus for a time on the individual and their issues. Action learning deliberately lasts over a number of set meetings. The 'projects' that members are working on take time to develop. In looking at expected outcomes from an action and then after the event exploring the results of that action, real learning can result. The individual has feedback of a direct kind and also indirectly through the perspectives of other set members. Over a cycle that typically lasts for a number of months, the set members learn about their ability to affect their environment and their ability to change themselves. Development like this takes time and it also requires confidence. The support of the set can generate in individuals the confidence to act in ways that on their own they would have been unable to contemplate. The action will be better thought through and therefore is likely to be more effective. Effective action brings its own rewards, not least in boosting confidence. This cycle of action, positive feedback from success and raised confidence is the key to development for an individual: confidence is a prerequisite for developing competence. Being able to manage others and being more competent feeds back into a raised level of confidence.

An holistic approach

Action learning is based on valuing the whole person. By this we mean that the process involves taking into account the thoughts and feelings of the individual as well as the tangible results of their actions. The process of action learning is intentionally iterative between the objective world of things and subjective world of feelings and works on making explicit links between them. In the set the focus is on the subjective – the thoughts and feelings of the individual towards the world and how they are experiencing it. In between the set meetings the focus is on action, inaction (ie, deciding not to act) and the environmental responses to this action. In the action learning set meetings links are made between the past, the present and the future through the processes of reflection, attention to feelings and action planning. Feelings are important because they give us feedback which helps in making sense of our thoughts. The simple question 'What did you feel when that happened', or 'What do you feel about that now' are excellent in exploration of the last events in relation to the project and they tell us different things from questions about thoughts. The action learning process engages both thoughts and feelings in moving towards a plan for action.

This chapter has introduced our view of action learning and its potential for much wider use. The following chapters unpack this further with an emphasis on practical aspects of action learning.

Chapter 3

How a Set Works

This chapter describes the process of a typical set. Sets differ in the numbers of people involved, in the motivations of the individual members and the nature of the issues that they bring to the sets, but here we will describe the essential features of all sets and discuss the nature and rationale for divergence from this norm. The essence of the set is to create the atmosphere and use processes that stimulate learning from action. The actions take place outside the set meeting and often away from other set members. The set provides the focus for the reflective part of the cycle leading to learning from experience and the formation of plans for action informed by this learning.

What does it feel like to be in a set meeting?

Set meetings are made up of a collection of individual time slots. They can feel rather like watching television with a number of episodes from different series running one after the other. Each episode is more linked to the same programme last week than to the previous half-hour of viewing. It is like this in sets where each individual is working on their project (issue or problem) and what is happening in an individual's time slot is related to what they spent time on at the last set meeting but is unrelated to the topics that other people spend time on during the set meeting. The difference from watching television is that there is no passive observer role; every set member is active all the time. Apart from the facilitator there are two roles in the set: presenter and set member. These roles are described more fully in the following chapters.

Each set member brings their own project to the set. As described in Chapter 6, projects being worked on by set members vary from specific organizational innovations to very personal areas of development and from those which appear to have clear boundaries to messier and more complex issues. What it feels like to be in the set will depend to some extent on the type of projects and issues that set members are working on. Because projects differ, the atmosphere in the set is likely to change as different individuals take the presenter role. A manager working on specific plans where she has a free hand to plan changes and where the project is about making the best decisions on how to introduce the changes, will create a different atmosphere from a situation where the presenter is undertaking a more personal project to change their relationships with colleagues.

How it feels to be in the set will also depend a great deal on the personality of the set members and the degree to which the set becomes an arena for emotional openness. Sets vary and set meetings of a particular set also vary. Sets develop their own culture and degrees of openness and trust. It is important that feelings as well as thoughts are acknowledged as a natural aspect of reflection but how these feelings are displayed will vary with the climate and culture within which a set works.

Time

There are three ways that time impinges on the work of a set. First, there is the overall time cycle within which a set works. This is the length of time over which a set will meet and is negotiated at the outset. A usual cycle would be six months to a year with a review positioned after the first four meetings and at the end of the cycle. Second, there is the periodicity of the set meetings; how long between each set meeting. Again this is negotiated at the beginning, with set members agreeing the meeting dates some time in advance. Third, there is the time-keeping within the set meeting and the overall length of the meeting. As action learning sets have a clear structural arrangement the time-keeping in the set meeting is important for the success of the process.

The suggestions made below should not be set in concrete. They are based on our experience, often in conditions of time scarcity. However, we are continuously surprised by the room for manoeuvre exhibited to find time for action learning. As a broad recommendation we would say: go for as much time as you can afford and then go for a little more – the benefits of a little extra time are potentially valuable for individuals and the set.

Further, while we suggest roughly equal time per set meeting for each set member, this is how we have tended to work. We are now, for one or two sets/ organizations, spreading set member participation over a few sets so that each set member has significant time in a particular session but each has rough equality over a few set meetings. Each set member still checks in on their progress/reflections following their time at an earlier set meeting. The key here is, once familiar with the basic processess of action learning then, as facilitator, staff developer or set member, you alter and experiment with what is useful and imaginative for you and your set colleagues.

The total time of the set at each meeting will require agreement by consensus, not majority. The set may agree to, say, three hours per session. The same agreement applies to the frequency of the meetings, for example, once per month. It is also useful to agree over what period the set will meet, at the end of which a review of the progress of the set and set members will be held. This period will vary. We have tended to use between six months and a year.

The timing issue is one that the set may not be totally free to determine since there may be constraints for an organizationally sponsored set. The set may also be an integral part of a course and its life therefore determined by the course programme.

Time within the set meeting is generally allocated evenly to each member and it is important to make sure that time-keeping guarantees equity and effectiveness for all set members. If the set consider that one member has a particular need for more time at a set meeting, then with the agreement of the set the time can be reallocated. If, for example, towards the end of a presenter's time he is in the full flood of expressing a deep worry, it is sensible for this to be recognized, so that they can deal with it, rather than slavishly keeping to schedule. Time can be given away from one set member to another by negotiation and this is often useful when there is an issue that causes a strong emotional response in the presenter towards the end of their time. A set member's offer to give away time should not be accepted lightly by the other set members. It may be that a set member is unconsciously avoiding having the focus on them and yet may need the time and be sorry afterwards. The set member may misjudge his need for time, particularly in the early stages of set work. A presenter may feel that she has little to say precisely at a point when the set could be most useful, for example, when confusion makes the presenter unsure about her progress with her project or confused about the issues facing her. At these times challenge and probe from the other members can be very helpful.

If the negotiated timing is not adhered to, the set can easily become cosy and sloppy and therefore less effective. In order to enable useful reflection and learning for each set member at each set meeting, time must be a focus of attention. There is no coasting time at set meetings. When not presenting, set members are contracted to help another member in a support role. When the set meetings are being most effective and helpful they can also be quite exhausting events. For this reason it is important to have a comfortable and appropriate environment for set meetings. Set meetings are not cosy chats about how we are all getting on, they are working meetings with important outcomes for the future action of each set member. As well as leaving a set meeting having reflected and learnt from past action and set new action points, a set member is likely to feel stimulated by having contributed to this process for others.

How long should the set meeting be?

The time allocated and the numbers of individuals in sets is best decided on the basis of needs of the set members as well as practicality. Three hours is very tight for a set meeting with over five people. A good rule of thumb is that an allocation of half an hour per set member plus half an hour for opening and closing is a minimum below which the depth of set work would be seriously impaired. There is often the need for a break between individual set members' time to reorientate the mind and for physical comfort. A change of scene over lunch at least provides the opportunity to take a walk to refresh from the intensity of the set process as much as for physical comfort.

These timings look specific and inflexible and they have to be like this to some extent. Time-keeping is an important factor in the success of set meetings because the overrunning of one set member's time eats into another member's time. Sets that have unlimited time are very rare and so are sets that have too much time. Overrunning is a potential problem. This structure works but it is tighter than it looks. It is very difficult to stop an individual's time on the dot. It is useful for the facilitator or another set member to look after the time and to inform the presenter when she has about five minutes left. There is always more to say, more ideas to be had and rarely has everything been explored. Another individual may be willing to cut their time in order to carry on with the discussion but this puts at a disadvantage those who come later in the session. One way round this is to rotate the times that people have at different set meetings. This is a good idea from the point of view of different energy levels, the 'after lunch' slot often being the least favourite. It is important that time within set meetings is organized and changed by negotiation with set members.

09.15–09.30	Arrival and coffee
09.30–10.00	Round of how we are feeling
10.00–10.25	Presenter 1
10.25–10.50	Presenter 2
10.50–11.05	Coffee
11.05–11.30	Presenter 3
11.30–11.55	Presenter 4
11.55–12.00	Break
12.00–12.25	Presenter 5
12.25–12.45	Review

Figure 3.1 *An example from an organizationally based half-day, monthly set meeting with five set members from different departments*

The importance of planning

We have found that one of the difficulties in working in sets is finding a convenient time to meet. Set meetings cannot be squeezed into an odd hour here or there; they require more dedicated time and the right environment. Getting people together for this concentrated period of time requires planning. We have found that planning meetings for up to six months in advance is a good thing to do and at a minimum to plan far enough in

09.00–09.15	Arrival and coffee
09.15–09.45	Warm up round
09.45–10.30	Presenter 1
10.30–11.15	Presenter 2
11.15–11.30	Coffee
11.30–12.15	Presenter 3
12.15–13.00	Presenter 4
13.00–14.00	Lunch
14.00–14.45	Presenter 5
14.45–15.30	Presenter 6
15.30–15.45	Tea
15.45–16.30	Presenter 7
16.30–17.00	Closure

Figure 3.2 *An example of a time schedule for a whole-day monthly set meeting with seven participants supporting a research degree*

advance to accommodate set members' normal planning cycles. Once in the diary a set meeting tends to be given priority above everything that is predictable. This is part of the commitment that members make when they join the set and can be written into the ground rules. Commitment and ground rules are discussed more fully later in this chapter.

Setting the tone

Space and comfort - appropriate settings

Although it is probably true that a set meeting can take place almost anywhere, there are distinct advantages to taking care about the venue and its facilities. First, the set needs privacy and relative quiet for its meeting. It may be that sensitive issues will be discussed and possible that emotion will be displayed. It would be uncomfortable and restrictive if this were impossible because the venue was too public. Although we have found people's places of work good venues for set meetings (eg taking turns at each set member's work and taking the opportunity to be shown round the business at lunch time), it is important that the meeting room is appropriate and not an office where interruptions are likely. We have also found that people's homes can be a venue for set meetings – they often provide a degree of comfort and a relaxed atmosphere that is hard to find in a work context. The freedom to make tea and coffee or lunch as required and in private – and so continuing the set interaction uninterrupted – can also enhance the meeting. This venue may not be appropriate or possible where families would have their movements restricted and children demand the attention of their parent. Different sets will have their views of appropriate settings but it is important to consider the environment for the effectiveness of the set. In one of our course-based sets where the set was in a peer-assessing role for each other's projects, they requested the more formal atmosphere of the office for the set meeting rather than a living room. Classrooms were sometimes found to have inappropriate furniture for the length of meeting and to be difficult to book for this amount of time and size of group.

Freedom from interruptions

It is important that the set meeting be free from interruptions. Phones are the worst culprits and should be discouraged inside the meeting. We have found pagers and mobile phones equally irritating and use the ground rules to ban their use within set meetings. However, it is often necessary for people to be available for urgent calls or emergencies so one compromise is to allow time for phone calls to check on these at break times.

Comfort and energy levels within set meetings

To promote an atmosphere of concentration and reflection, nurturing and energizing must be important elements. Our experience is that the availability of tea, coffee, biscuits, etc can make a great impact on the success of a lengthy meeting. In set meetings, getting this right is important. Figures 3.3 and 3.4 describe ideas about how energy levels change over time and can be modified through attention to normal patterns of human interaction.

Communication between people in formal meetings can be greatly enhanced by the recognition that they are fundamentally the same as any meetings between people and can therefore gain much by the mirroring of normal human contact.

Everyday contacts between people have a pattern that establishes the beginning, middle and end of meetings. Aspects of this pattern can be easily transferred to more formal meetings, workshops and set meetings to enhance their effectiveness and make them more enjoyable for participants. A useful cycle to go through in any meetings is:

connecting – eg, hello, shaking hands, hugging, etc;
nurturing – eg, having coffee ready, asking 'how are you?';
energizing – eg, sharing latest events, short interesting game/joke;
working – eg, individual time slots;
rewarding – eg, thanking and offering outside set support;
leave taking – eg, checking on action points, next dates, goodbye.

These stages provide the programme with a feeling of wholeness and completeness which is missing from many group meetings but which can make a big difference to the effect of the meeting on the individuals. Working is the key reason for being in the group but working becomes more effective where it is built up to and reinforced as part of the total process of the meeting.

Figure 3.3 *Energizing meetings*

46

Beginnings

The beginning of a set meeting is important. We have found that setting the right tone at the beginning and finishing off the business well at the end are two of the main factors in having a fruitful set meeting.

Ground rules

In action learning sets we formalize the ground rules that all set members will agree to at the beginning of the process. These ground rules will then last for the duration of the set (six months or so). Most ground rules have

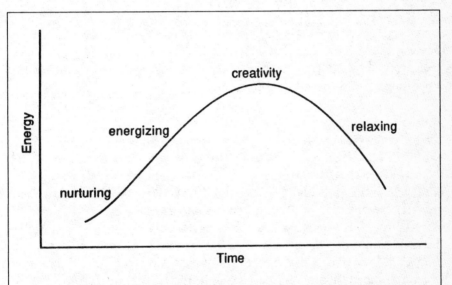

This cycle shows that energy-flows over time require periods of nurturing and relaxation. As well as the set meeting as a whole becoming more effective with the use of an approach to the event taking into account different stages within it, throughout the meeting energy will come and go. Keeping energy high for each individual may be greatly aided by periods of nurturing and relaxation. These periods do not have to be long to be effective but ignoring the need for them by rushing on to next business will make the meeting as a whole less successful. This cycle applies to the whole set meeting but also to the presenter during her time.

Figure 3.4 *The creative cycle, adapted from Randall and Southgate (1980)*

- All set business is confidential to the set
- One person speaks at a time
- Really listen to each other
- Don't make fun when I'm trying to be serious
- Aim to attend all meetings
- No smoking in meetings
- The ground rules can be changed through negotiation
- Don't phone at work about the project

Figure 3.5 *Example of a typical set of ground rules*

confidentiality as their mainstay but there are many other rules that people may want to suggest. Each set generates their own ground rules specific to them and may want to review these after a period of time. A useful process for generating ground rules is brainstorming.

Brainstorming

Brainstorming is a technique for generating ideas quickly in a group. It has two distinct phases: the recording of all ideas on the topic or issue, and second the analysis and ordering/organization of the ideas. In the first phase the group appoints a note-taker and then everyone says whatever comes into their mind on the topic. It is important that the note-taker writes everything down as it is said even if it seems irrelevant. No one should comment on anyone else's thoughts but they can of course add thoughts of their own that were stimulated by earlier ideas. There is no turn-taking; everyone simply says what they think of at any time (so long as the note-taker can keep up) until all ideas are collected or nothing new appears to be being added to the list. It is useful if the list is on a flip chart or white board so that it is visible to everyone the whole time. The second phase is the collation, analysis and organization of the material generated to make more sense of it. Here the group comments on the ideas and takes issue with them in order to find the final set of ideas, or clusters of ideas, to use for the purpose intended.

Ground rules must be agreed by consensus and the set members must feel comfortable to revisit them, to add to or change them as they wish as the meetings go on. They can provide a useful way to introduce a review of each meeting by asking the question, 'How well have we kept to our ground rules?'

Rounds as a way of starting a meeting

In other types of meeting we come in with our own agendas. We don't know anything much about the state of mind of the other people in the meeting and we often don't acknowledge them as people at all but simply as colleagues to be worked with for this particular time. We also know that the thoughts and feelings which a person has can be the biggest influence on how people are at this meeting. A set member having a preoccupation about something important unrelated to the project will make their contributions less effective in a set. This distraction is unhelpful. The set should, however, acknowledge the right of set members not to share their preoccupations.

In order to help each individual to feel closer and more able to reflect upon their state of mind and emotion we can do two things – (1) provide a forum for individuals to express their current state (often to acknowledge my preoccupation can release me from worrying about it for the duration of the meeting); (2) do something which links the individuals into the set: a set is more than a group of disparate individuals.

A round to begin
1. What's on top?
The simplest of rounds can be very effective. One we have used a great deal is just to ask everyone to spend a minute or two making a statement about what is on their mind – 'What's on top'. The other members simply listen and it is important not to comment or begin a conversation. It may be what is on top leads into what the individual wishes to bring to the set so comments should wait until later.
2. Trauma trivia and joy (this is described fully in Chapter 7)
These rounds should be voluntary in that a set member may say 'Pass' or leave a part incomplete. Rounds are most effective when they establish connections but do not run on too long. Allow between 10 and 20 minutes according to numbers and time constraints.

Negotiation of time within the set meeting

The main approach is to allocate time to individuals and to introductory and closing phases. Some sets like to take a more formal approach and prepare the agenda beforehand. One example is given in Figure 3.6. This proforma is used regularly by a number of sets which meet monthly as a way of helping to get into the meeting more quickly. Each member circulates their notes on

My previous action points were:

What I have done since the last meeting

What I want to spend time on at this set meeting

Time I think I need

Figure 3.6 *Proforma for preparation of a set meeting*

the proforma to every set member before the set meeting. Time and ordering of the time is then negotiated very quickly at the beginning of the set.

The presenter's time – the key to the process

What is an appropriate project to bring to a set?

By 'project' we mean anything that a set member works on in order to generate action points. A project does not have to yield anything in the form of tangible outcomes; the aim could be, for example, to raise confidence or to produce a major report. Some projects are problems – how to improve a working relationship that is difficult or how to bring a small business into profit in a declining market and so on. Anything can be worked on with the help of a set so long as the individual wants to progress with it. The will to act is often the first thing that a set can help the presenter to reveal. Action learning is about harnessing energy to develop both personally and as the result of our actions. It does not work magically; it requires from set members attention and effort. If a set member generates action points in a set meeting but never finds time to take the action, the result will be restricted to having reflected on the past. The most powerful action learning is making the link between past experience and future action. So it is best for set members to bring a project to the set that they really want to work on.

Another useful rule of thumb is that the project should not be trivial. If the set member could progress the project on her own, is clear about what to do next and has the will to do it then she has little need of the set to help her. A set can be most useful when the issue has been identified but the steps to progress are unclear, or when the presenter feels some discomfort with an aspect of life or work and is confused about exactly what the issue is. The presenter does not have to be precise about the project at the outset. Working with the set will help clarify thinking, sometimes in unexpected ways.

Although it is important to have a non-trivial project, it is also best not to work on too large a project. It is easy to take on too much and then become frustrated at the lack of progress. In thinking about the scope of the project, set members need to consider the time between set meetings and let that be a guide to the nature and scope of the project. Each set member needs to set action points that are possible to undertake in the time between set meetings. In set meetings presenters consider not just what the next step will be, but also the time period required for the actions to be undertaken. Where the actions take place beyond future set meetings, however, the set will be unable to generate reflection time. Wherever possible set members should choose a project that will be current for them over the anticipated life span of the set, although there need not be a one-to-one relationship between the span of the project and the length of the action learning set cycle. To some extent the nature of the project brought to the set will be related to the context of the set. If the set is formed to support a course, the projects will be related in some predetermined way to that course and similarly where a set is part of a working environment the nature of the project will relate crucially to that environment. These issues are discussed in Part III. Some sets are formed without such clear contexts and in these sets the nature of projects can be widely spread.

Allocation of time to individuals

Allocation of time to individuals is an important feature of an action learning set. A set differs from a 'normal' meeting because there is not a free discussion of topics but rather an acknowledgement of the issue as tied to the individual whose issue it is. The issue remains the 'property' of the individual and the other set members' task is to support her in discovering appropriate actions in relation to the issue. In the set no one will take the problem away, rather they will support the individual who has the problem to work on ways to solve it or dissipate it. Set members will not resolve the problem; only help the presenter to decide what action to take (if any). The set members may challenge these action plans but they do so in order to help the presenter refine and specify the most useful action points. When the presenter is happy with her action plan the other set members can feel that they have done a good job in the set.

A set is not working as a set if individuals do not have their own time. But how they use this time can vary from person to person.

How can I use my individual time as presenter in a set meeting?

The usual approach to using set time is to report on the action taken as a result of the previous set meeting, so a useful format for a presenter would be to refer to the action points from the previous meeting and to reflect on:

- what I did
- what happened
- what was different from what I expected
  and/or:
- what I did not do – why – what I did instead
- what can I or have I learnt from this?

From this is generated a list of still-to-do action points carried forward, with set members questioning whether they are still appropriate or need refining, whether the time allocation is realistic, etc. The report can lead straight on to other action points that the individual thinks of – what I think I should do now – with set members asking questions like, 'What makes you think that is a good next step?', 'What would you expect to happen if you do that?', 'How will you go about that?', 'How long would that take you?', 'How important is that?', 'What do you expect to happen when you do that?' etc. Then the presenter can continue with:

- what is the issue now
- what actions could I take now
- what would be the best thing (specific) to take as action points.

This format is most useful when the individual is in the middle of a project which is going smoothly. The balance would be different in the first meeting of the set cycle when there were no previous action points or when the scope of the project is not fully explored. It would also be different at the end of the project when more time will be spent on exploring the future rather than in reviewing the past, or in generalizing the learning from the project as a whole.

Types of process that sets can use

There may be occasions when a presenter wishes to use their time as presenter in a particular way in order to meet specific needs. As set members become more familiar with the action learning set they become more aware of how they can use their own time in the set most effectively.

A presenter can come prepared with a particular aspect of the project that he has identified as being a significant current issue and one that the set can really help with. The focus on a part of the project rather than all of it encourages deeper understanding from the set members and talking through in more detail with the set will help the presenter to open up ideas and see things from different perspectives.

A further strategy for using time is where the individual presents a problem to the set and then remains silent and asks the other set members to talk about the problem and to discuss ideas in relation to it for ten minutes. The presenter may learn more from this discussion while not being part of it as they do not steer the discussion. This may free up the discussion and open new avenues not thought of by the person whose problem it is. This phase must be very accurately timed with a cut off; it is followed by the individual asking for clarification or responding while the others remain silent, and generating action points as part of the response. This is a useful strategy when the presenter is lacking ideas on how to proceed.

There are varieties of this last approach, eg, the presenter talks about the problem with one other set member acting as an interviewer and the other set members play the role of observers, each taking a different observer role – looking at feelings, what is said, where there is a will to act, energy levels, body language, etc. There must be time for feedback with this strategy – its power is in the feedback given to the presenter which helps to uncover ways of thinking about the issues in a new way, eg, feedback like 'when you said that you frowned' can really reveal to the presenter an access to their feelings that are otherwise denied.

Another variant of this is the reverse, when the presenter wants to talk through things and have the other set members say nothing at all. This is often useful when the individual is confused about the project or experiencing strong feelings about it. Just to talk can be valuable and help to open up the issues involved. A listening, attentive audience can be soothing and safe when things are tough. Often at the end of the time the presenter finds that action points are more obvious. At this point the set members may be allowed to make suggestions for action points.

Sometimes a particular issue is so 'hot' that the set member can see nothing else and it is obvious that this must be the object of the presentation. At these times the atmosphere of the set can be emotionally charged. One of us facilitated a set where a member's line manager had put a block on the project and the time was naturally spent on the implications of this and what the member could do about it rather than on the next steps of the project itself. Similarly some crisis at home has sometimes meant that work on the project has come to a temporary halt. The set works on how to enable the set member to cope with the situation as it is rather than ignoring these important contexts. In these cases the set is dealing with exactly the issue that is stopping progress with the project although the ideas and discussion may not be about the project at all. Here it is possible to see the value of set work at its broadest – it is not just about progressing a project but about helping an individual to develop in relation to the project and to their life in general. Sets often become very close support teams for the individuals involved alongside project progression.

The process of set work is increasingly in the hands and control of the presenter who can, with some thought, construct their time to their best advantage. Different strategies will suit the presenter at different times and sets will discover their own patterns which work for them. Sets quickly have their own life and where one set will find multiple strategies are useful, other sets will be happier using a regular formula.

Ending

Action planning

The action plan is one of the main features of the set meeting. It is the tangible outcome. The aim is for each set member to leave the meeting with specific action points for their project that they have decided to do before the next set meeting.

The action points are the result of the time allocated to the set member and are decided upon on the basis of the discussion. They are, however, decided by the individual himself – they are not in any sense given to him by the set although they may have been taken on from suggestions made by other set members.

To be powerful, action points need to have certain features: first, they should be specific. Compare the following action points:

- I will talk to a few colleagues about the project.
- I will ask Jack and Mary to read and comment on my report suggesting a new marketing strategy and arrange a meeting to discuss it by the end of next week.

The second statement allows the results of the actions to be implied by the way they are described. It is easy to see what has been decided and therefore the results of the actions will be more easily seen. The advantage of specific action points is that they say how the action will be done rather than vaguely saying that something will be done. The formulation of action points allows the support members of the set to question the value of the action in relation to the issue. This questioning enables the presenter to draw up a list of actions that are clear and specific.

Second, action points need to be feasible in the time between set meetings. The most usual form of action points refer to actions that will be undertaken before the next set meeting. Thus progress on the project is kept up through a constant cycle of experience and reflection. If action points are taken which are unrealistic the effect of not doing them or doing only part of them will be demotivating. So one question for all set presenters is – although you think this is the best thing to do next, what is it that you can feasibly do in the time between this set meeting and the next one? What priority does it have and what competing things do you have to do? They are sobering questions – it is easy to become enthusiastic during a set meeting and to forget the restrictions of time and energy that affect us the rest of the time. We can't always get the balance right but one of the best ways of supporting a presenter is to look for the most effective action points in the time available rather than the ideal action points: What will make the most impact in the time available? What is the best thing to do first?

Two very effective time-management suggestions are the following (see for example, Bliss, 1976):

The Salami Technique says that in order to complete something you have to take it in stages – to eat a salami sausage is daunting but to eat a few slices is appetizing.

The Pareto Principle (or 80–20 rule) says that it is 20 per cent of our effort that generates 80 per cent of the results. Thus it makes sense to think about what things you do that are most effective and what things are not worth as much effort.

Recording the actions

It is important that each presenter makes a note of their own action points and checks these with the set at the time so as to ensure that they are specific and understood. We have found it useful for a set member to make a note of all the action points and to circulate these under confidential cover fairly soon after the set meeting. This acts as a spur to action and is useful to feed into the next set meeting as part of each presenter's agenda. This simple rule encourages the set to focus on action rather than on discussion and the service to the set can be rotated among set members or taken on as a task by the set adviser.

Reviewing each meeting

Because action learning is essentially about reflection it is important to reflect regularly on the process itself. We normally spend a short time at the end of each set meeting making sure that action points have been adequately recorded and checking to see that each person feels that they have gained something from the meeting. Ideas on how to improve the process and ideas for other meetings are exchanged at this time and the allocation of roles for the next meeting is made – who will arrange the venue, who will send out the action points typed up, who will time-keep, etc. This review feeds in to the start of the next set meeting but it does not fully cover all the process issues that may be there. For this reason a more thorough review is needed periodically. Reviewing is discussed fully in Chapter 5.

The set progress

As the set becomes more established, members become more self-critical and critical of the process. New ways of running sets may be explored. The set members may feel more like taking risks and giving more explicit and directed feedback about interaction in the set. The exercise in Figure 3.7 has been used on courses where action learning is a basic process of learning and where the set has continued over an extended period of time or where set membership has changed at the end of one project before leading into a second project. The feedback is given in order to help all members understand how their work in a set is seen by other set members. It adds to an evaluation of the process and can lead to the establishment of new ground rules for the set.

Leaving and joining

When is a member of a set no longer a member? One person missing can alter the dynamic and because getting to know people is an inevitable part of set life, not getting to know some people because of their absence can provoke difficulties when that person returns. Keeping up to date with what is

Using the following list of statements, each set member takes it in turn to ask for feedback on one of the statements. This process of both asking for and giving feedback should be voluntary.

How do you find my set interactions in terms of statement number . . .

1. Helps me to find useful action points
2. Sometimes gets defensive
3. Talks too much
4. Listens attentively to what I say
5. Makes suggestions that are useful
6. Challenges me too much

A variant of this would be to base the exercise on a list brainstormed by the set members.

Figure 3.7 *Feedback exercise*

happening for people can enhance the effectiveness of the set and therefore not doing so can hold up the set progress for everyone and not just the individual who has not attended. To work well sets need commitment from their members. Set members often display a remarkable degree of care for each other beyond an interest in the project that individuals are working on. Rather like the best of colleagues, they want to help when times are rough and not just when things are running smoothly. When I feel that I have no time to spare for the set meeting can be exactly the time when the set could help me most.

Sets evolve in other ways – particularly in the ability of set members to take control of the process for themselves. The set advisers will model the facilitator process and develop the set so that the adviser becomes redundant to the process. Whether the set adviser remains part of the set beyond this time will depend on how far their own needs can be met in the set and how far the set feels that the adviser has become a set member. The ideal is for sets to learn how to listen actively, how to give support and challenge, how to receive ideas and how to ask for the type of help they need so that the facilitator is out of a job. This happens more or less quickly depending on the skill of the set and set facilitator and the attention given to reflection on the process through reviews. We have found that the set adviser quickly becomes part of the set and, as time goes on, less different from other set members. The facilitator leaving the set becomes more possible as time goes on, in that the set members can self-facilitate adequately. This can be an unpopular move, however, and may require some acknowledgement of a stage change in the life of the set, for example by setting aside time for review and celebration.

Closure

Even where the end point of a set cycle has not been predefined, at some time there will be a natural end for the set. Individuals have completed, with the set's help, the projects they brought. Becoming independent is an inevitable and natural result of set process. Actions produce results and take away the need for the set. Of course, often we have other projects that we could bring to a set, but the same group of people may not be the most appropriate for the new set.

It is important to acknowledge the end of a set and not let it drift into closure. Membership of the set has, most likely, been significant for the participants and they will have witnessed and shared their excitement, joy, laughter, anxiety, frustration and even tears. The life of the set is characterized by stages similar to life in general: growing through tentative beginnings, through awareness and understanding, to maturity and eventual end. It is rare to find a working group that develops this closeness and it is therefore fitting to celebrate the process at its end: to mark the closure of the set as an event in itself.

New beginnings

Time and time again we have witnessed people who have been introduced to the experience of action learning in one setting, and gone on to join or set up new sets. The need for support is a natural part of life and the set experience is easily transferable to most contexts. Action learning sets have a very basic structure with some important key elements but beyond these it is a flexible and robust process. It is important to us in writing this book that without losing the simplicity and power of the action learning process we liberate it from becoming a preserved area for the very few. We hope that the description we have offered in this chapter will be seen as somewhere to start and that future users will experiment and extend the limits of the processes as we have done. This chapter has set the scene on how a set works. In the next chapter we discuss more fully the role of set members and how their interaction can foster effective action learning.

Chapter 4

Being a Set Member

The action learning set gives a particular structure to a group which, although very simple, radically alters the normal flow of conversation. The simple rule is 'one at a time'. Generally, time is shared within the set so that each participant is for a part of the time the 'focus' of attention. Their perspective and their issue is worked on by the whole group and in this time they control what happens. During this time as *presenter* the person presents his or her issue to the set in order to reflect on it and to design new ways of progressing with it. The outcome of this time is a set of 'action points' that the presenter decides to take on and which he or she intends to complete before the next set meeting. During this time the other set members act as *supporters*; listening, observing, commenting and questioning the presenter with the aim of helping in the exploration of the issue and in forming the new action points. The third role, that of *facilitator* is to enable this interaction to be most useful to the presenter. Because in 'normal' interaction in groups people rarely concentrate on one issue at a time and almost never work on one person's perspective on the issue at a time, controlling the process can require skill. As set working becomes familiar to set members so they take on the roles of supporter and presenter more easily and the role of the facilitator declines (see Chapter 5 for a fuller explanation of this role).

The aim of this chapter is to explore the roles of presenter and supporter and to make explicit what people do in these roles. The chapter will describe in some detail helpful aspects of communication within the roles and also things that are destructive to the process. In many ways being a helpful set member is the same as being a 'real friend' but more so. Friends listen actively and, through empathy with the individual and the context they are in, find ways of supporting them and enabling them to move forward. Friends also 'know' each other well and rarely pull their punches when important issues are at stake, whereas an acquaintance might collude with a pretence or 'front' put on to cover up important issues. The essence of an action learning set is to enable each set to learn from experience so that their actions can be effective.

What do set members do?

Action learning sets provide a safe, supporting and challenging environment characterized by trust and confidentiality where set members work on issues and solve problems through a process of reflection and action. The individuals in the set may or may not have personal investment in each other's projects but in either case it is not necessary to know details of the projects of other individuals. They contribute to the development of the other set members' projects only in so far as they help them to discover actions that they can take to progress the project. It is rarely necessary to know details in order to help someone to help themselves: listening can often be the key to helping another person solve a problem for themselves. As well as learning from their own projects, however, set members learn a great deal through their view of other set members' projects. Set members often have insights into their own projects while other presenters are having their time. There is also a more general development of understanding from the variety of projects and contexts that are brought to the set.

In action learning, set members aim to help each other to make progress with their projects but the members do not attempt to become directly involved with the projects of other members. (The only time this would not be true is where there is a set with a shared project. Here the time would be used to explore the individual's relationship with and progress on the project rather than a general discussion within the project team.) It is a key element in the success of the action learning set that ownership of the project, problem or issue remains with the individual who brings it to the set.

> I arrived with an issue I wanted help with. I expected help and to some degree I thought that help would be other people telling me how to do it but in fact what was much more useful was that I was helped to find my own solutions. The other set members didn't change my mind about what I intended to do so much as help me to see that my aims could be achieved more easily in quite a different way. (Set member at review.)

One of the features of action learning sets is the 'one at a time' convention. It is not only that members attempt not to talk over each other but that they share time so that at any one time one member's issue is the focus of attention.

Because each member is assured of this individual attention for their own issue at each set meeting an atmosphere is promoted where the giving and receiving of help is effective. The set members focus directly on the issue as it is perceived by the presenter and thus interaction is not a generalized discussion about 'the world' but focused on the person and their context. In the next section we consider the role of presenter and then move to describing the role of the other set members in the supporting role. Facilitation is the subject of Chapter 5. The skills introduced in this chapter are revisited in more depth in Chapters 8 and 9.

Presenting

The first question facing the presenter is always where to begin in describing the project to the set. The presenter knows she needs support and advice but how to involve the other set members in her issue and how to explain the context can be tricky. A good guide is to 'start from where you are'. Unlike most conversations, the set members can be relied on to listen while the presenter has false starts, repeats herself and presents disjointed and unformed ideas. They will not expect her to have the project in a nice neat package nor will they move on to another issue out of frustration or irritation with her inability to express herself clearly. On the contrary, they will see her stumbling words as an incentive to listen more closely, to mirror their observations and to reflect back what she has said in order to help her to get her story straight. They are indeed like the very best of friends who will not judge and will always give the benefit of the doubt that what is being disclosed is important and that they can help.

It is the *story* and not history that is important (Egan, 1973). The distinction is about the here and now as opposed to the past. I can describe the past as if it is remote from me and does not have any direct bearing on what I am doing now. Alternatively, I can describe the past as I view it from here – in this latter case the past becomes part of the story about what I feel now. We contrast story and history in more detail in Chapter 9.

Feelings can be the best place to begin the story. It is in the here and now that new actions can be discovered and not in the past. It is what the presenter feels now that is the important information in this exploration the set will make. What is felt can provide a very rich source of questions for the supporters to ask and for the presenter to explore. Feelings express authenticity. The more that feelings are explored the easier it becomes to discover useful action points.

Where the project remains external and does not arouse any emotions it is unlikely to be a very important project to the presenter or to others. The nature of action learning is that it involves action; learning is not confined to the theoretical level: what I think may remain hidden inside me, but what I do is usually very visible. Where a project is seen as involving me as a totality rather than me only in my work role detached from the rest of myself and my life, then there is a real opportunity for personal growth and development through the project. The cycle of action and reflection becomes a personal exercise demanding more of me than the completion of a few objective tasks. When I take on issues of real importance to me, action learning provides the encouragement to take real risks and to make real progress. Where I opt for an easier route, not allowing myself to face up to deeper issues involved in the project, action learning will help only with completion of the surface project. It is up to the presenter how deep they want to go. What is on offer is the chance to have the kind of support for change that is rarely available. It seems a shame to waste the opportunity on something trivial.

Learning to receive

Just as the main skill in being a support is to actively listen, there is an equivalent for the presenting set member in really listening to the questions that are asked and the ideas posed. It is easy to keep on the blinkers of our own ideas and quite hard sometimes to accept that there may be other ways of doing things. The presenter has nothing to lose and everything to gain from having an open attitude to the responses and questions of the supporting set members. Really listening to their challenges and giving real consideration to their ideas can enhance the presenter's future actions greatly. If the presenter decides to reject their ideas then she will have done so from a point of full consideration and her own ideas will be strengthened by having considered alternatives. Learning to receive is also about receiving support. Learning to trust the support members to really want to help is often difficult when we are used to relying totally on our own resources and feeling that it is weakness to admit that we need support. Sets can be truly supportive only if allowed to be so. If the presenter allows herself to be vulnerable in a set meeting she will take great strength from the support of the set members. The great promise of action learning sets is their non-competitive spirit. Learning to rely on the support of the set happens over time and is part of the establishment of the set

Time	The presenter's role	The support role
Beginning	Describing	Observing/listening
Middle	Exploring	Reflecting back
	Questioning	Offering ideas
	Listening/thinking	(but not presciptions)
End	Exploring future actions	Asking 'what if' questions
		Specifying action points
		Questioning action

Figure 4.1 *Example of the progress through a presenter's time*

culture. Set members do not deal with the issues and problems for the presenter, rather they enable the presenter to decide for herself the next actions to take in relation to her project. She does not go to the set to do the project, but rather to learn from the experience of doing it.

Asking for what you need

The set process is responsive to what the presenter needs according to their current state of mind and the type of project. At times the presenter might need to be supported and encouraged in order to progress. At other times the best support may be fairly tough challenges to the presenter's way of thinking, to help her re-evaluate her situation. Whatever the other set members think about what the presenter is doing, she remains the best judge of what progress means to her. By that same criterion, the presenter is responsible for helping the other set members to give her the kind of support she most needs. This means that the presenter can increase the empathic responses of the supporting set members by being explicit about the kind of support required. Asking for appropriate support becomes easier as the set gels and the process becomes more familiar. Presenters learn what kinds of support help them best at different times. For example, a presenter whose action points last time resulted in a crisis may feel vulnerable and want to be listened to with little challenge, while someone who is very sure about what they want to do next may want strong challenging questions in order to check out their ideas.

Taking control of the process

There are many appropriate and useful ways of spending one's time as a presenter other than strictly presenting. A presenter may ask for a brainstorming approach or he may ask to be a spectator while the other set members discuss his project. It remains the responsibility of the presenter to ask for the type of help they would find most useful.

The presenter must therefore make it clear when she is being helped and when the support offered is not helpful. If the presenter expresses herself clearly on this, the process will more likely develop towards a satisfactory conclusion: it would be useless to spend time discussing something that will not help her to generate her next action points even if the topic is generally interesting. For best results the presenter must keep the focus on her real issues. The other set members are trying to help and they can do so more easily if they get feedback on what is and isn't useful. Helpful statements like, 'What I really need is . . .', and 'That's interesting but I would rather move on to . . .', can cue the set members in to the real focus. Supporters would be within bounds, however, to occasionally question the presenter about changes in direction. Sometimes this may be an avoidance strategy and worth a challenge.

Action planning

In forming an action plan there are two distinct areas of concern. The first is whether the action is appropriate to the problem and the second is whether the action is possible in the time allocated. Perhaps the most important thing a presenter does is to generate action points to be worked on before the next set meeting. 'Good' action points have a number of important characteristics. They are:

- specific
- clear
- feasible
- consist of the most important next steps.

Being specific and clear is easier after the issues have been fully explored and alternative actions discussed. The action points are likely to be more feasible if the context, including the constraints within which a presenter works, have been taken into account in their generation. The task of the presenter with the set's support is to try to meet these criteria as a result of their set time – it requires the full cooperation and energy of the whole set and it is the essence of good set work.

Sometimes the focus of the set develops and changes over time. One model would be the traditional project process: project definition, exploration, diagnosis, action, evaluation and review. At other times progress over time can move from one project to a redefinition of the project and to a refining of the focus for the project such that the initial description of the project is nothing like the description later on:

> I began work on a career plan for my future and moved through investigating my skills and past feelings about work. The project ended up being about me – about what I want from my life and how I want to spend time. It became much more personal than I had envisaged and I gained a great deal more from it than I had first anticipated.

> My project started with an aim to bring in a new computer system for management information; it grew into a reorganization of the management structure of the whole company.

Whatever the process over time the main criterion for success is that individual set members (and sometimes their line managers and companies) feel that progress and development is taking place.

Supporting

'Is what I am about to say helpful to the presenter?'

A very useful question that set members can ask themselves in the support role is, 'Is what I am about to say going to be helpful?' This question will weed out those questions and comments which would only serve his own purpose – to give him information he wanted for himself or to make him look knowledge-able, etc. It is easy to underestimate the discipline involved in asking this question but the rewards for the presenter are enormous. To cultivate the attitude of real attention to being helpful is the key to effective set work.

Recognizing that each person is the world expert on their own problem

Only by believing that people can take responsibility for themselves can we really take part in action learning. If a set member describes his experience believing it is the same as that being described by the presenter, while the presenter is thinking that her experience is different, the advice will be useless, however powerful it was for the supporter's own situation. The important effects are when the responsibility for solving the problem starts and ends with the person whose problem it is. The task as support therefore changes from being how to help solve the problem to being how to help the presenter to solve her problem, requiring a different approach to support. Instead of suggesting the solution that would appeal to him, the supporter spends more effort helping the presenter to come to their own conclusions about what to do next. Advice is offered only rarely with the belief that what any set member would do is not necessarily what the presenter should do. When advice is offered it will be offered with a different spirit – 'What do you think would happen if you . . .', rather than 'I think you should . . .'.

'What does it feel like to be that person with that problem?'

In order to help most efficiently it is useful to cultivate an attitude which is curious and thoughtful about the way the presenter feels about the problem being discussed. It is usually the case that each person in the set would have a different reaction to the same situation so it is less than helpful for a set member to describe what he would do in that situation. It might be better to think himself 'into the shoes' of the presenter and think about how it feels for her. Some of this can be done through observation. If I look closely at how the presenter is responding to questions and listen carefully to the words they are using to describe the situation, I can often understand the emotional attachment that she invests in the project. Often a good question can start with 'How do you feel about. . .'. The answers are often surprising and revealing and can lead on to probing important issues in the situation that help in generating action points. This attitude is best described as empathy: the ability to share another person's feelings. Empathy is perhaps the most important attitude for set members to have as it provides the best data on how to help the other person. Remembering that I don't have to help solve the problem can be a liberation here. My responsibility as a set member is rather to help the presenter to help herself.

A spirit of trust and confidentiality

One of the first actions of a set is usually to set its own ground rules (see the example in Figure 3.5, page 48) and one of the most important ground rules is confidentiality. Sets work best in an atmosphere of trust where members feel able to disclose their feelings and thoughts to others without judgement and in confidence. Lack of trust can make the set impotent as individuals are unlikely to focus on real and important issues where they feel they will be ridiculed or that others will discuss their issue outside of the set. A ground rule of confidentiality can give a feeling of security and intimacy required for openness and frank discussion of difficulties and help to make action points make a real difference.

It is often said of learning in formal educational settings that 'you get out what you put in'. Similarly, in action learning the effects will become more important if you are prepared to work on an important issue.

There does seem to be a relationship between trust and personal risk-taking such that a person is more able to take risks with new ideas or new experiences when they feel supported. There is a relationship between risk-taking and development in that development requires us to stretch our abilities and skills to move into areas that are untried. One analogy would be learning to ride a bicycle. There is always a risk that the child will fall off, but with encouragement and support the balance will come. Balancing without the aid of a third wheel or a steadying hand requires courage and will to succeed. The parent cannot ride the bicycle for the child; he or she must learn the skill through practice and trial and error with help and guidance from an encouraging onlooker. So, if the presenter is to act to solve the problem or move forward their plans, they need encouragement and support to take the risks that are involved.

Listening

In most human interactions the convention is evenness. If I say 'Hello', I expect a similar reply. It is also characterized by turn-taking. I talk a bit about my idea and then I listen while you talk a bit about your idea. Occasionally this turn-taking is deliberately altered. For example, when I have had an interesting holiday, you may wish me to talk more than usual. At other times the discussion is not even because I talk too much and you 'can't get a word in edgeways'. In this latter case you are unlikely to find the 'conversation' rewarding. In discussions with larger groups the situation is compounded. Our interests are unlikely to be equally served by any one solution. We may have a clearly outlined topic for discussion but have very different orientations or objectives in relation to the discussion of the topic.

People have different styles of operating in a group discussion: some talk more than they listen, others like to observe the rest and think about the issues silently. All of us are capable of operating with different styles depending on our relationships with the other people, our interest in the topic under discussion, our anticipated beliefs about the results of the discussion and so on. The balance between how much we talk, observe, listen and think will depend on the mix of these various factors.

If I want to really support someone I need to know what kind of support they want; where they are with their thinking so far and what they feel about things. I can get this information mainly from two sources – listening to what they say and observing the way they say it and the non-verbal cues they give which reveal feelings and attitudes involved in what they are saying. Listening is a very important skill which we all have but in many situations we choose to use it only minimally. In communication with others our own agendas and our own thoughts often dominate while others are speaking and so we are not really attending to what they say. In the worst cases we are simply waiting for an opportunity to speak ourselves. Really listening means having the right purpose in listening (see attitudes, above) and it means much more than leaving silence for the other person to speak. This type of listening is often called 'active listening' because it requires a great deal of attention and effort that we do not normally associate with listening.

Much can be gleaned from observation as well as active listening. People often reveal their feelings in the way they look as they speak and in their body language. An observation like 'When you said that, you frowned', can generate feedback to the presenter that helps her to articulate her feelings and therefore helps her to uncover important aspects of the problem she is describing that can otherwise remain hidden.

Learning to give

A really effective set is one where members are willing to give support and challenge to each other. Learning how to give support and challenge is, however, not a trivial matter. We describe this here as 'giving' because the key is the spirit in which challenges are made and support offered. Useful challenges are made when the presenter is helped to think through her problem and come to a clearer understanding as a result. Useful support is where the presenter is enabled to move forward from where negative feelings were blocking her progress. The best help is when there is an appropriate match between the presenter's need and the type of support offered by other members of the set. In some ways support can be seen as the opposite of challenge, ie, when I am confident and clear about the issues, challenges can minimize the risk that I may be working with blinkers on. A challenge at a time of robust activity can be thought through and worked on without depression. If, however, a challenge is made when I am feeling insecure, I am unlikely to rise to meet the challenge but rather to cave in under its extra strain. It is in times of insecurity and anxiety that I need support and gentle encouragement. People differ in their response to supporting and challenging statements or questions. It is important that set members and set advisers are sensitive to individual differences. What can be a useful perspective to one person can feel threatening to another. Set members attend closely to what the presenter wants from the set and do not attempt to give them what they believe to be 'good for them'. Although the set process is about learning, the set members do not take the role of teacher or parent or manager in relation to each other. Their role is accurately described as supporter where the initiative remains with the presenter and the set members contribute their support to this process. The skills involved in doing this are described more fully in Chapters 8 and 9.

Recognizing issues underlying the problem presented

One of the best ways in which the presenter can be enabled to progress with their project is when the problems being faced are explored in some depth. The presenter may be unable to articulate very clearly the problems and issues that are confronting her. If she is asked open and searching questions, however, she will gain insights that she could not generate on her own. For example, a problem that she first described might turn out not to be the real problem at all:

> I came with one project and ended up with a totally different project. The best thing was that the set helped me to realize that the project I first came with wasn't important at all. The real issue was buried underneath the project and once I looked, it became like the layers of an onion.

Thinking of the problem as an onion with layers on layers can be a useful analogy. A group of people working collectively can bring many different perspectives to help uncover the problem. A new angle can release a whole set of new possibilities.

Learning how to ask good questions

What is a good question? Answer: one that helps the presenter to learn more about her problem, herself or the context within which she is working. A good question is selfless – it is not asked in order to generate an interesting response or information for the questioner, rather it is asked as a way of opening up the presenter's view on their situation. There is a variety of good questions.

The open question – one which cannot be answered with a 'Yes' or a 'No', but requires explanation – is open in that it opens up the area for discussion. Open questions are exploratory and ask the respondent to go deeper into her world in order to bring forth an adequate answer.

A reflecting back question is one which is half-way between the noncommittal – 'Can you say more about that?', and the more formulated question asking for particular information. In this technique the listener interjects to recap some of what the presenter has just said. This can be by way of a summary or a mention of what the listener has taken to be the main points. This acts as a check to see if the listener has 'heard' correctly but it also acts as a check for the presenter who can think more about whether what she said was accurately conveying her meaning; saying what she meant to say. This type of interjection can be powerful in helping the presenter to share her issue with the other set members as it allows her to review her 'story' as she tells it. It is very useful towards the beginning of the presenter's time when the issue is being outlined and the listeners are trying to understand its implications.

A related technique is one used often by a skilled interviewer – it requires a reiteration of the last few words of the previous response and asks for clarification of meaning; thus: 'When you say . . . what exactly do you mean?'

A simple question that can bring forth many goodies is the question of the innocent 3-year-old: 'But why?' 'Why' questions, however, get answers that are rationalizations – 'Because . . .', and asking 'Why?' can seem like an interrogation. The presenter may not have an answer to the question 'Why' but will usually feel impelled to invent one. It is often better, therefore, to translate the 'Why' question into a 'What' or a 'How' which asks for an easier descriptive form of answer, eg, 'Why is that important?' becomes 'What was important about that?', asking for a description rather than an explanation. It follows that other powerful questions can also start with 'How', 'When', 'Where', etc – questions which require more clarification of the situation.

Good questions are rarely leading questions such as, 'If I was in that situation I would do XYZ – what do you think about that for your situation?' This can however be appropriate towards the end of the presenter's time when she is searching for action points. It is easy for this to become a bit of advice in another guise and direct advice is seldom the best thing to offer, particularly in set time. Advice may be best offered after the set meeting rather than using time to describe your own situation in someone else's time. Effective questioning technique is further examined in Chapter 8.

Giving time for reflection

It is easy to fill time with speech, even if this is kept strictly to one at a time. This can work against the presenter who may have far too many thoughts to deal with at once. Leaving space for thought between questions and comments is a very useful strategy. This means that supporters must support each other by allowing the presenter adequate time to consider the comments of other supporters. This can be a frustrating experience. Most people have something they can offer and to remain silent while there is a burning issue to explore is not what we usually do. The presenter, however, may find silence the most liberating and useful part of the whole exercise. To be allowed, for example, to really consider carefully an observation made about her demonstration of anxiety can be the lever to gaining control of a difficult problem. If another set member immediately offered another question the presenter might lose the thread of her thoughts completely and the impact of the observation would be lost. The inclusion of silence can mean that, in a presenter's time, some of the supporters may not speak at all. Counter-intuitive though this may seem, this might be the most helpful thing that they could do.

What room is there for manoeuvre here?

As in all problem-solving there are some solutions which feel impossible to take because they are too radical, the costs are too high or they are unethical, etc. Where any one person draws these lines will be an individual decision. Although it is important that a presenter is challenged about her chosen actions and radical suggestions are not outlawed, it is also important that a practical approach is taken to the future actions people take. Some problems can seem intractable and it is up to the set with its collective creativity to let the presenter find the 'eye of the needle'. When the presenter is feeling gloomy and despondent, set members can help by being with her and keeping a positive approach. There is always *something* that can be done however small. What are the alternatives? What scope is there for change? If I can't do it alone, who can and who will help? Finding the scope within which a presenter has control, both contextual and in terms of personal willingness, is one useful focus for the set at such times. One warning, however: do recognize as real the difficulties that the presenter faces. The feelings of disempowerment are real to them. A good friend will help me to overcome negative feelings to feel refreshed, ready to tackle things. This does not happen through trying to pretend the difficulties are not there but rather through listening attentively and helping me to discover for myself that I can do something about it.

How to help someone to generate their own action plan

There can be as many good questions asked about suggested actions as there can be in exploring the problem. Don't let the chance slip by to question whether an action will be appropriate. Again the simple question, 'What do you *want* to do?', can be most powerful here. Another good question at this time is to ask, 'What do you expect to happen if you do that?' Other questions can be about the feasibility of the action – time available, the power and influence to perform it, etc. Another good question here is, 'What would happen if you did nothing?', and 'What would happen if this works to its most ideal?' Both these questions help in further defining the action points and assessing their feasibility. It is important that the set leaves sufficient time to concentrate on helping the presenter to specify action points before moving on to the next presenter's issue.

Preparing

Following the initial meeting action learning sets can begin more easily if everyone comes prepared. The simplest and quickest preparation is to read through the action points that were generated at the last set meeting. Each set member will have worked with his or her own, but to read through those of others will help to get thoughts in tune ready for the set. Set members remind themselves about other people and think through where they might have got to with their projects. This helps set members to be ready for each presenter's time. Some sets arrange to have more structured preparation, eg, phone calls in between the sets or sending round questions asking for a synopsis of the work done since the last set meeting. Suggested headings for such a form could be:

- Describe the main issues arising for you since the last set meeting.
- What do you want to concentrate on in your presenting time?
- How much time would you like for this?
- What other issues would you like discussed?

The most important preparation, however, is for each set member to have completed the action points from the previous set meeting or, if not, to have thought through the reasons and to be clear about what they want to discuss at the set meeting. Nevertheless, at the beginning of the set meeting other issues may surface, to do with very recent events. This can make preparation redundant and it is usually more important to respond to these 'on top' issues than to stick to previous arrangements. For example, if one set member arrives in a state of notable elation (or depression) it may be inappropriate to wait until it is technically his turn and set members may agree to let him have his presenting time first. Alternatively, a set member may not be clear what they want to say; it is often the role of the set to help the presenter explore her issues or problems. Although one key to set working is the clear structure of the meeting, flexibility is a key concept in responding to the individual, the project and even the maturity of the set.

Another level of preparation for the presenter is to consider what type of help she would like from the set members in her own time. As set members become more experienced it is easier to think of the best way to use time as presenter. A presenter may want to use her time in different ways according to the type of issue she is bringing to the set and her stage of development in thinking about it. There is a continuum between one extreme where the presenter takes all the time talking, to the other where the presentation is very brief and the set members question, comment and make suggestions for most of the time. There are many varieties of process that are useful in the set (see examples in Chapter 3). Experimentation can help in finding which ones work best for each set. When set members think through the process that they want to use, prior to the set meeting, they are likely to greatly enhance learning in the time available.

Reviewing

Most set meetings will end with a brief review of the meeting to ask, 'How do set members feel now?' Has each presenter a record of their action points? The most important review question for the individual is 'What did I learn?' This question is encouraged throughout the set meeting in reviewing past actions but is also useful to ask as a periodic check on the set. What has each of us learnt about our projects, about ourselves and about our group process?

Sometimes the review is more substantial, focusing on issues of evaluation of the group process and interaction between set members. A useful review period is after about five meetings. The more honest the feedback, the more likely that the set will develop into a positive experience for everyone. Feedback to the facilitator is also important. The role of the facilitator is the subject of our next chapter.

Chapter 5

Being a Facilitator

Sets can have a facilitator (sometimes referred to as a 'set adviser') or they can be self-facilitating. This chapter sets out the role of facilitators and examines how facilitators can contribute to making the set effective. We will examine what sets need to be effective without a facilitator in Chapter 6 on types of action learning. To prevent unnecessary duplication, users of this guide are referred to Chapter 3 on the basic processes of how a set works and to Chapters 8 and 9 for personal and interpersonal skills used in a set.

Overview

The key purpose of the facilitator of an action learning set is to enable each set member to work on and with their own real issues. The facilitator encourages each set member to take responsibility for defining their issues, for action in overcoming a problem and pursuing an opportunity or task. This key role is also taken on by the other set members for each other as modelled by the facilitator.

For this main purpose to be fulfilled, an important subsidiary purpose is necessary. In addition to enabling set members to achieve their 'tasks' the facilitator has the initial responsibility of ensuring that the set works or functions as a set. Action learning sets are a form of group working. Maintaining the set as a group is crucial to enabling the main purpose. If the 'process', how the set works, is not attended to then the set will go into decline or destruct. However, in our experience the nature of action learning is one that promotes an effective group process.

The value of the facilitator to the set is underlined in another way. All set members take their issues, tasks and problems to the set. The facilitator does not take her issues to the set. She can therefore give undivided attention to the effective operation of the set and set members can, initially, give regard to their own and other set members' issues.

As set members become aware of the process that underlies action learning – how the set works – they begin to model the facilitator and integrate her facilitation and process skills into their own set practice. For example, the set members will soon begin to enhance their capacity to listen by implicitly recognizing how the facilitator attends to the presenter. Set members will come to action learning with personal, interpersonal and group process skills with varying levels of sophistication. The structured nature of action learning fosters the acquisition and enhancement of these skills.

Thus the facilitator's 'expertise' in facilitating the set is acquired by the set members. This transfer is important. The aim of the facilitator is her own redundancy! Action learning is about empowering people to take responsibility for action on the issues of their lives. For the facilitator to create a dependence in the set members is to limit the potential for that empowering; hence the placing of quotation marks round expertise. It is an expertise to be acquired and taken on, not to be subordinate to.

The facilitator plays a crucial role. She takes initial responsibility for the set working together through regard for the process. She ensures that each set member can pursue their issues. But what does this mean? How does the facilitator enable this to occur? There are two aspects to this process. The facilitator models how to *give* support and enables the set member to *receive* support from the other set members.

Getting the set going

Sets as a group

An action learning set is a type of group activity. Group working calls for good basic interpersonal skills which until recently have not been addressed in schools and post-school education. It has been suggested (Egan, 1976; Heron, 1989) that in British and American cultures we do not give much explicit attention to the development of our interpersonal skills. We would endorse that general view and discuss it in more detail in Chapter 8.

The way the group is organized is important. Groups can be classified in a number of ways. One is along a continuum, from being unstructured to groups that are structured, the distinction based upon the rules or norms that are made explicit about how the group operates.

Unstructured   Structured

Facilitated Sets

Self-facilitated Sets

Figure 5.1 *Group organization*

Action learning sets fit on the continuum towards structured forms of groups. The structured nature of facilitated sets derives from the basic procedures adopted for action learning outlined in Chapter 3.

Life of the set

Like all groups, sets have a life that starts, matures and ends. Acknowledging sets as having a life helps us understand the set in terms of the feelings that set members and the facilitator can have toward the set. The facilitator's sensitivity toward that life of the set will enable the set members to deal and cope fruitfully with that life.

Facilitating a new set

The facilitator at the introductory or first set meeting conveys the basic format of how sets work and how each set member can most appropriately give support to other set members and also best receive support during her time.

Rather than repeat them here we recommend that facilitators follow the guidelines set out in Chapter 3. It is important for the facilitator to keep the format details to a minimum to avoid giving the impression that the facilitator is going to be a talker or instructor. If brevity is paramount in order to get the set working (doing it is better than lengthy description) then we would simply emphasize the following points.

Most of the guidelines below are actually minimum ground rules for a set to operate. The ground rules can also be referred to as a contract. Additional ground rules will emerge which the set can agree. Whilst the guidelines are considered elsewhere (Chapters 3 and 4) they are included here for the facilitator to give primary attention to in the early stages of the set's life.

Warm up

At the initial meeting ask each set member to say who they are (if they do not know each other), what they do, together with a warm-up activity like:

- something no one here knows about me;
- trauma, trivia and joy (see Chapter 7);
- what is the best thing about my work or studies and what is the most difficult.

The effect is to ease any tensions that there will, quite naturally, be in the group. It is important that the facilitator engages in this activity, perhaps as a model by doing it first on this occasion. A warm-up activity is also useful to get the energy of the group moving (see Figure 3.4 on page 47).

Confidentiality
The set members may or may not know each other prior to the creation of the set. It is critical that the set contracts to maintain confidentiality about other set members' contributions to the group. Material protected by confidentiality and not to be taken outside the set includes:

- what the other set members say about themselves, their content, how they may feel, what they may intend to do;
- how a set member operates in the set – whether it is positive, negative at times, or whatever.

It is perfectly legitimate for a set member to take their own content – how they felt, what they intend to do – outside the set. It may well be helpful and necessary for the set member to do so.

Conveying how the set is working outside the set may be appropriate, but with a caution. Set members tend to develop their own commitment to the set. How set members relate to the world outside the set requires some care. Those who are not members of a set, particularly in an organizational setting, could develop feelings of envy depending on how a set member projects the set. Mistrust or anxiety could be felt by those who are not members of a set. The set could be regarded as a type of 'in-crowd'. The formation of sets is an important consideration (see Chapter 2).

Timing and future meetings
The use of time is critical to effective set working. We examine the use of time in relation to the overall cycle of meetings, how frequently they meet, the length of time of each meeting and how time is used within the set in Chapter 3.

Making 'I' statements
When a set member takes her time and begins to relate her story (refer to Chapter 8, page 147 for a useful distinction between 'story' and 'history'), it

is important to suggest that she (and all set members), when talking about herself, uses the word 'I' when describing something that she has been doing, how she felt and what she intends to do. This avoids the use of words like 'you' (meaning 'me' or 'I'); one (ditto), and people (ditto).

The benefit of using 'I' is that it becomes clearer that what the set member is saying is not only about her, but that she 'owns' what she is saying. Contrast the following where the set member is ostensibly talking about herself:

- 'If you get into our office late, you feel that you have let the others down.'
- 'If I get into the office late, I feel that I have let the others down.'

A simple change in words from 'you' to 'I', but we now know that she is talking about how she feels rather than pushing it 'out there' where she can avoid actually expressing her own feelings and create an ambiguity about whether she is talking about herself, the others in the office, or both.

Another common example is, 'It's not fair', when what we probably mean is, 'I feel unfairly treated because . . .'. It is important that as facilitator we model the owning of our statements.

The relationship of the facilitator to set members

The purpose of action learning is to enable the participants to take responsibility for their learning and actions and to develop and/or enhance their autonomy. Inevitably, in the early stages of a set the facilitator is going to take a significant role in guiding and directing how the set works. The aim of the facilitator is to move away from this dependent relationship to one where the set members achieve greater autonomy.

Heron's (1989) three modes of facilitation are useful to convey how the facilitator can move along a spectrum, as shown in Figure 5.2.

Hierarchical mode

Initially the facilitator is in *hierarchical* mode, directing the learning process, exercising power over it and doing things *for* the group. She leads the set for it is usually a new way of working with which the set members are unfamiliar. We are continually struck by how new a way of working it is to set members. This comes out at reviews when set members comment upon the effectiveness of the process and how unusual it has been up until that point to work in that way.

At this initial stage, adopting the hierarchical mode is entirely appropriate. To adopt another approach would be to abdicate the responsibility the facilitator has for the successful launch of the set. This mode of working means that the facilitator will clarify and interpret questions about procedures, the aims of set working, appropriate and inappropriate behaviours and interventions.

Hierarchical	Cooperative	Autonomous

Figure 5.2 *Mode of facilitation*

However she is also, even at this stage, modelling practice that will enable set members to take on a more participatory active role – ideally from the first set meeting. For example, she will encourage set members to support, clarify, question and challenge a set member. In this way participation is encouraged and set members learn not to let the facilitator alone interact with the set member whose time it is.

An important example is the tendency for a set member to give the facilitator eye contact to the exclusion of the other set members. The non-verbal and usually unwitting effect of this is to exclude the other set members from the dialogue and to focus the interaction on one set member and the facilitator. Whilst the facilitator may try to cast her eyes around the group during the interaction to non-verbally encourage the set member to include the set in his interaction, she may consider it more effective to be explicit and say that we do tend to fix eye contact on the facilitator because of their initial influential and hierarchical role. In this example we have the facilitator being in hierarchical mode about a process and behavioural issue – eye contact – designed to lead to a less hierarchical outcome – shared eye contact – from that point onwards.

Cooperative mode

As the set becomes more confident with the procedures, processes and norms of the set, our facilitator can move on to Heron's second mode – the *cooperative* mode. Here the facilitator shares her power over the learning process and different dynamics of the set *with* the set members and the latter become more self-directing in their interactions within the set.

Set members no longer require only the facilitator's interventions to prevent imbalancing or disorientating the process. The set is more like a rowing boat where the crew (set members) are integrated and maintaining the system of an effective set. If there is a tendency to go off course, a set member will intervene to make the 'correction'. The facilitator is becoming one of the crew.

For example, in a set one of us facilitated, the set had been in existence for six months when, at one meeting, a set member picked up a point made by the presenter and began a monologue about the need for the law to be changed in the area of the presenter's issue. This was picked up and pursued by another set member. A previously silent colleague intervened to say that we were in danger of getting into a discussion that would not be of use to the presenter, detracted from the presenter's immediate concerns and was also using up the presenter's time. This was a brilliant intervention made without disabling anyone in the set and without any intervention by the facilitator.

The facilitator may still act as a prompt and support the set when set members are not going to pick up something that is happening that is militating against the progress of a presenter or the set. For example, a presenter may be saying he wants to do something but is conveying non-verbally that there is no will apparent and the lack of will is not being noticed. Should the facilitator intervene? If other set members are not picking up the signals then it may be appropriate to intervene and ask the presenter what it is about undertaking an action that may inhibit or promote the action.

Autonomous mode

The next mode beyond the cooperative is the *autonomous* mode. Here the facilitator respects the total autonomy of the set members. They are now on their *own way*, using the set to meet their needs as defined by them. Our facilitator may still be with the set but she is giving more space to the set members to determine their direction. Here the main responsibility is to subtly create and support the conditions within which the set members can self-determine their own learning.

The fullest example of this is when the set becomes self-facilitating and our facilitator has withdrawn. We shall examine the working of self-facilitated sets in the next chapter.

Summary

These three modes deal, in Heron's words, with the 'politics of learning'. We adapt this term to mean the management of the set, who makes the decisions and how the decisions are made about what is learned and how learning takes place. We are also conscious that there will be swings back and forth along the continuum until the point where the set becomes totally autonomous. There may be external constraints. The set may be an integral part of an academic course which prevents the set moving beyond the hierarchical–cooperative modes. Similarly with a set in an organizational context, management may require facilitation to be a condition of the set's existence.

Core qualities of the facilitator

Given the above modes of relating to set members, what core qualities do we as facilitators bring to the set? The purpose of being in a set for the participant is, through the task, issue, problem or opportunity he is addressing, to release and enhance the set member's capacity for understanding and managing his life and development. The key question is, what climate can the facilitator model and encourage in the set that is conducive to that development?

The facilitator has to keep in balance the needs of the individual set member and the maintenance of the group. These needs can be addressed in two ways. First, what qualities does the skilled facilitator bring as a person to the set to encourage a developmental climate for set members? Second, how does the facilitator create a learning and developmental climate for the set as whole? The latter is the subject of the next section.

For the individual qualities we draw on Rogers (1979) who considered the core conditions for a climate of developmental growth. The first is that the facilitator is genuine, real and congruent. She is herself. As Rogers puts it:

> There is a close matching, or congruence between what is being experienced at the gut level, what is present in awareness, and what is expressed to the [set member].

In practical terms this means that when the set member is expressing a feeling or an attitude, the facilitator is aware of the feelings or attitude and in being genuine and congruent is in effect being with the set member. The facilitator is enabling the set member to be himself as he is. If the facilitator is saying in effect, here I am as I am, then this conveys that it is perfectly legitimate for the set member to *be* as he is.

The second condition for creating the appropriate climate for development and change is acceptance, or caring or prizing: Rogers' 'unconditional positive regard'. Rogers calls it a non-possessive caring. However, this unconditional caring is not a 'should'. It cannot be a contrived regard for then it would not be genuine. The condition provides a 'nurturant atmosphere not a forcing one' (Rogers, 1979).

The third facilitative condition is empathic understanding. This means that the facilitator senses accurately the feelings and meanings the set member is experiencing and she (the facilitator) communicates this understanding to the set member. The purpose of empathizing is to understand where the set member is coming from and is. This enables the set member through his response to gain a clearer understanding of his world and behaviour. The empathy enables the set member therefore to have more control over his world. We consider empathy in more detail in Chapter 9.

Given the above conditions, an important proviso needs to be made. The facilitator and the set are not working in a social vacuum. We all bring our values to the set and it is important for the set to consider the processes by which they wish to work, like the relationship between facilitator and set members. In addition, facilitators and set members are increasingly concerned with challenging the many ways in which complex patterns of domination and inequality are maintained. An example can be drawn from Weil and McGill (1990):

> The onus for raising . . . issues is also often put upon those who have most to lose. For example, in largely male or white groups, it is common for members of oppressed groups to be seen as 'the problem', or as 'having a problem' that is not 'the group's' concern. Equally, when women or black people try to highlight aspects of their own experience, which may differ from that of others in the group, they can be seen as disrupting the status quo.

Therefore, if a set member or the facilitator feels that an assumption is being made about them that needs to be challenged, the conditions exist explicitly in the set for the challenge to be made without the challenger being made to feel outside the norm. We refer to this in greater detail in Chapter 14 under the sub-heading 'Personal relationships development and empowerment'.

Creating a learning climate

What climate is our facilitator endeavouring to create in the set? By 'climate' we mean the most effective conditions for learning by set members. Such a climate enables:

- each set member to achieve whatever tasks they bring to the set – the set makes a difference;
- set members to acquire and enhance their personal, interpersonal and group facilitation skills;
- the set becoming collectively an effective learning community;
- (optional) the set becoming an effective self-facilitating set.

For the organization sponsoring action learning we could add:

- benefits to the organization in enabling individuals through the use of sets to foster change and organizational learning.

We have discussed the other specific contributions facilitators can make to encourage effective set working. We have also indicated how set members can contribute to the quality of the set (Chapter 4).

What does the climate look, sound and feel like to the set? Climate is, we hope, a helpful word but we could also use the word 'culture'. In defining culture, McLean and Marshall (1988) admit that:

> It is not easy to define culture . . . we are familiar with it, know of its existence, recognise aspects when they are pointed out and yet find it very difficult to say very clearly what it is.

However, they draw on management writers who have attempted to define it in organizational contexts. Here are a few:

> . . . how things are done around here (Ouchi and Johnson, 1978)

> . . . the taken for granted and shared meanings that people assign to their social surroundings (Wilkins, 1983)

> . . . the collection of traditions, values, policies, beliefs and attitudes that constitute a pervasive context for everything we do and think in an organisation (McLean and Marshall, 1983)

Most of our experience of sets has been in organizational contexts, in which the set members bring with them their own backgrounds, together with the way in 'which things get done around here' including their perceptions of the history of the organization, its primary tasks, size, where it is geographically and its current senior management which reflects aspects of the power base.

Action learning set culture

Set members are part of the culture they work in and they bring that with them to the set. The set, however, even if created with the agreement of an external (to the set) senior manager has the opportunity to create its own culture. This cultural opportunity could be said to be a sub-set of the culture of the main organization or it could differ from the main organizational culture. Indeed it could be argued that if a newly created set were simply to replicate the culture of the organization, what would be the point of creating it in the first place?

Thus we have a cultural justification for the creation of action learning sets. If sets are about the development of individuals in an organization, then sets should have a climate or culture conducive to set members' development. This is a good reason for using sets in organizations in order that employees do not get stuck in 'the social glue that holds the organisation together' (Baker, 1980, in McLean and Marshall, 1988) where the social glue paralyses individual and managerial development. Any organization which adopts action learning is at least espousing that it wants to support development of individuals, organizational learning and change.

This cultural justification for creating sets based in organizations leads us to the culture or climate that can be created for action learning sets.

The conditions for the learning culture

Clearly, the intention should be to create a learning and developmental culture. This is obvious when stated, but what are the characteristics of a learning and developmental culture in the organization that is a set? Here we draw upon and adapt Hawkins and Shohet (1989). For us a learning and developmental climate or culture is one that:

- Emphasizes the potential that all different work situations have for learning, both individually and collectively. A set's work can take any learning opportunity that is relevant to the set member and create the conditions for learning.
- Problems and crises are seen as important opportunities for learning and development. Major crises are seen as growth points, and the culture of the set is one where it is safe to take risks. Failure is seen as an event to be learnt from, rather than to be depowered by. An example is of a set of colleagues working for the same organization, one of whom was under threat from a resident on an estate. The set member felt frightened and immobilized by the situation. This was shared by colleagues in the set who could empathize readily in the same role. The set could have become immobolized by the feelings expressed. However, the expressed feelings gave energy to the set members that enabled them to move on to reflect about the context of security in relation to the new roles that they had with the organization.

Learning came through that shared concern, a realization of effective but simple security needs adopted by the organisation as well as specific actions by the colleague whose experience triggered the shown learning

- Good practice emerges not from reaction to crises but from set members balancing all parts of an activity, from action, to reflection, to new thinking, to planning and then back to action. This is what happened in the example above. There was not simply a reaction to a very real crisis. The set member whose problem it was initially moved from an emotional reaction to the event, through her meanings of the event in collaboration with other set members, toward new meanings and actions. It was a process involving set member feelings, reflections on concrete experience, new and challenging thinking, shared planning, a range of options and subsequent actions.
- Individual set members take time out to reflect on their effectiveness, learning and development. This becomes a cooperative process rather than an individual one or one that happens rarely for the individual.
- Making explicit and working with the emotional and political aspects of learning and development in the set (see Chapter 10).
- The set encourages feedback both from other set members and back in the daily workplace.
- The set encourages emulation of good set practice elsewhere in the organization so that a learning environment is transferred.
- Time and attention is given to individuals. The starting point is where they are coming from, recognizing their individual needs.
- Learning and development are seen in the set as active concerns which results in action and further learning.

The conditions set out above for a learning culture in action learning are the espoused conditions. We can say that these are the conditions that should prevail. Whether they do or not will be up to the facilitator in the first instance, and as the set gathers experience the whole set will embrace it by putting the above desirable conditions into action. It is the difference between *saying* what should happen and actually *doing* it (Argyris and Schon, 1978).

Reflection and review

Reflection and review can take a number of forms.

- Reflection, evaluation and feedback at the end of a presenter's time.

- Review of a set meeting at the end of the meeting.
- Review of the set after a period and series of meetings
    about the set process
    about the norms of the set.
- Review of the achievements of individuals in respect of
    achievement of the tasks undertaken during the period
    learning about self, the set process and relationship to others outside the
    set.

We distinguish the above from the process of reflection that happens for each set member as presenter that is part of the learning cycle which we outlined in Chapter 2, page 30 and refer to in more detail in Chapter 10.

Individual reflection, evaluation and feedback at the end of a presenter's time

At the end of the presenter's time a brief opportunity can be taken for the presenter to reflect with the set upon the process by which he came to his actions. He may give feedback about which questions, facilitations and interventions he found helpful and less helpful. He may also ask for feedback about how he reflected upon his issue – the content. The reflection about process is the means by which the set learns about set (and group) working.

In this way the set and its members build up their learning from experience – they learn how to use their learning to each person's and to the set's advantage. At the same time they are creating the climate for learning.

Set meeting review

Set meetings usually concentrate on each set member and the time allocated to each. In the early stages of a set's life it may be appropriate to spend 10–15 minutes near the end of the set meeting reviewing how the set has been for set members. A set review can include the following headings for consideration:

- One thing that I have gained from being in the set today.
- One thing I have gained/learned about the way the set works.
- Something I would like the set to consider that I am not yet sure about.
- Something I want to share that I have difficulty with when I am presenting and/or when I am a set member giving support to another.
- Something I want to say about the set, myself, the set adviser, another set member.

These headings are a suggested range from which a facilitator and set members can select or indeed add to. They are not intended for use all at once and certainly would be overwhelming and not containable in the time allocated above.

The feedback (see Chapter 9 on giving and receiving feedback) to the set will provide positive impressions of what is being gained and learned by set members. It will also provide the set and the facilitator with an indication of the impact that the set is having upon set members. For example in one set the most significant impression for one set member was that:

> For the first time in a group I have actually been listened to and heard without anyone interrupting and contradicting me.

In the early life of the set it is better to engage in the doing of action learning than to discuss what action learning is supposed to be about. There is a tendency in our culture to go into discussion and abstraction about an activity rather than just doing it. The doing of action learning will very soon provide a huge resource from which to review and reflect. Let the practice and doing emerge before reflection; otherwise there is little 'material' on which to reflect!

Periodic review

When this takes place is up to the set unless there is an organizational requirement for an 'in-house' review. To let the set get into the flow of action learning is very important. If the set has agreed to run for one year with 10–12 meetings we would suggest a review at the end of six months and at the end of the year's cycle. The six month review could use the time allocated to the set meeting or allow one or two hours after the set meeting.

Figure 5.3 shows a typical review used by us for set members belonging to one organization. The action learning set was an acknowledged and integrated part of their management development.

We will take the numbered questions in Figure 5.3 to identify the reasons for each set of questions.

Question 1 gives the set member the opportunity to reflect upon the impact of the set from the standpoint of the set member personally, in relation to her personal working practice and interpersonal relations. Typical responses under this heading have been the following:

> I have found a place that I can unload my burdens.
> I feel that I matter.
> I now plan my work in a much more effective way.

---

1) What have I gained/learned from the set or done differently as a result of the set:
   - for myself
   - for my work in relation to:
     my personal work practice
     my colleagues and staff?
2) What have I gained/learned in terms of my understanding of the *process* of the set that I have applied in my work?
3) What have we gained as a group?
4) How can I/we improve the operation of the set to make it more effective?
5) How do I wish to utilize the set in the next year?
   and/or
   Where do I go from here?
   and/or
   What issues do I wish to bring to the set that are important to me and my work?
6) How may we link up, and to what purpose, with the other staff in the department who have experienced/are experiencing action learning?
7) Are there any implications for the department as a result of the operation of the set/s?
8) Any other issues you may wish to raise.

Figure 5.3 *Action learning set review*

I am now more confident in managing my staff and have learned how to challenge staff who were previously not pulling their weight.

Question 2 is about making the processes inherent in action learning sets explicit. Processes refer to *how* the set works to enable the set to be effective for each set member. This aspect of the review is very important. Set working employs interpersonal skills (see Chapters 8 and 9) that are central to being an effective manager. For example, a manager has a basic requirement to be able to listen to colleagues and staff who are responsible to her. Simple enough. But we rarely get the opportunity to get feedback and to reflect on our capacity to listen effectively. The process of action learning provides a kind of living laboratory to get that feedback, reflection and practice. For many of our sets, participants have remarked along the following lines about this:

I never realized how important it was just to listen.
I now give my staff the time to really listen to them.

When we asked Question 2 initially we found that some set members were a little non[illegible] basic lack of clarity on the distinction between [illegible] distinction between task – the content of what is [illegible] member's project, task or problem – and process – how the set works to enable a set member to address their project [illegible] rs. This led us to provide supplementary material to support and prompt their reflection on this question with a statement of the basic skills they employ in the set that are part of the process. This is set out in Figure 5.4 and considered in more detail in Chapters 8 and 9.

Figure 5.4 poses questions about the skills used in set, the opportunity to reflect upon how the individual set member works in the set, what may be transferable to other situations and what values are identifiable that could be emulated elsewhere.

Question 3 moves from the individual to the group. Whilst this is a personal

There are a number of basic (but sophisticated) skills that we bring to all interpersonal situations. An action learning set places significant emphasis on some of these. Examples include our skills of:

- listening and attending
- reflecting back and questioning
- disclosure and assertion
- empathy
- giving and receiving feedback
- reflection
  - of my practice – on what I bring to the set
  - of the process of the set – the way the set works
- time management
  - my own time
  - managing the time of the set
- personal planning

How has your use of these skills changed/enhanced as a result of the set process?

Another key to the review/reflection of the set is identifying the values that underpin effective working of the set. How might you carry those values (if you wished to) to other areas of your work?

Figure 5.4 *Action learning set reviews: process skills and reflection*

reflection on the set member's view, it can be incorporated in a collective reflection at the review meeting. Examples include:

> Trust occurred amongst the group. This helped me and others open up and deal with things I felt vulnerable about
>
> As a group we have become more powerful. Powerful in the sense that we are better equipped to provide solutions to problems rather than just moaning. It has also been useful for individuals to tackle problems after sharing them in the group. (This was a set where the set members all had the same job, but worked separately.)

Question 4 is designed to bring out set members' ideas on how they think the set could be improved. It places them in constructive critical mode. The question is designed to elicit positive suggestions rather than whinges. Question 5 invites a set member to ask how she wishes to use the set in the period following the review.

Question 6 is appropriate to organizations using action learning sets as a vehicle for management development where sets have been created. The question is designed to supplement any intentions senior management or those responsible for the creation of sets may have. Question 7 is linked. Action learning may have implications for the organization in terms of its capacity to collectively learn and therefore to transform itself.

Question 8 is a self-explanatory sweep-up question for set members.

The review process can be undertaken by the set members and the facilitator alone. However, in an organizational setting where set members are sponsored by their line managers, it may be appropriate to have the review with the line manager(s). In the above example the review took the following stages.

- Agreement by the set members and facilitator (one of us in our capacity as consultant facilitator to the organization) to undertake the review and to invite the chief executive to the review.
- Agreement of the chief executive to take part in the review. It was agreed that the feedback would be provided at the commencement of the programme of action learning for this group of managers.
- Two-page review designed by the facilitator (Figure 5.4 in an A4 format with spaces for completion of responses) given to all set members at least one week prior to the meeting with the chief executive.
- The review meeting takes place using the responses as an *aide-mémoire* for the set members.

- Review meeting led by the set members presenting their analysis to the chief executive as a lead-in to a dialogue about the effect of the set on them and their work.
- Facilitator at the review meeting to listen to the presentation and dialogue with occasional contributions.
- Agreement of outcomes and negotiation of next stage of the life of the set – to continue for a further year with the facilitator, to have a further review with the intention of becoming a self-facilitating set beyond that point.

Reviewing the norms of the set

At the commencement of the set the facilitator guides the set and establishes, with set members, the basic ground rules upon which the set will be organized and run (see Chapter 3). Setting the ground rules means that the set has created explicit ways about how it wishes to work. For example, a basic ground rule will be that one person speaks at a time; simple, yet crucial for effective set working.

As the set progresses over a few meetings, other ways of working begin to emerge that may be obvious to everybody and articulated, for example, 'Have you noticed that we are tending to slip over the time allocated for each set member with the effect of diminishing the time available for whoever takes the last slot?' This can then be considered and the tendency modified.

However, not all ways of working are articulated or apparent to the set. The facilitator has a responsibility, because of her greater experience, to focus on what is happening that is not being said, but she may also not be conscious of all that is happening.

Examples of ways or patterns of working that can emerge without the set consciously realizing it include the following.

- One set member tends to ask fewer questions of a presenter than the others.
- A set member tends to come in first and quickly after the presenter has made his initial commentary.
- The facilitator gets into 'rescuing' a particular set member when the latter is struggling to find her own solution.
- A set member regularly avoids making specific the actions that he will take on between set meetings and talks generalities instead.

What is happening within the set, which these examples convey, is that the set is not noticing that some patterns of working are emerging that may implicitly limit the effectiveness of the set or the work of a set member.

1) The unwritten rules of this set are . . .
2) What I find it hard to talk about in this set is . . .
3) What I think we avoid talking about in the set is . . .
4) The hidden agendas that this set carries are . . .

Figure 5.5 *Exploring the norms and dynamics of the group*

Sets can, like any group, begin to unconsciously develop unstated patterns or norms, some of which can limit the effectiveness of the set. The set can begin to collude and become not just a safe place, but too safe a place. The set may get into a position where it never challenges a set member who is perhaps unconsciously seeking collusion in his way of seeing the world.

These patterns or norms of behaviour need not be limiting. For example a norm may emerge that set members start to bring a 'present' to the set, like biscuits. Such norms can 'oil' the set and help to make the interactions more effective and relaxed.

How can the set uncover these implicit norms and review them to assess their value to the set? The set can agree to put aside time in a meeting or outside to consider the norms and dynamics of the group. Figure 5.5 provides a few open-ended questions for set members (and the facilitator) to consider individually and then to discuss in the set, an activity adapted from Hawkins and Shohet (1989). This activity is one where safety and trust need to be present.

A way of helping to foster an additional sense of safety may be to carry out the following activity first.

Hand three small cards times the number of set members plus facilitator to each person and ask them to record on each of the three cards one positive thing – a word or short phrase – about each person in the set. (If there are five set members plus the facilitator, each person should have 15 cards with one attribute per card.) On the other side of each card print the name of the person the attribute applies to. The cards are not signed by the author. The cards are placed in the centre, name side up and shuffled. Each person in the set is then given their cards name side up.

Each person may say how they feel if they wish to – but not to ask who wrote what!

Figure 5.6 *Positive feedback activity*

92

Review of individual set members' achievements

Here we are referring to additional reflection and review where the set member has completed a project for a client in the set member's organization and/or a project that has been completed as part of a course leading to a qualification. The project may have been documented. However, it is valuable to ask a set member to compile a reflective document which highlights what she has learned from undertaking the project and what she has learned about learning in the process (see Chapter 10 on levels of learning).

Chapter 6

Types of Action Learning

In this chapter we emphasize the flexibility of action learning and how it may be adapted to the needs of organizations and individuals. We distinguish two particular types of action learning. In addition we identify the nature of the issues that individuals may bring to sets.

First there are sets initiated and supported within an organization. These are distinguished from sets initiated by colleagues created without the support of an organization. *Organization initiated* action learning includes sets formed for management development purposes. Action learning sets are now used in educational contexts as part of a diploma, degree or postgraduate programme. *Independent* action learning sets can be found within or across organizations or may be organizationally free. Independent sets are formed by the participants themselves (hence our term) with their personal and management development aims.

Second, action learning sets can be *facilitated* by a facilitator (set adviser) as seen in Chapter 5 or be *self-facilitated*. With the latter, responsibility for facilitating the set is shared by the set members themselves.

Both types can overlap, as shown in Figure 6.1. The diagram shows that sets can be organization initiated or independent and be facilitated or self-facilitated. We will consider the purposes to which sets may be used by organizations and the use of independent sets by individuals. The remainder

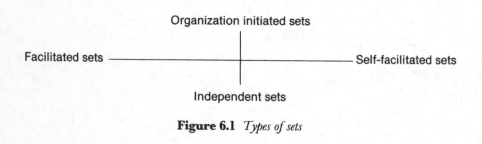

Figure 6.1 *Types of sets*

of the chapter will indicate the particular requirements of self-facilitated action learning sets.

Sets sponsored by organizations

Taking initiative and gaining commitment for action learning

Two groups of people may initiate action learning within an organization. The first group are those who have responsibility for development and wish to use action learning as an important means of enabling staff and management development to happen. The second group are the people who wish to be participants in sets for their personal and management development. Both groups of people have responsibilities for ensuring that the sets are created and maintained.

The key here is the source of influence for initiating the creation of sets. For organizational support, there is a need for a champion in the organization to make action learning happen. This is particularly important where resources of time, finance and project initiatives are required. The champion may be a managing director, head of staff/management development, trainer or someone who is an enthusiast to make action learning happen. Ideally the champion will be familiar with the use and effectiveness of action learning, what it is like to do action learning and the personal/managerial and organizational benefits.

Determining issues brought to the set

We discuss particular applications of action learning in organizations in Chapter 12. Here we consider the basic approaches organizations may take as to how they expect participant managers and staff to use sets.

The continuum in Figure 6.2 can be used to describe the range of ways in which sets can be used by set members. With organizationally initiated sets it is important to clarify for the sponsors, set members and facilitators (in facilitated sets), at which ends of the continuum sets are expected to work.

The person responsible for initiating action learning can take a stance along the continuum. Let us call him the development manager. At the left end of the continuum the development manager negotiates the parameters of a project with the set member, 'client' (considered below) and a set adviser. There is shared 'ownership' if the project and accountability by the set

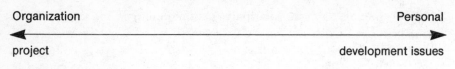

Figure 6.2 *Organizationally initiated set continuum*

member is maintained mainly through the project. At the personal end of the continuum the set member is left to decide the issues she brings to the set. Responsibility rests more with the set member to use the set for her development. The set member is accountable for her development in reflection with her line manager and the management developer responsible for creating the sets.

The organizational project

At the project end of this continuum the development manager will require staff joining sets to undertake a project that is directly geared to the needs of the organization. The member of staff joins a set to enable her to gain support while undertaking the project that has direct pay-offs for the organization. The project may be directly geared to the organization's strategic purposes or be a one-off problem-centred issue for resolution. A project could be based on an operational or a developmental problem. An operational problem would be one that concerned the way in which a product is currently produced or a service delivered. The problem becomes a project to resolve or at least to reduce its incidence. Examples include:

- low morale in a front line customer service department of an organization;
- reducing the number of return visits by clients in order by deal with their needs more effectively first time.

A developmental issue or problem would be one that takes the organization and its members beyond the operational into new pathways of potential action; some examples are:

- implementing a management development system;
- planning and implementing a monitoring strategy to reflect equal opportunities policy;
- developing and implementing a new marketing strategy;
- introducing performance measurement into customer care programmes;
- identification, design and implementation of a staff development policy.

Enabling management development through project work via action learning sets has two crucial aspects.

First, the problem tackled must be one for which there is not a prescribed solution. If we know how the problem can be resolved it is not a problem. We just need to get on with it. However, 'I' may have a problem doing it. This is a different matter. 'I' may have a problem in undertaking the task I am addressing. An example would be where 'I' lack the confidence to do a particular task. We will address this below at the personal development end of the continuum. An organization, in agreeing an organizational problem for resolution through a project, will want the project to be one that is at least intractable initially. Otherwise, resources are being wasted. If we know how a problem can be resolved, go ahead and do it!

Second, there is the 'ownership' of the project. The project has to be owned by its initiators to ensure the planning, implementation, and outcomes of the project. The 'ownership' of the project is shared three ways, the first two of which are essential:

1. The person in the set, the set member, who will have ownership in wanting to undertake the project to completion over a period of time. If the set member pursues a project without really wanting to do it then a lack of commitment to the project may mar its successful progress. The desire to undertake the project will be negotiated with:
2. The second person, a 'client' elsewhere in the organization for whom resolution of the problem is also important. This person will act as the client who will negotiate with the set member the purposes of the project, its implementation and a review of its outcomes.
3. The third interested person with some ownership in the project. This person may be responsible for management development, the set member's line manager and/or our management developer in the organization who will wish to be assured of the development of the individual beyond completion of the project.

The set adviser and set may have an additional and useful contribution. They provide a focus for the set member to decide the feasibility of the project within the set framework. The set member takes any problems to the set so that she can think them through with the support of the set and the set adviser.

Group project

This guide is primarily about projects and issues undertaken by individuals progressed with a set. A variant is a group project, where the members of the set are undertaking a group project for the organization. In this form the set divides the project work between members of the set. It is important to recognize and distinguish two features here which, if a facilitator is present, will need to be highlighted for the set. There will be team issues which the set members will wish to resolve and work on. There will also be individual issues that each set member may wish to bring to the set to reflect upon and progress. It is appropriate for the set to work on the latter. Where the issues are team ones, it is better to go into team mode. For example there may be conflicts in the group over the progress of work. The facilitator and members can aim to keep the distinction clear so that the action learning set method is used for progressing individual parts of the project.

We have found that some trainers and managers confuse action learning with team improvement and team building. We stress that the two issues are kept distinct for the reasons outlined above.

Personal development issues

At the other end of the continuum, the 'personal development issues' end, the set becomes the forum for staff to bring their issues to the set with the simple rule that the issue is one of significance to set the member. Sets are formed with staff who will potentially benefit from action learning; who voluntarily wish to become members of a set with other colleagues in the organization; and who do not have direct line relationships to each other. The sets commence, leaving the participants in the sets to address their own issues, problems, and opportunities.[1]

In this way participants start from 'where they are coming from' with their issues, problems and concerns. Examples could include:

● personal motivation towards work;

---

[1] We are sometimes asked why we use the terms: 'issue, problem, opportunity' when inviting set members to bring what is pertinent and relevant to them to the set. We do this partly because we used to ask set members to bring a 'problem' to the set. The danger of using this term is that it might convey they may have a problem and they may not, that they may feel that they should have one and/or that they are a problem! There may indeed be a genuine problem, eg a sticky relationship with a 'difficult' colleague. However, by using a wider range of terms we avoid centring on problems *per se*. Further, an opportunity might be, say, an advertisement in the press for a post to which the set member is considering applying but is uncertain because it is not in their immediate purview. This is not a problem – at least not at the outset. Similarly, a person may have a project they are pursuing which they bring to the set.

- line relationship as a manager with colleagues for whom the manager is responsible;
- completion of a research degree with field work in the manager's employing organization;
- prioritization of work for self and staff;
- future work direction.

As at the organizational end of the continuum, the set member could design some of the above issues and problems as a project with specific targets in respect of planning, implementation and review. Other problems may require more short-term attention and once resolved go on to other issues. For example, a set member may bring her desire to improve her working relationship with an 'awkward' colleague to the set, attention to which may be resolved fairly quickly. However, to the set member this relationship may be *the* intractable problem facing her at the time.

The choices along the continuum

Both ends of the continuum are justified but do start from different perspectives. At the organization end is the view that any initiated project should have direct organizational benefits. The manager, as set member, gains her personal and management development en route. At the personal development end is the view that the manager has her 'baggage' of skills, qualities, attributes and 'ways of seeing the world'. This is the starting point. Enable that person to work on her issues. In this way her management development will derive from those issues most significant to her. Between the ends of the continuum are combinations of the above. For example, once the personal development issues have reached a degree of resolution, wider organizational issues and projects can be negotiated with clients elsewhere in the organization.

Both ends of the continuum have their disadvantages. At the personal development end, the manager and other set members may stay in a 'crisis'-centred mode, always returning to operational issues of concern. In the example above we gave the instance of a set member addressing the operational issue of working with an 'awkward' colleague. The set member could stay in the mode of always addressing issues like this one so that they recur in one form or another. The set may, even with a set adviser, collude with this mode and the set member may not rise above the parapet to look at developmental issues.

At the organizational project end, the manager may address the issues of the project, 'safely' ignoring her personal developmental issues by immersing in the content of the project.

Independent action learning sets

'Independent' means that an organization is not involved in the creation of an action learning set, in determining the parameters of the set, or providing direct resources for the set. Members form sets for their personal needs without the support of or constraints imposed by an organization.

An independent set has advantages of being released from the constraints, demands and expectations of an organization. This freedom can be positive. There is usually a sense of commitment and responsibility to make the set function, to meet, to continue and to ensure that the set works for each member. The negative side may be that maintenance of the set imposes a responsibility of time and resources that the set member cannot provide, that an organization can.

In an independent set, members can bring issues to the set that they may not bring to one supported organizationally, particularly where the organization requires a client-based project. This leads us to another continuum, shown in Figure 6.3. In contrast with the organizationally sponsored set, the set member has complete choice and total responsibility for what she brings to the set.

In Figure 6.3 by project/task we mean:

- producing a report or project to a deadline
- how to work with a 'difficult' colleague
- how to overcome being reactive in work.

A reflective issue or problem brought to the set could include those examples given above in an organizationally sponsored set at the personal development end. We could add more here:

- What am I doing this work for anyway?

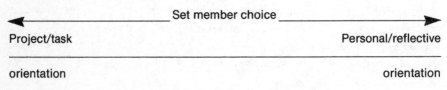

Figure 6.3 *Independent sets continuum*

- What makes me do what I ought to do as opposed to what I want to do?
- How do I balance my work with the rest of my life?
- Where am I going in my life?

A set member may start at the task end but gradually (and even deriving from the task end) move to the more reflective/personal development end of the continuum.

Another advantage of independent action learning sets is that they enable those not attached to an organization to join a set. Here we include people who are home-based, not in paid work, or self-employed who would like support plus action from a set. With an independent set each member can decide what to bring to the set without any accountability to external providers. The only accountability is to themselves supported by the other set members!

Sets created and supported by an organization benefit from having a champion. She can obtain agreement for this form of development, the resources of time allocation, funding of set advisers and possible cover for set members' work. Independent sets require to be their own champions in creating and maintaining the sets. This appears a more daunting task.

Consideration of the need for a set adviser to facilitate an independent set may be an impediment on grounds of cost for the set adviser's time. However, as we show in Chapter 5 and below, depending on the skills that set members bring to the set, a facilitator may not be necessary. Alternatively, a set adviser could facilitate the set for a short period to enable take-off to self-facilitation.

Self-facilitated sets

We define a self-facilitated action learning set as one that operates without using a facilitator (set adviser). In self-facilitated sets the set members take responsibility for the facilitation role and action learning process.

We recommend that readers refer to particular chapters that support the running of self-facilitated sets. In Chapter 3 we outline the set process, the basic insights, procedures and processes by which a set works; Chapter 4 conveys the essential roles of set members as presenters and enablers of the presenter; Chapter 5 considers the role of the facilitator, giving the self-facilitated set member an insight into the skills and attributes of facilitation; Chapters 8 and 9 underpin the skills required for effective set interaction by addressing skills development.

We use the term 'self-facilitated action learning sets'; some writers and practitioners have referred to 'self-development groups' (Pedler *et al.*, 1991). We would distinguish a self-facilitated set from a self-development group by the former using explicit action learning processes.

We also make a distinction between self-facilitation and unfacilitated sets. It is a small but crucial point. Self-facilitation means that all set members consciously take on the role of facilitation to progress the set meeting. Each set member takes and shares responsibility for facilitation as part of their set membership. Only when being presenter will they relinquish that responsibility.

The Brighton experience

Our initial experience of action learning was through participation in self-facilitated sets. In the description below we will draw upon that experience.

Our interest in this form of action learning derived from our work on experiential learning and enabling student learners to have much greater autonomy in their learning. Action learning provided a promising vehicle for postgraduate courses in management for part-time students.

We met as an action learning set to begin the process of building up an experienced team for the postgraduate management courses. If we were to ask students to use action learning methods we needed to be familiar with the process too! At its formation the set comprised five persons: all were white and able-bodied; four had academic and one had administrative responsibilities; two women, three men; ages ranged from 32 to 47.

Rapidly it became clear that action learning could be used much more widely than originally thought. Action learning offered staff as well as students a means of addressing and learning from their own concerns and problems.

From the outset there were three important ways in which this set differed from the traditional notion of an action learning set. First, action learning sets in organizations tend to have a 'client' outside the set to whom the set members are responsible for the progress of the task or problem. Although each of us was working on real problems directly pertinent to our job responsibilities, we did not have a client. We were our own clients using the set for our purposes, although there would be a benefit to the organization for those of us concerned with pursuing tasks based on the organization. An example of this was taking a postgraduate management development programme from an interesting and rather novel idea through to successful validation and implementation. The novel idea was the use of action learning as the major vehicle for learning! Hence the desire for some of us to do action learning if we were going to prescribe it for those embarking on our courses.

Second, and in our view most important, we decided to work without a set adviser. We would do that task ourselves. We will look at the implications below.

Third, we set up our particular group voluntarily. While we all worked in the same organization the set was not formally recognized by the organization. We met in our own time. We were a self-facilitated and an independent set simultaneously.

We have continued to be members of self-facilitated sets. It is from these experiences that we draw our ideas for their successful operation.

Benefits of self-facilitated sets

We started our own self-facilitated sets using the action learning approach because it gave a coherent structure and way of working that combined individual action and reflection and was an effective means of maintaining the group. Often, when people get together in groups that are unstructured the result can be failure or group destruct. The action learning process has a sensitive format that meets the needs of members and the group as a whole. The action learning way of working in groups does not guarantee success, but it does reduce the chances of failure. Action learning methods are also very explicit and clear. This makes it easier for learners new to group working to practise, reflect and add to their repertoire of skills.

Effective use of private and public sector resources
We believe organizations will use self-facilitated groups more frequently as they move from hierarchic and rigid forms of working to flatter, more flexible structures with people across and between organizations.

Developmental activities for staff can be resource-hungry and can be wasteful if the activity does not lead to pay-offs for the organization and the individuals experiencing the development. Later in this chapter we show how an organization can use self-facilitated sets to promote staff and management development. An external facilitator may initiate the process. In Chapter 12 we show how sets, whether facilitated or self-facilitated, contribute to the learning process for the organization.

Continuous professional development
Professional development presupposes qualification plus experience with a need to continue to enhance in a structured way the professional's

development throughout their career. Development can be isolated and lonely. Structured development can be expensive and lonely! The use of action learning can provide structured development that is collaborative. The use of self-facilitated sets or, with experience, a gradual move from facilitated to self-facilitated sets can keep the cost down as the need for a facilitator is reduced and eliminated.

The use of action learning sets enhances the set member's understanding of task and process. Facilitation skills develop in each set member that are valuable as the professional moves forward in their career.

Structured group learning in higher education
Throughout the UK and in the industrialized nations there is a trend to mass higher education. This is happening without a commensurate matching of staffing. Teaching staff face higher numbers of students from a greater diversity of backgrounds. The one-to-one or one-to-few tutorial or seminar is going to be less common. Learners are going to rely much more on their own resources of time and application than in the past. Learning how to learn will be the premium challenge for the learner and their teachers. For learners to become flexible and self-managed learners will require methods that enable that to happen. Self-facilitated action learning is one path through higher education expansion, ensuring the experience of learning in higher education is a positive one where real learning is enhanced rather than diluted by numbers. Teachers can use action learning methods to enable that positive experience to happen. Facilitated sets are a transition to self-facilitated sets. We explore the potential in greater detail in Chapter 13.

What does a self-facilitated set need to be effective?

Potential set members
Personal commitment is important for a set member in a traditional set. That commitment is even more important in the early stages of a self-facilitated set. Drawing upon Heron's (1989) modes of facilitation, this form of action learning is at the autonomous end of the spectrum. Set members share responsibility for the maintenance of the set, its procedures and processes. There is no facilitator to take responsibility when the set is not achieving its purpose. Each set member in a self-facilitated set *shares* the responsibility otherwise vested in a facilitator (see Chapter 5).

When creating a self-facilitated set, the set members need to gain commitment that is voluntary. We do this by ensuring that the first meeting is a 'taster'. At the first meeting of the set it is open to anyone to say that it is not what they anticipated and that they may choose not to come to subsequent meetings. This is similar to facilitated sets. A potential set member should not feel obliged to join a set just because it has met, or feel any group pressure to continue. It may mean that the set is stillborn. As long as there are sufficient people who wish to continue, the basis for real commitment has been identified.

Drawing upon the initial Brighton set (McGill *et al*, 1990) we saw that:

> For each person, personal commitment to the set and the way it worked was a priority. Being at the set was very important compared to other activities associated with our work. This generated a feeling of protectiveness towards the time of the set. Something that required so much effort to protect and sustain could not fail to attain significance.

Procedures

At the first meeting of a set, basic procedures and ground rules are agreed. These can be modified at subsequent meetings to suit the set. These include:

- *Life expectancy of the set.* The set agrees the length of time for which it will hold a cycle of meetings. It may meet for six or nine months, or a year. The set reviews its progress during and at the end of the designated period. (See Chapter 5 for review processes).
- *Frequency of meetings.* This is dependent on the needs of members. However, meetings once every two to five weeks enable set members to maintain momentum and to fulfil actions between set meetings.
- *Set numbers and duration of set meetings.* There is a relationship between the number of members in a set and the duration of each set meeting – usually two to three hours dependent upon the number of set members. A small set of three or four can get through business in two hours. Five to six members will need three hours. We do not recommend sets below four unless there is a degree of action learning experience among members. Occasionally, the set may agree to have a day meeting to give set members more time, to review the set process and to celebrate the set.
- *Time allocation at meetings.* This is usually divided equally after allowing sufficient time for informalities (how we are feeling today) and common business (diaries for subsequent meetings). The set may agree that a set member has more time if there is a felt need.
- *Time-keeping and note-taking.* Without a facilitator these key functions are allocated between set members. Time-keeping is necessary to prevent time

drifting with the effect of reducing another set member's time. One person also needs to maintain a note of set member actions for circulation amongst the group so that recall is prompted by the note before and at the next set meeting.

- *Review of the set.* The set may wish to review its effectiveness for each member by allocating time either at the end of a presenter's session or near the end of the meeting.

- *'End' of set review meeting.* The set may determine to end after the review meeting, continue for a further period and/or add to or alter the membership. This final review stage is an important learning process. The finite period of meeting also provides an opportunity for all set members to make a judgement about whether they continue or not.

Applications of self-facilitated sets

The self-facilitated Brighton set described above provides a useful example of how sets can be extended in organizations. As it happens we started as an independent set. Over a period of about three years it led to more independent sets being created, then the organization creating sets for course delivery purposes. There are an infinite variety of ways in which sets can be created in organizations, with or without the organization's support. Below we explore some which we have experienced.

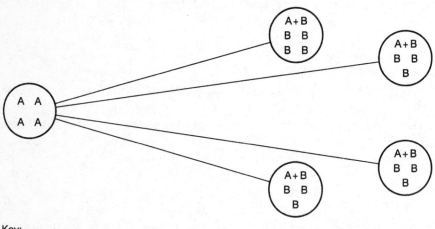

Key:
A = original set members
B = second stage new set members + an A

Figure 6.4 *Extending self-facilitated sets*

From that first set we each went on to invite other colleagues in the organization to join a new set; this is shown diagrammatically in Figure 6.4.

The new sets were created by each of us inviting potential members to an initial meeting preceded by informal conversations. People had heard about the first set and wanted to join. Starting new sets seemed the logical next step. Not all new members remained but the effect overall was to put action learning on the map in the organization. It was recognized as an effective form of self-development among colleagues. The experience outlined above took place in a university business school, an organization interested in the learning process and in developing effective methods of student learning. The independent sets helped create a culture by which staff with personal experience of sets began to use them on their courses as a key learning method for postgraduate courses. These staff now acted as set facilitators guiding managers on management development programmes. As a result, the model shown in Figure 6.4 became like that shown in Figure 6.5.

The above example shows how an organization can make effective use of limited resources and achieve development of its staff. We are not advocating that those responsible for staff/management development in organizations

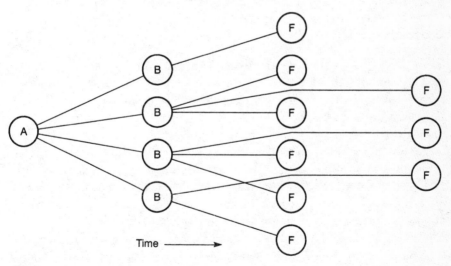

Key:
A = the original set and its members as in Figure 6.4
B = self-facilitated sets initiated by set members from A
F = sets facilitated by set members from B

Figure 6.5 *Organizationally supported facilitated sets*

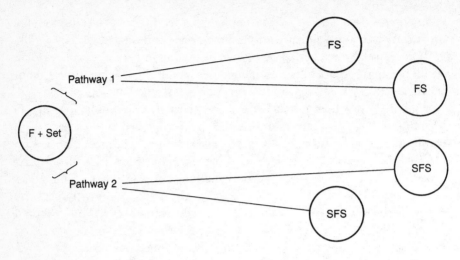

Key:
F = facilitator of the first set
FS = facilitated set
SFS = self-facilitated set

Figure 6.6 *Development with action learning: pathways*

leave their staff to start sets themselves as a cheap way of encouraging development of staff. However, the model is adaptable to organizations that take responsibility for using action learning as a part of their developmental repertoire; see Figure 6.6.

In Figure 6.6 the organization appoints an external set adviser. She facilitates a set consisting of members with little experience of group facilitation who gain, over time, an understanding of the set process. Over a period of, say, one year, those set members who are willing and are confident of initiating a set move on to new sets consisting of staff who are invited to join and wish to become set members for their own development.

This second stage has two possible pathways. Pathway one is where the original set members become facilitators for the new sets. Pathway two is where original set members merely act as initiators and all members of the set move into self-facilitation mode. We recommend the latter when new set members have some experience of group work.

Both pathways require the initial resource of time from the set members plus the costs of employing the set facilitator.

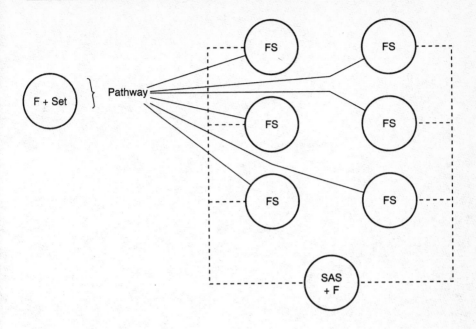

Key:
F = facilitator of the first set
FS = facilitated set
SAS = set advisers' set for the facilitators of new sets, with F as set adviser for facilitators
     of the other sets

Figure 6.7 *Support for internal facilitator*

Finally, if the organization wishes the 'new' internal facilitators as in pathway one above to have their own support, the original set facilitator may act as set adviser to the facilitators, as shown in Figure 6.7.

PART II
DEVELOPING ACTION LEARNING SKILLS

Chapter 7

A Workshop for Introducing Action Learning

Our purpose in this chapter is to describe an approach to a workshop that conveys a real sense of what action learning is to potential users of the method before they fully commit themselves to working in action learning sets. An organization or group may decide that action learning may meet some of its needs and purposes. As advocates or consultants we have the task of convincing potential users of the advantages of using action learning.

We are addressing two potentially overlapping groups. The first are managers, trainers and staff developers, who may be considering using action learning for professional, managerial development of their staff. This group could also include educationalists and teachers who may wish to use action learning as a vehicle for learning in courses. The second potential group are those staff, managers and students who may be the participants in a set for their developmental and learning needs. The latter would also include those considering an independent set.

We believe that the most effective way to convey the potential value of action learning is to *do* it. We have found that those who wish to use action learning may have read about action learning, may have had action learning described to them but they may still remain sceptical because of an unfamiliarity with this way of working together. There are severe limitations to the verbal description of the process because the description lacks the key ingredient of people actually engaging together. *Doing* action learning overcomes these problems and gives them a real feel for the process – how it works for them.

Uses of the workshop

This workshop method and approach can be used for the following purposes:

- To introduce participants to action learning as a vehicle for their personal and/or management development who are unaware of the process of action learning. Participants may then follow through with planned programmes of action learning sessions.
- As above but with the intention to follow the session with a programme of action learning that is self-facilitated, ie, without a set adviser (McGill *et al*, 1990). Here the set adviser models practice that is later emulated by all members.
- With participants who are familiar with action learning but who wish to become set advisers. The workshop gives participants the opportunity to observe the process of action learning.
- As a basis for 'cascading' in organizations. Once action learning becomes an organic part of the development of staff in an organization, the workshop can be used to introduce staff new to the method.

Workshop benefits

The workshop conveys the nature of action learning. The method has the following advantages:

- Experimentation before commitment. The method acknowledges that participants at an introductory workshop may not yet have fully committed themselves to joining or starting a set. The participants can therefore obtain a close understanding of the process before fully committing themselves.
- Working with a large group of potential action learners. We are also frequently asked to introduce action learning to a significant number of people who may form more than one set. The workshop method enables us to reach a wide number of interested people. We have had as many as 40 engaged in this initial workshop but the more usual number is between 12 and 20 participants.
- Convey more accurately the *how* of action learning. The workshop enables potential action learners to get an idea and a feel of what it is like to be in a set. The key to action learning is in the process as well as what is dealt with

at the set – the content. The process is about *how* a set works. An analogy might be learning about a new activity, say, cycling or swimming. You can read about it, have it described to you but it is not the same as doing it. Similarly with action learning – doing it makes all the difference to understanding and feeling what it is like to be a member of a set.

- The workshop method works. The method serves its purpose and engenders enthusiasm beyond that associated with merely having action learning described.
- Self-screening. The workshop has a benefit once action learning sets are created, for it means that there is a greater likelihood of the set(s) continuing and maintaining itself. 'Self-screening' can occur at the workshop stage. This is useful as it reduces the number of those who may join a set but subsequently decide that it is not really what they expected and then leave. When such early withdrawal from a set happens the numbers in the set may be reduced so that the set is no longer viable. This in turn can be dispiriting to the active and committed set members. A new set that has experienced the introductory workshop method is thus more likely to take off successfully, maintain its numbers and be effective for each individual and as a set.
- Cost effectiveness. The workshop is cost effective in reaching a wide number of potential users and ensures that the sets that are created are more likely to maintain their numbers and use the process of action learning more effectively and at an earlier stage. We have used the approach in universities, local authorities, companies, and at conferences and workshops. Participants have been professionals, managers, academics, administrators, students and self-support groups, the latter wanting to go further than just being support groups.

How the introductory workshop is organized

The workshop has four phases which may be modified according to the time available. A full-day workshop will enable all phases below to be undertaken. It is possible to adapt the workshop to fit a minimum time of three hours. In this description we will assume a day for the workshop. The phases are as follows:

1) Introduction to action learning.
2) Concentric circles.

3) Practising action learning in sets.
4) Reflection and moving on.

In Phase 1 we aim to give a brief overview of the purpose of the day, a description of what action learning is, how it can be used and in what contexts. Phase 2, concentric circles, is the key to the workshop and the core activity. This phase conveys to the whole workshop the nature of action learning through *doing* it. Phase 3, practising action learning in sets, gives all the participants a more direct experience of action learning by running sets concurrently for part of the workshop. Phase 4, reflection and moving on, enables all participants to review the workshop and reflect upon the potential of action learning. We will detail the activities within each phase. The phases are shown in Figure 7.1 which could form the basis for a workshop programme.

Prior briefing

The facilitator may also be a consultant or adviser to the organization wanting to use action learning. It is assumed in this chapter that the

Prior briefing with the organization or sponsor

PHASE 1
Introduction to the day:
Purpose, structure and format

Working in Triads
Plenary debriefing and reflection on triads

PHASE 2
Concentric circles
Plenary reflection on the process
One-to-one reflection on the process

PHASE 3
Practising action learning in sets

PHASE 4
Workshop reflection

Moving on
Ending

Figure 7.1 *The phases of an introductory workshop*

organization as client will have determined with the consultant/adviser the purpose for which action learning is to be used. This is critically important, not only for the success of the developmental intentions of the client, but also will underpin the success and *raison d'être* of the workshop.

In the briefing the facilitator should determine the background of those attending, including their familiarity with working in groups, participative forms of learning and working together, and the skills that are a particular emphasis in action learning. Participants who are not familiar with group work and experiential learning may well feel some caution about the process. The facilitator needs to be sensitive to these feelings and adapt the workshop accordingly. The length of the workshop is also critical. A day workshop allows more scope for gradual entry to the use of concentric circles. More limited time may mean that some of the phases need to be sacrificed. The key is to create a safe environment using time with effect and sensitivity. By the end of the workshop participants should be aware of what action learning can be like and what they may potentially achieve.

Phase 1: Introduction to action learning

This phase includes a description of what action learning is, how it can be used and in what contexts it is appropriate. Further, an outline of the structure and purpose of the workshop will enable participants to clarify what they will wish to achieve.

The workshop starts with introductions and a useful warm-up activity that is appropriate for the group. The warm-up is designed to create an environment that contributes to developing trust and support. The activity will ensure that everybody gets to know each other, their first names, roles (if appropriate), their expectations of the workshop and something that the group do not know about 'me' that 'I' am willing to share with the group. This is just one format for starting the workshop. There are many others. This is followed with an outline of the purpose and structure of the day. It also useful at this point to ask participants what each of them wishes to achieve by the end of the workshop and to put these on a flip chart. These can be reviewed at the end of the day. Here it is emphasized that we will be experiencing individually and collectively action learning and related activities. To undertake the experiential activities effectively requires an atmosphere of confidentiality and trust in a safe environment. Through the remainder of this chapter we aim to convey the kinds of conditions which facilitators and participants can follow to ensure those requirements. Each phase and activity needs to convey the conditions for creating safety, confidentiality and trust appropriate to that activity.

We follow the brief warm-up with the participant in groups of three in an exercise known as 'triads'. For participants with little experience of interpersonal skills training or group activity we find this is a valuable entry to action learning work, enabling each participant to present an issue with another giving attentive listening. Triads take about one and a half hours and are very effective in introducing participants to the process of enabling individuals to work to some purpose on their issues or problem as well as heightening participants' sensitivity to the skills of presenting, enabling and observing which occur in an action learning set. The triad process is a 'safe' activity because, as its name suggests, three people work together for the designated period before working in a larger group in Phase 2. The triad is a stepping stone to the next phase as it enables participants to use and acknowledge skills in a small group as well as creating the conditions for trust to be engendered.

Participants in triads frequently say how unusual it is to have such undivided attention. To be really listened to as a presenter is an important ingredient of action learning as is the complementary capacity to listen on the part of the enabler.

The workshop participants are each given a written description of the triad activity as well as having it described by the facilitator. (The description is shown below.) After describing the activity and before they go into their groups, participants are asked what conditions they would wish to prevail in the triads. These are flipcharted and then become by agreement the ground rules for work in the triads.

Participants are divided into groups of three (or four where there is not a multiple of three). The groups can be self-selecting with a suggestion that participants work with those whom they least know or do not know. Alternatively the facilitator can with agreement count round the group to divide into groups. Sometimes, this 'random' approach makes it easier for participants who are little known to each other. They are then invited to engage in the process set out below.

After describing the activity and before they go into their groups, participants are asked what conditions they would wish to prevail in the triads. These are flipcharted and then become by agreement the ground rules for work in the triads.

Confidentiality is the most significant. By confidentiality we mean that each participant in the triad agrees that the content of each other person's issue and their feelings will not be disclosed outside the triad. This agreement encourages trust and greater disclosure. The participants in the triad are also asked to do their own time-keeping to ensure all have the opportunity of each role. The times given are broad indicators. A triad may find that one or two of their number may require more time to consider their issue, in which case they can negotiate the allocation of time between them. Participants when acting as observers are also asked to give specific feedback. This feedback is given within the triad group and is confidential to the members of the triad.

Triads: task/problem/issue resolution

Divide into groups in the following roles:

Presenter
You are to think of a task/problem/issue that you face in your role at work and discuss it with one of the group. Try to be brief and specific. The 'task', 'problem' or 'issue' should be of *real* concern to you.

Enabler
You are to help the presenter with his or her 'problem' by trying to get the presenter to think through his or her issues. Ask open questions (How do you know? What does this mean?). The object is to enable the presenter to define or redefine the problem/issue and their relationship to it in specific terms for the *presenter* to take some steps towards solving it. Try to focus on what can be done *by* the presenter – not what others ought to do. Some helpful questions may include:

- What could you do . . .
- It sounds as though you are feeling . . .
- How does that make you feel . . .
- What do you think is really going on . . .
- What do you think would happen if . . .
- Do you think that . . .
- How would you know if . . .
- How can you . . .

Observer
The observer listens to what is being *said*. You observe the verbal interaction and consider what questions/responses were more/less helpful in enabling the presenter to move forward his or her issue. The observer also listens to/senses what the *feelings* of the presenter are in relation to their issue.

Finally, the observer also listens to/senses what the presenter has *invested* (or not) in the issue. What is the presenter's *will, commitment* or *motivation* toward the issue and its possible resolution?

Further points the observer may wish to consider include:

- is the enabler providing solutions for the presenter?
- is the presenter focusing on what they can do?
- is the presenter avoiding resolving the problem?
- is the presenter's proposed action specific enough?

Take 20–25 minutes between presenter and enabler. After the session and a pause, the presenter and enabler convey how the experience was for them. The observer then gives feedback for 5 minutes to the 'enabler' on how their behaviour aided the presenter, followed by 5 minutes to the presenter, and then the presenter and 'enabler' may wish to add their comments. Change roles in order that each person can take the role of enabler and presenter.

During the triad activity the facilitator may go round some of the groups and give feedback from observation that may not have been already covered by the observer to the presenter and enabler.

At the end of the activity, when all participants have experienced each role, the workshop participants are invited into a plenary circle to reflect on what they have gained from the activity and how it felt doing the activity. Each person should be given time to convey their thoughts and feelings. The facilitator can draw on the reflection to make comparisons with the process of action learning.

The round of reflection is useful to enable participants to understand the value of the process of the triad, the skills that are being harnessed and that the activity embraces some of the skills and roles that are found in action learning. The plenary reflections can commence with the flip charted conditions that participants wished to prevail before they went into triads. They can be asked to comment on whether the conditions did prevail or not, and if they wish to add or modify any in the light of the experience.

As presenter, the participants gain experience in having specific time for an issue or problem that is relevant and of concern to them. The presenter may be very clear about the issue being raised or start with only a tentative idea or a feeling about something; either way they are given undivided attention to their issue. The key here is that the enabler is able to attend to the presenter without having a vested interest in the presenter's issues. The enabler gains experience in the act of attending to another person and is given feedback on their skills in listening, questioning, empathizing, challenging and confronting. Participants state how rare it is to get feedback on their use of these skills; they also convey in the plenary reflections how difficult it is not to try to provide the presenter with solutions! As observers, participants gain experience in a role which is rarely exercised in this form. In normal circumstances of interaction with others they are not usually 'detached' from the interaction.

Following the plenary reflection using triads we can now move to the central phase.

Phase 2: Concentric circles

This phase conveys to the whole workshop the nature of action learning through *doing* and experiencing it. This is the key to the workshop and the core activity that would be the basis of a workshop even with more limited time.

This phase commences with a verbal and, if helpful, a flip chart description of the way in which the concentric circles work and how participants can prepare themselves for the activity. The concentric circles consist of an inner circle of participants who work as an action learning set with a set adviser (the facilitator) and an outer circle of participants acting as observers of the action learning process taking place in the inner circle. The concentric circles are shown in Figure 7.2.

The inner circle is for the 'set' with a spare chair left vacant. The outer circle is for observers of the process and content. Participants as observers in

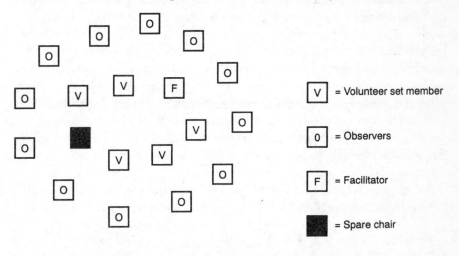

Figure 7.2 *Introducing action learning with concentric circles*

121

the outer circle have the opportunity to take the chair when appropriate.

At this point it may be helpful to explain the reasons for using the circles method. Action learning requires to be experienced in order for each participant to get near to understanding its potentiality. If there are more participants than can be accommodated in a single set the use of circles can enable some of the participants to experience working directly in a set whilst the other participants can observe the process. As with the introduction to triads, the facilitator may wish to ask participants what conditions they would wish to prevail for the circles activity, perhaps adding to those used in the triads. This can also form the basis for reflection after the activity.

The participants are then asked if some will volunteer to work in the inner circle. Four to six volunteers are invited from the whole group who will form the 'set' with the facilitator of the workshop as set adviser. Volunteers are asked to think of an important, unresolved but real issue/problem/ opportunity that has no obvious solution, which they are willing to talk through in the 'set' and with the outer circle of participants observing the process. Depending on time, the volunteers are also informed that we may only be able to take one or two of the 'set'.

Those who form the outer circle are asked to observe the content of the set discussion and, more importantly to observe the *process*. The content is the presenter's issue or problem. The process is what is happening in the set whilst the set is dealing with the issue – the *how* of action learning. The prior triad session provides a useful introduction to the role of observers in this session.

The volunteer set members can also be asked if they are willing to receive personal feedback from a participant who is acting as an observer in the outer circle. As facilitator, it is usual in inviting this additional form of feedback to suggest that the set member requests someone from the outer circle. That person may be someone they know or do not know but feel comfortable with. All observers then observe and make notes of the process, content and some observers additionally observe one person in particular in the set. It is emphasized prior to the action learning activity that the observer will give the feedback to the set member on a one-to-one basis privately after the plenary feedback on the whole process, providing a safer environment for the set member to receive feedback.

Two circles of chairs are formed for the 'set' and observers. In the inner circle an additional chair is left for any of the observers in the outer circle to occupy, for a moment only, to pose a question about content or to convey a process observation that may enable the 'set' to progress. The vacant chair is a useful device for it usually commits the interest of observers without losing sight of their main role. We will return to this type of intervention later.

The set then proceeds like a normal set. Ideally two facilitators run the workshop, one of whom will take the role of set adviser in the inner circle and model the role of set adviser as outlined in Chapter 5. The other facilitator joins the outer circle as one of the process observers. If there is only one facilitator, she should take the role of set adviser. In this chapter we only emphasize those particular tasks for the set adviser that enable the set to operate in this 'unusual' context.

The set adviser will aim to relax the volunteer set members who may initially feel some natural anxiety about being in the middle and under observation. Our experience is that once we get going that concern reduces significantly. Again a warm-up is beneficial to allay that concern and also help the forming of the set. One particular activity here that does not take too much time is called, 'Trauma, trivia and joy' and is set out below. This is a very useful activity for it enables the members of the set to convey how they are feeling with an informal immediacy.

Trauma, trivia and joy (adapted, with thanks to John Southgate)

Each person in the group is asked to convey briefly an event or incident, one of which could be termed a trauma, another a trivia, and one a joy that has happened to them in the last day or so. Each member of the set takes a turn describing their events, including the set adviser who may start and therefore model the activity.

There is no discussion of the events. Other set members usually convey their empathy and feelings with the occasional word or feeling, the effect of which is to create a warm and supportive atmosphere, relax the set members and help the set to get to know each other a little. Set members are asked not to invent events if they have not actually occurred. If a set member has just a joy and trivia that is fine. If a set member wishes not to be included in this activity and 'pass' that is also legitimate. Most participants find the activity light and energizing.

Moreover, the activity may trigger an issue that a set member wishes to address and/or the event may unwittingly become a key part of the issue.

The activity will take about 5 to 15 minutes depending on the numbers participating. It is important not to rush an individual but to convey the idea that it is a brief 'warm-up' to get us going.

With the warm-up completed, set members are then asked to describe in cameo form the issue that they would like to bring to the set. This is an important moment. As set adviser it is necessary to remind the set members that we will only have time for one person's issue or two at the most. Asking each person to convey the issue they would like to bring to the group is important in two ways. First, it conveys to the set and the outer circle of observers the range of issues that the volunteer members of the set would like to bring to the set. This immediately conveys to all present what individuals consider they could bring to the set that could be useful for them. In terms of conveying the potential of action learning, hearing examples of what could be brought to a set is instructive. Second, hearing the issues that could come before the set helps the set members to make up their minds on which person's issue they would like to consider. A set member may decide that another's is more pertinent than the one they raised. Describing the issues also conveys some significant openness and courage to all those listening. Examples of issues that volunteer set members might bring forward could be:

- organizing my time over the day (week or any period) at work;
- balancing my priorities of work with the rest of my life;
- deciding whether to register for a postgraduate qualification;
- how can I ensure that my 0.5 job share stays at 0.5 and does not become a near full-time job?
- being new to the post how can I get support without conveying the impression that I am not 'up' to the job?

Note that the issues are critical to the person conveying them. What is brought to the volunteer set will depend on the degree of trust and therefore safety the volunteer feels towards the people in the circles. It is appropriate for the facilitator to emphasize that volunteers only bring issues that they feel safe to bring to this unusual situation, particularly in organizational settings. Once a normal set is in operation the safety is usually enhanced and the trust enables more openness and disclosure of more sensitive and personal issues.

It is important that the set adviser lets the set members come to agreement about whose issue is considered. In the event of stalemate when the set members cannot agree whose issue should be taken the set adviser may have to resolve it. In our experience this has only happened once. At the suggestion of the set adviser it was amicably resolved with the toss of a coin! This, incidentally, ensured that the set adviser was not steering what should be discussed and who would bring their issue, only the process of moving on.

Guidelines for the 'set' members

Here we give only a brief indication of the main guidelines for a set in the workshop as full details are given elsewhere (see Chapters 2, 3, 4 and 5). Also, when facilitating a set in the workshop, we aim to minimize the verbal description of the process.

Once the set has agreed who will volunteer, the set adviser re-emphasizes briefly that the presenter has 40 minutes in total as their time – the initial, say, 10 minutes of which is for the presenter to convey her thoughts on the issue to the set as listeners. Following her introduction to her issue, the set members and adviser can ask questions that seek to clarify what she as presenter has conveyed and to check out their understanding of her thoughts and feelings. The set adviser also emphasizes that the questioning should be supportive of the presenter in enabling the latter to focus on their issue. The interaction should be supportive yet challenging for the presenter. The interaction is not an interrogation!

The aim of the set is to enable the presenter to reach her own solutions, not for the other set members to present their solutions to her. This is the key to the whole process of interaction between the presenter and colleagues in the set. This enables the presenter to begin *taking* responsibility for her actions.

During the time taken by the presenter, she may say something like, 'I ought to do this because . . .'. It is often very helpful to ask the presenter what she means by 'ought'. This enables the presenter to distinguish between 'oughts' and 'wants' and to clarify their thoughts and feelings on an issue. Complementary to this is drawing the attention of set members to the danger of 'oughts' hidden in questions that may be designed to be helpful to the presenter but are actually solutions they consciously or unconsciously wish to impose on the presenter.

Further details of the operation of the set are given in Chapters 3 and 4. As facilitator of the introductory session and as acting set adviser it is important to convey to the 'set' and the observers just sufficient information to get started. Otherwise there is a danger of the facilitator doing the very thing he or she wishes to avoid, namely talking about action learning as opposed to giving participants experience of the process of doing it. The above indicators by the set adviser are therefore the minimum to get the set working and avoid inadequate outcomes in terms of the learning about the potential effectiveness of action learning.

As the volunteer presenter nears the end of her issue she is asked to convey how she would like to take her issue forward following the meeting and possibly to 'contract' with another person on the workshop to ensure action occurs. The contract is simply an agreement to contact the other person within a given period of time (say, a month) to convey the presenter's progress on action she agreed in the set. Undertaking a 'contract' of this kind replaces the usual arrangement set members have between one meeting and the next – a crucial aspect of set activity which the workshop cannot replicate.

One or two volunteers will have taken about one hour. It is important to judge the total length of time so that there is sufficient range of the process without losing the attention of the observers.

Reflection on the process by the participants
Before completion of Phase 2 it is necessary for the workshop to reflect on the process of the inner circle or set. The workshop participants then form one circle. Following a short break, it is important to enable the inner circle 'set' members to start by conveying their initial feelings about the process. We usually suggest that the presenter(s) is last in this part of the reflection. The presenter should also have the option to opt out of this, as should all the inner circle, if they wish to. This is simply to recognize that the set members and particularly the presenter may well have become very engaged in the process and have feelings and emotions that they wish to gradually lighten but are not yet ready to reflect upon.

Going round, each person in the outer circle who observed the process then relates their description of the process. It is in this reflection stage that participants gain their understanding of what action learning is really about. There is a tendency for the observers from the outer circle to re-engage with the content as opposed to conveying their feedback about the process observed and what was significant in that process. It is unhelpful for the presenter to have the content 'opened up' after she has agreed her actions. The only exception here is if a reference to the content is necessary to make a point about process.

Participants may wish to follow up the process discussion by highlighting the main points on flip chart for reflection, building on the conditions agreed at the beginning of the activity. Following the plenary reflection on the process observed by the outer circle, those observers who additionally observed, by prior agreement, a set member, give feedback in confidence to that person on a one-to-one basis.

Phase 3: Practising action learning in sets

Phase 3 gives all the participants an experience of action learning by running sets for part of the workshop concurrently. This part of the workshop will depend upon the number of participants and facilitators and the experience of the participants. Sets are created with five or six participants per set. Participants can be facilitated with set advisers if there are enough for the number of sets required or there can be a combination of facilitated and self-facilitated sets.

Facilitators and participants in sets in this part of the workshop will again be constrained by time. The same process as for the inner circle in Phase 2 will be applied. One or two volunteers will be invited following an appropriate warm-up and brief summaries of each person's issue described to the set. The major difference in this stage is that all participants are engaged as direct participants in the sets without external observers. In this phase all participants integrate the role of observation into their role as set members.

Timing of the set is left to the set adviser with an indication of when the sets will come back into plenary for the final reflection. Time available will determine whether there are one or more presenters within each set. Ten minutes or so is appropriate at the end of the set session to enable each person in the set to convey within the set how the process felt for them.

Phase 4: Reflection: gains from the day and moving on

With Phases 1 to 3 completed, the workshop can conclude with an overall reflection on the day. The purpose of this stage is to enable participants to reflect on what they have gained and learned individually and collectively. Before engaging in the reflection it is appropriate to use a short period for any factual clarification by participants of any aspects of the action learning process and the potential uses of action learning.

How can this important stage be organized for maximum effect for each participant? Participants can be asked a range of questions that enable them to reflect upon the workshop with a view to its relevance and future use for them. Working individually, then in pairs, participants could be asked to reflect upon the following questions:

- What have I gained/learned from the workshop today:
  for myself
  in my work (if applicable)
  in relation to my colleagues and friends?
- What personal changes will I undertake/implement myself and with colleagues?
- Where do I/we go from here?

- What actions am I going to take:
  from my work in the 'set' (if the participant had this opportunity)
  to enable me to influence the forming of a set and/or create a set?

The responses to the above questions will depend upon the nature of the relationship of the participants at the workshop. For example, if the workshop is organizationally based, the focus may be on a structured response to the creation of sets for staff and management development purposes as outlined in Chapter 2. The manager responsible for staff development can then move on to devising a programme of development using action learning sets with the knowledge of those who wish to engage in this approach.

If the workshop has been organized round individual responses to attending then the questions may require participants to assess how they may get sets going in their work, amongst voluntary groups or with colleagues and friends. Sets may also be based on gender or ethnicity to enable participants to work on issues common to them.

Following the pairs work, participants can then share their ideas and feelings in a final plenary. This ensures a cross-fertilization of the ideas and can act as an energizer for each participant. The workshop can then conclude with an appropriate round such as a single phrase which sums up the day for each of the participants.

Chapter 8

Skills Development: The Basics

The purpose of this and the next chapter is to enable set members to consider the interpersonal skills they use that make for effective working of the set for themselves and for other members of the set. Facilitators may wish to use some of the activities to focus on a skill that could be developed or enhanced by members of the set. Chapters 8 and 9 are also intended for action learning practitioners to reflect on their current use of the skills. We would like to emphasize that these chapters are to be used as a resource when particular set members and facilitators wish to give attention to a skill(s) that they wish to practise and/or reflect upon.

Groups: working together

Group working calls for good basic interpersonal skills that have only recently been addressed in schools and post-school education. It has been suggested (Egan, 1976; Heron, 1989) that in British and American cultures we do not give much explicit attention to the development of our interpersonal skills. We would endorse that general view. Egan (1976) stated it this way:

> when I suggest to some people that they may profit from involvement in a . . . group, they respond (at least non-verbally) as if I had asked them to take a trip to Antarctica. They don't feel prepared for a group experience because their lives have been devoid of similar experiences.

The educational experiences of most of us in our culture will have centred round the teacher with the occasional 'group discussion', but we are rarely asked or enabled to be personal in a group or to share ourselves with any degree of openness.

Heron's (1989) view, in a UK context, is that we tend to lack basic human skills:

> skills in handling (our) own feelings, skills in interacting with other persons, skills in self-direction and collective decision-making.

We would agree with these statements with a reservation – that we have and try to use the skills but that they are not consciously developed.

Until a few years ago, although we have been called teachers, lecturers and tutors, we had not paid much attention to the development of our interpersonal skills, and if asked to engage in such an activity to explore and enhance those skills we would have found a way of avoiding the situation as potentially embarrassing and very exposing. At the same time, we as tutors would be asking students in higher education to work in groups on assignments or projects, somehow expecting them to do it without doing it ourselves in other contexts or modelling effective group practice with students. Similarly, we would expect managers to work in groups assuming they found group work straightforward.

Our personal experience was a common one in higher education and in many other organizations. Developed skills in this area were the preserve of some of the 'caring' professions like counselling, therapy and social work. The notion that such skills were the preserve of these professions only deepened prejudice about their use in other contexts. Fortunately the enhancement of these basic skills is now seen as a prerequisite for personal effectiveness as managers, teachers, lecturers, retailers and in most working (and personal) situations. As colleagues in work we can make for better working relationships by enhancing these skills.

For a number of years now we have believed, and put into practice our belief, that interpersonal skills and personal effectiveness in groups are very important. Few of us live and work in isolation; so much of our experience in work and life rests upon being effective in the presence of and with other people. Having knowledge about something may be useless if we cannot convey, act, interrelate, in a manner that is effective for the purpose.

Groups that are facilitated inappropriately or insensitively can, partly because of the facilitator's lack of skills training, actually compound the difficulty for participants. Shock stories then move on to the rumour track and frighten off more people from group-based work.

Demystification about how sets work has been a major purpose of this book. Action learning is a particular form of group working that is highly structured and supportive of participant set members. The structured way in which the set works is particularly important in the early life of a set when participants may be apprehensive about working in groups. The way the group is intended to work in an action learning set creates a very supportive group environment. Yet with practice and some continuity it can be a challenging and non-collusive environment beneficial to its members. A productive balance of challenge and support can be achieved within a set by judicious use of interpersonal skills, and in this chapter we will review the range of skills which may be deployed by set members. Chapter 3 describes the basic processes of a set meeting. If these procedures are broadly adhered to then the set can begin to work safely. Set members may like to refer to Chapter 4 to complement the skills addressed in this and the next chapter.

Interpersonal skills

This review of interpersonal skills is designed to enable readers to focus on their current interpersonal style and possibly modify it in order to enhance their interpersonal effectiveness. We distinguish between basic and additional interpersonal skills. Listening, reflection and disclosure are basic skills. These basic skills provide the foundation for assertive behaviour and the effective use of higher level skills. The latter include the expression of emotion and empathy. Using these additional skills effectively produces a rapport among set members which enables giving and receiving of feedback. Set members, by actively listening, reflecting back, and offering empathy and feedback, can effectively help focus and specify those actions the presenter wishes to take.

The remainder of this and the next chapter will address the following skills:

Basic Skills:
Listening and attending
Reflecting back and questioning
Disclosure and assertion

Additional Skills (Chapter 9):
Management of emotion
Empathy
Giving and receiving feedback
Shoulds and oughts
Generalizations
Specifying actions

We will continue to use the term 'presenter' for the set member conveying her issues to the set. The listener is any set member or the facilitator. We will also, where appropriate, use an example drawn from experience, of a woman as presenter conveying issues which are important to her, to other set members and a facilitator. We will refer to this example in the text to develop the significance of the skills in use.

Listening and attending

Listening

When an action learning set is working effectively as a set, in particular for the person presenting, the whole set is *really* listening. We regard this as one of the basic skills brought to a set. It is a basic skill but probably the most important upon which the remainder of the skills we address in this chapter depend. By listening we mean the ability of the listener to 'capture and understand the messages [presenters] communicate, whether these messages are transmitted verbally or nonverbally, clearly or vaguely' (Egan, 1990).

People spend much of their lives listening, unless they have an impediment in their hearing. It is a very familiar activity. However, despite the significance of listening, people experience *not* being listened to. We still are surprised by the commentary from a set member that has this refrain:

> It really is a luxury to be listened to, really listened to. In my work I can go through the week with colleagues without them knowing what I am feeling or thinking. I suspect I am the same with them.

or

> This is the only place where I have the space to be listened to. No one listens to each other in the department.

Set members when reviewing how their set has worked over a cycle of meetings refer to how affirming it is to be listened to by other set members. Affirmation of the person expresses that person's essential worth as a human being just as the opposite behaviour can undermine that essential worth. This is easy to say, but there is a tendency for us to lose what a person has said because we may listen very inattentively. We may lose a significant part of what is being said simply because the act of verbal communication is itself complex even though we take it for granted. See what happens when A communicates with B in the example below.

Losing the message

A has a feeling or an idea she wishes to express.
A finds words that may or may not accurately reflect her idea.
A transmits her message.
B receives physical sounds and visual signals and decodes them.
B relates the message to her own feelings and ideas, may make judgements, create arguments, perhaps while A is still speaking, and may miss part of the message.
At this point B may decode incorrectly for all sorts of reasons:

- lack of understanding
- parts of the message are lost
- confusion caused by conflict between verbal and non-verbal information
- having a negative or positive 'fix'.

By the word 'fix' we mean the tendency for selective listening – only hearing what we want to hear. We often evaluate the listener as they are speaking, eg, when a politician of a different persuasion to ourselves speaks, we may 'switch off' and only hear what we want to hear. Similarly with a politician of our own persuasion! The listener evaluates the message as it is transmitted, judges it and rejects or accepts it without critical analysis. Whilst this is common it can lead to poor interpersonal relations in work, in relationships and certainly would be less than useful in an action learning set.
There are many ways in which the message can be lost!

How can we reduce this loss of what is transmitted? We can do so by *attending* to the presenter, suspending our responses to enable us to reflect on the presenter's message, and checking internally that we are with the presenter in a non-judgemental way.

Attending

Attending refers to the way in which we can be *with* our presenter (in the context of a set meeting) both physically and psychologically. A feature of a set meeting where listening by the whole set is happening is the sense of the presenter being attended to. By this is meant the quality of the attention the other set members are giving to the presenter. Egan (1990) has characterized this with the useful acronym SOLER to convey the minimum requirements for a listener (set member and facilitator) to attend to a presenter.

S – face the presenter *squarely*, that is with a posture that conveys involvement, reflects the presenter in a positive manner and indicates that you wish to be with the presenter. This is not meant to be in a threatening manner but just one that suggests you wish to be with them – inclining towards the presenter. The posture shows that you are not distracted.

O – adopting an *open* posture. Crossed arms and legs may convey a closed stance towards the presenter. Such a posture may not necessarily mean that you are closed toward the presenter, but it may convey it non-verbally to her. The key question to ask is to what extent is my physical posture conveying an openness and availability to the presenter?

L – at times it is possible to *lean* toward the presenter in a way which suggests engagement. We can see this when observing people in pubs and restaurants leaning forward, leaning back or away.

E – maintain *eye* contact with the presenter. This is a useful indicator of involvement which does not have to be continuous to be effective. It does not mean 'eyeball to eyeball' either!

R – be relatively *relaxed* in your behaviour. This means not being physically distracting or fidgety. It also means being comfortable with the presenter so that your body can convey non-verbal expression.

A commitment to listening to the presenter, utilizing SOLER, ensures authenticity. Contriving a physical stance will convey messages that are counter-productive for the presenter. Negative or uncomfortable messages might include staring, getting too squared up so that it becomes threatening, looking out of a window continually or tapping a pencil on a table! Being aware of the effect of your physical and emotional presence is the key. SOLER is useful to convey the basic features of attending. To the reader unfamiliar with the approach it may appear that to adopt the features could suggest a lack of genuineness or manipulation. It is designed rather to highlight what we all do naturally when we are authentically attending.

Active listening

Effectively attending to the presenter means that set members are in a position to listen carefully to what the presenter is saying verbally and non-verbally. Egan (1990) expresses active or complete listening as involving four things:

first, observing and reading the [presenter's] non-verbal behaviour – posture, facial expressions, movement, tone of voice, and the like; second, listening to and understanding the [presenter's] verbal messages; third, listening to the whole person in the context of the social settings of life; fourth, tough-minded listening.

In observing non-verbal behaviour it is important to recognize that we are still listening to presenters in a way that deepens our understanding of what they are trying to convey. It is helpful in forming an overall picture of where the presenter is. It is inappropriate to fix on an expression of non-verbal behaviour and then to create a total impression from that single piece of information. However, see our note on feedback in Chapter 9.

Listening to and understanding the presenter's verbal messages are part of the whole picture. At this point the listener does not form her responses to the presenter but listens.

Engaging in the attentive behaviours described by SOLER will enhance the development of the skill of creative listening. An example would be where a presenter is telling what it is like for her, working in an office where there is a manager continuously baiting her for not adopting the norms of the office, which include late working in a predominately male work force. The listener may have some views about how he would cope in such an environment. For example, he may think, 'I could cope with that' or, 'It would not be a problem for me'. But if he listens to his own thoughts on coping, he may detract from how she is thinking, feeling and being in *her* environment. The key is for our listener to 'put aside' his own responses to her situation and listen from the presenter's standpoint – where she is coming from. As we shall see below, even when the listener responds, it is necessary to work with where she is and not give his own solutions to her predicament. Any responses should empower her to deal with her situation in a manner that is enabling for her.

Our listener will, if effective, place himself (as far as is possible as a man) in her context. That is, he will endeavour to understand what it is like to be a woman in a mostly male environment, to tackle a prevailing norm that she feels oppressed by. Rather than get trapped in his own contextual picture, what is her picture that he needs to understand to enable her to deal with it? In this way he will be endeavouring to get into her social context – how working life is for her.

Tough-minded listening requires that our listener places himself in the frame of the presenter so that he really understands where she is coming from. It also means that he picks up what is perhaps being distorted by the presenter. For example, our presenter may be talking about going for a promotion in the organization and how she is well qualified for it. However, she is also conveying less explicitly through her voice tone, demeanour and some of her words that she may feel that she is not confident to do the job if promoted. This is turn may affect her will to apply for the post. It is for the listener to pick up this inconsistency and hold it until it is appropriate to offer it as an observation.

Hearing, active and passive listening

Contrast the distinction between hearing, passive listening and active listening. If you close your eyes you can hear what is going on around you (unless you have a hearing impediment) as well as inner sounds inside you. Even though we close our eyes we may well be interpreting what we are hearing from the sensation of the sounds – we will place meaning on the sounds through our listening. Even when we close our eyes we may listen by paying attention to what we hear. We could also be passive in simply not trying to grasp meaning from it or not really caring what we hear. Now with our eyes open we listen to somebody such as our presenter.

Listening actively is not just hearing what is being said but is a two-way process involving both sender and receiver skills. So, in the example of our presenter conveying her message about her work and promotion prospects, I as listener need to convey to her that I have received what she has tried to communicate. This is why active listening is a tough-minded process. We have to really work at it and if we are really listening it shows! The sender (presenter) is aware of the listener really listening.

Active listening also involves listening to the whole person, not just the words they may be using. Our culture emphasizes listening to what people *say*. We tend to listen at the level of our intellects. But active listening also includes observing what a person's non-verbal messages are saying – *body* messages. In addition, as senders of messages we convey our *feelings*, that is the emotional content of our message. Lastly, we have another level which can be called our will, commitment or *spirit*. Let us take our example of the presenter talking about her potential promotion.

She is saying that she is considering going for the promotion because she is well-qualified for the post. Her body is sending out messages that convey something about her feelings toward the post, as is her tone of voice. Underlying these messages is another that is transmitted about her will or spirit to go for the promotion. If as listeners we merely went by what she said we would conclude that all she needs to do is to get on with the application form. However, by actively listening and observing we are picking up more complex messages.

Contrast passive listening and the signals that are conveyed between the sender (presenter) and receiver (listener or set member). With passive listening the listener conveys, often non-verbally, that he is not really listening. Go through SOLER again and think of situations in which you have been on the receiving end of passive listening. Recall situations where you have given out the signals of passive listening to a person who wanted your attention!

Further aspects of effective listening

Apart from being passive towards the presenter there are other ways, which can overlap, that can impede the effectiveness of our listening.

Evaluative listening
When we listen evaluatively we may impose our own values upon the presenter's message. In our example of the presenter considering promotion, we may do any of the following whilst apparently listening:

think that she really hasn't a chance (or that it is a walkover);
feel jealous (why am I not going for it?);
feel dismissive (who would want the job anyway?);
make a judgement that she should not go for it.

The listener is judging what he is hearing whilst it is being transmitted instead of putting the thoughts to one side in order to hear what she is conveying. It is very difficult to put judgements aside entirely. It is important to recognize where they are coming from, however. Evaluations of the situation may be helpful at a later stage provided they enable her to move forward.

Inattentive listening
This occurs when as listener we are distracted by tiredness, our own emotions, or our difficulty with differences of culture, gender, race, sexual orientation or ability which 'get in the way' of listening.

Filtering listening according to the listener
Similar to the above, but more specifically the listener is filtering what the presenter is saying according to the listener's view of the world.

How shall I respond?
A listener preoccupied with this question (and it is understandable when we

first become conscious of our responses) may stop listening and therefore attending to the presenter. However, really active listening will not require any preparation for the listener is already likely to be at one with the presenter.

Listening with sympathy

A common and human response, but sympathy can get in the way for the presenter. For example, if at a later meeting our presenter reports that she applied for the promotion but was 'pipped' to it by another candidate, we as listeners could offer our sympathy and model what we consider to be her feelings of sorrow and loss at not getting the promotion. If we collude in this or even foster it we, as listeners, are merely getting in the way of the presenter moving on to future action. We could be disabling in our effect. Being with her empathically is different, as we shall see in the next chapter.

Listened to without interruption

Interrupting a person who is conveying her thoughts and feelings is a common trait in conversation arising from enthusiasm, boredom, having something to say ourselves, not being able to wait, emotion, or insensitivity toward the person speaking. In action learning sets one of the earliest reflections given by set members is, 'It is such a change being listened to without interruption'.

Given the time for each member of the set (25–40 minutes), a set member, when presenter, can use the early part of that time for herself. It is almost sacrosanct. It is for the other set members, as listeners, to take their cue from her before intervening.

One of the few exceptions to this is where the presenter has the need to take time to talk a matter through using most of her allotted time without receiving responses. The set adviser or other member of the set has to intervene to say that her allotted time has been used and that to continue will require agreement of the set members.

Listening with 'silence'

At times the presenter may pause or not want to express words. There may be a tendency for a set member to fill the silence or space with a question or a response. There is, in fact, no silence – it is just that the presenter has stopped using words! That 'silence' can be precious for the presenter and for the set in being with the presenter without words. The time is the presenter's. It is space for her. If that space includes silence, it is to be respected.

Reflecting back and questioning

Reflecting back

Much of listening is communicating to the presenter non-verbally that we really are listening. However, this section is distinguished from the last in that the listener now responds to the presenter in order to clarify and confirm that what the listener has received is an accurate reflection of what the presenter conveyed.

Given that non-verbal reflection has been conveyed, the listener may respond with an 'um' or 'ahah' during the presenter's commentary. This may not be the case in a set situation where there are five to seven people. An 'um' response is more likely in a one-to-one situation. However, the set will still give that confirmatory nod or whatever to confirm the presenter.

Once the presenter has conveyed that she has concluded her story, any member of the set may respond. Indeed when used effectively it can mean that the presenter benefits from having a group of people attending to her with what may be called a 'collective wisdom'. One member may attune to the presenter more closely than others and follow it through with reflecting back what has been conveyed, along with clarifications.

Given that the set member will wish to reflect back what he thinks he has heard, he may wish to start with phrases like, 'What I think you said was . . .', or 'If I have understood you properly . . .'. The purpose here is to *accurately* reflect back to the presenter what the listener thought she said. Using the presenter's exact words in 'reverse' may be helpful, if the meaning is unclear. An inappropriate response would be to:

- give an interpretation of what was said rather than an accurate response;
- make and convey an assumption beyond what was said.

This description may appear simple, obvious or even banal as set out on this page. It is stated here because of our social tendency to assess and interpret and think what we are going to say even before the presenter has finished. It is an important process to disentangle so that we really are attending to the presenter and not imposing our own view of her reality.

The listener in responding should aim to do so in a way that is not pedantic or interrogative. The tone of voice is important. A tone which suggests criticism or a lack of caring or agreement is not helpful. The aim is to reflect back what is being said – the presenter's words and meaning; her emotions, her feelings; her will or spirit.

The reflecting back does not have to repeat the words our presenter used exactly. It is useful to paraphrase so that she can respond with say, 'Yes, that's it', or 'Not quite, I would put it like this', until there is assent between presenter and listener. Moreover, by paraphrasing the listener is also going beyond simply saying, 'I understand' when in fact he may not and he has not demonstrated to the presenter that he has and she does not really know he has understood. The use of the notorious phrase, 'I hear what you say' may also convey the same lack of real understanding between listener and presenter!

Questioning

Questioning has been defined as:

> one of the most widely used social skills. . . . A question can be defined as a request for information, whether factual or otherwise (Hargie *et al*, 1987).

The use of questions to enable learning in an action learning set carries with it status and control issues relating to common uses of questioning. In many social interactions the majority of questions are often asked by persons with power and status in relation to the person being questioned, eg teachers, lawyers, doctors, etc. The tendency is for these 'higher' status persons to ask most of the questions to elicit information from which they can draw conclusions.

However, for a set member, questioning is for the benefit of the presenter. That is, questions aim to *enable* the presenter to broaden and deepen her view of the situation or issue she is addressing. Hence set members may need to adjust their usual style of questioning to ensure that the day-to-day eliciting/interrogative function of questioning does not supersede the enabling function in the set.

Deeper appreciation of an issue can be achieved by questions that are open, affective, reflective, and probing, rather than closed or leading.

Open questions

These are phrased to give the presenter a high degree of freedom in deciding how to respond. For example:

> How do you get on with your colleague?

is an open question inviting the presenter to consider the nature of a relationship. This type of question allows the presenter to express opinions, attitudes, thoughts and feelings. Responses to open questions are known to contain more self-revelation and to be significantly longer than responses to closed questions.

Closed questions
These are useful to elicit information that may help a set member to clarify or seek further understanding. Closed questions can usually be answered with a yes/no or a few words. The following question would probably yield such a response:

Does your colleague work many hours more than you?

Affective questions
These questions invite the presenter to share her feelings about an issue. Because of cultural bias against emotion (referred to below) open questions are more effective here. For example:

How do you feel about working with this manager?

By its nature the question is open yet probing, so caution and care are needed when asking. In particular, the set member will avoid *leading* and/or rhetorical questions like:

You don't like him, do you?

which may distress the presenter or cause her to withdraw (see Chapter 9).

Probing questions
These cause the presenter to stop and wonder about the issue in possibly a more insightful way. The presenter is having a problem with her colleague. A set member asks:

What aspects of your behaviour do you think might be relevant here?

This invites our presenter to consider her own contribution to the issue.

Checking questions
These are a helpful version of closed questions and are used to help the set member ensure that he has understood the responses so far. Examples:

What you plan to do is. . . . . Is that right?

So what you want to achieve with your colleague is. . . .?

Reflective questions
This type of question is useful to enable our presenter to reflect more on

something she may have said, to encourage her to elaborate more on a phrase she may have used. Examples:

You say there are difficulties with your colleague; what sort of difficulties?

In what way were your colleague's questions confusing?

This type of question ensures that the person asking it does not make assumptions about the 'difficulties' or what was 'confusing'. Such questions are usually said in a supportive tone and manner.

Multiple questions

A string of questions put together in complex sentences simply confuse the presenter who may also be unsure which question to answer. To be avoided!

As has been noted in Chapter 4 on being a set member, the key skill of silence, pausing to allow the presenter space to consider the issues, is crucial for effective set work.

Active listening, observing, reflecting back and questioning are key skills which underpin empathy, another important skill considered in the next chapter.

We will now move on to another aspect of interpersonal effectiveness between set members - disclosure.

Disclosure and assertion

Disclosure

A key condition for a set to be effective is that there is an atmosphere of trust amongst the set members and facilitator. By trust we mean that set members are willing to talk about themselves and disclose themselves in a way that is helpful to them. Having the rule of confidentiality is crucial to that sense of trust existing and being enhanced within the set.

In our interpersonal relations we vary the extent to which we are willing to convey what we are thinking and feeling. This variation is partly about trust. How far and how much we disclose may also be related to differences in culture, gender, class, race, sexual orientation, and disability. It is also about the nature of the relationship, for example:

• a loving partnership

- a working relationship as
    colleagues
    manager and managed
- doctor and patient
- woman to woman
- man to man.

Any disclosure will be transmitted through messages between the sender and receiver (as we saw in the example, 'Losing the message') and subject to the same loss and potential misinterpretation.

   In a set it is potentially useful for a set member to be open in their interactions with other set members. What does it mean to be more open in this context? Disclosure as a skill is intentional. It is a presentation of some

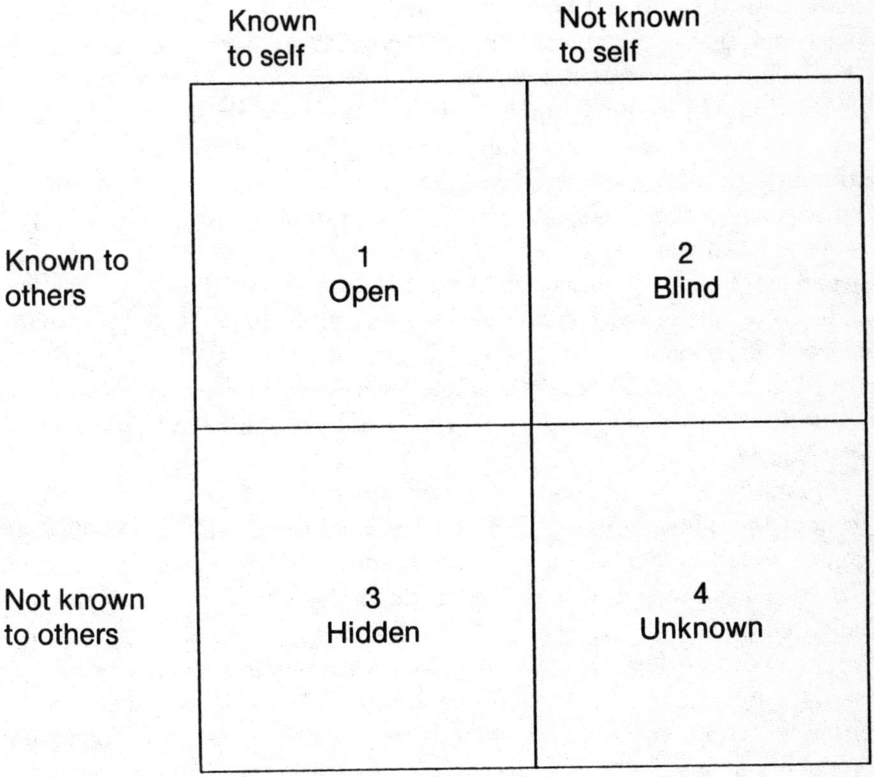

	Known to self	Not known to self
Known to others	1 Open	2 Blind
Not known to others	3 Hidden	4 Unknown

Figure 8.1 *The Johari Window*

aspect of self which is *owned*, (that is, 'I' statements are used), containing some feeling or emotion as well as factual material, which is *unknown to others*.

Johari Window

A very useful insight into how we may relate to people is the diagrammatic representation known as the Johari Awareness Model or Johari Window (a name derived from the authors' names) (Luft, 1984).

Interaction between two or more people depends on the extent of openness as well as the context in which it takes place. The square or window describes the possible forms of awareness of behaviour and feelings in a relationship. We will examine each quadrant in turn. The window represents a person we will call 'A'.

Quadrant 1 – the open quadrant, refers to the behaviour, feelings and motivations that 'I' (A) know about myself as well as others who see my behaviour. This is the window that A (and all of us) open to the world. It is the basis of most interaction that we willingly display.

Quadrant 2 – the blind quadrant, is that which refers to behaviour feelings and motivations that others see but which 'I' do not. This is the window A 'displays' to others without being aware that he is displaying it. In an interaction, person A displays himself as quadrant 1 – his public self. The person to whom he displays himself, person B, sees the public A but may also get an insight into A through quadrant 1 into quadrant 2 that A cannot 'see' or be aware of. For example, A may interact with B but not realize that in the interaction he inadvertently makes a sexist remark to B. Only if B points out the remark to A, will A be aware of it. How B conveys the message that A has made the remark and how A reacts to it will influence how A gets to know that particular blind spot.

Quadrant 3 – the hidden area, is that window which refers to behaviour, feelings and motivations which 'I' know about but which I am unwilling to convey to others. For example, A may be unwilling to disclose to C that he likes him, even though C may observe manifestations of that liking through A's window 2.

Quadrant 4 – the unknown area, is the part of ourselves that we do not know about, and is not known by others either. This window will contribute to our behaviour but neither we nor others normally see that part of ourselves. We may gain insights into it through our dreams when we sleep or even in the occasional day-dream, or we gain insight through therapy, and that is the place for it.

	Known to self	Not known to self
Known to others	1	2
Not known to others	3	4

Window a: unchanged

1	2
3	4

Window b: disclosing

Figure 8.2 *Disclosing*

The total window is drawn to scale in Figures 8.1 and 8.2 for ease of representation. Luft (1984) suggests that quadrant 4 is much larger than displayed.

Using the Johari Window we can see how disclosure works in an action learning set. Figure 8.2 represents a presenter, A.

In window a in Figure 8.2 we have a starting point, say in a new set. In

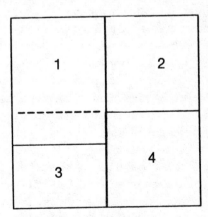

Window c: more open

Figure 8.3 *Disclosure and personal insight*

window b the presenter begins to disclose some of that which is hidden from the view of others from quadrant 3. The result may be for A, a new presentation to the group represented by window c in Figure 8.3 with enlarged quadrant 1.

In relation to an action learning set it is possible to recognize how this could be happening for others in the set, even if not symmetrically. The effect is that disclosure may encourage disclosure across the set as well as an atmosphere of being able to give and receive feedback, which is described in Chapter 9.

Self-disclosure

The section on Johari has shown how, in an atmosphere of trust, in a set and with confidentiality we may offer to disclose ourselves to other set members. How do we go about saying what we wish to say?

'I' statements

In Chapter 6, we refer to how 'I' statements enable a person to *own* what he is saying as opposed to words like 'you', 'one', 'we', 'that', 'it'. When you wish to be clear about a message you are conveying, whether it is about your thoughts, feelings or actions, it is unambiguous when you start with the pronoun 'I'.

Telling it like a story

A useful distinction is between telling a message in the form of a story and telling it like history. We acknowledge the origins of the distinction in Egan (1973) and have adapted it to the set context.

'Story' is involvement; 'history' is non-involvement. History is a statement or message which is analytical, factual – it ticks off the facts of experience and even interpretation of these facts but leaves the person who is the revealer untouched, relatively unknown. The presentation can be long and even boring. The presenter is detached and uninvolved, taking no risks. The presenter treats herself as *object* rather than subject who is 'there and then'. Generalities may be disguised by the use of words like 'we', 'one' or 'it'. History does not reach or engage the listener. It is flat or boring because it is divorced from the person. It is not really disclosing the person.

'Story' on the other hand is not analytical. It is authentic self-disclosure – an attempt to reveal myself as a person and to reach the listener. Story involves emotion. Story is a signal of invitation – the presenter is opening the door to others in the set. It is a story if it is a description by the set member about themselves expressed, for example, as 'I felt really good about the way

I challenged my manager on the way he addressed the staff as "girls", without making him feel inferior or blamed.'

Again, a story may start as a story but because the individual has worked through an issue it is no longer really an issue for her. One of us recalls taking time in a set to discuss what we considered to be important – it was about the use of time at work – and being challenged by another set member as the latter felt there was no real will or commitment about what was being described. The story had become history.

Another way of categorizing the difference is contrasting the words below:

Story	History
I	Them; it; people
Feeling; affect	Fact
Actual	Abstract
Real	Abstract; detached
Interesting	Boring; a turn-off

In other words, when we are expressing our feelings (the affective part of us) as well as the cognitive and conative, we are likely to be in story mode and disclosing something about us that has its basis in a real meaning that will make connections with the listeners.

Story is selective in detail – not necessarily complete in communicating fact, but complete in communicating self. The 'story' teller is taking a risk and knows it. By so doing the presenter requests support from set members. In a set, self-disclosure is a leap of trust – and demands dialogue 'here and now'. It is unusual not to be engaged when someone is telling their story. It is usually interesting. The presenter may have taken a risk, made herself vulnerable in the process but will not lose the set members' engagement. The set members will seldom be bored by such a story with sincere self-disclosure but they may be embarrassed.

The embarrassment can be a cultural bias against self-disclosure and the expression of emotion, seen in some contexts as a weakness at one extreme or exhibitionism at the other.

Orbach (1994) suggests that:

Emotional illiteracy exists because we have no shared language for emotional life. Words like love, hate, jealousy and competition reveal little more than the tip of an emotional experience whose depths we are unused to exploring.

Self-disclosure peaks in childhood and is seen as a passing phase that goes with oncoming maturity. In the fullness of time we become fully locked-in mature adults! However, as human beings we do not lose our emotions, they remain in us and can be a barrier to our development or can enhance that development. Self-disclosure is often associated with the psychiatrist's couch – we must be weak and in need of 'treatment'.

Fortunately, this model (a medical model) is becoming outmoded with our increasing understanding of ourselves as having subjective feelings which impinge on our everyday lives. For example, our presenter earlier in this chapter wanted to go for promotion. She was inhibited by a sense of lack of confidence which she was not really aware of. Getting feedback about how she was unaware of her demeanour in a supportive way enabled her to work on her confidence as a means of taking action. She may have known inside her that she was lacking confidence and trying to hide it. But to the set the demeanour showed (quadrant 2 in the Johari Window). The facts which she wished to hide were revealed in non-verbal clues.

Thus, telling it like a story is more likely to convey congruence between what we are saying and what we are feeling and what our thoughts really are. It is more likely to create bridges of understanding than taking no risks which can lead to misinterpretation.

Appropriateness of disclosure

Too much self-disclosure is embarrassing. Too little and we may find we do not relate to others and reduce our capacity to reflect upon ourselves in the set. Quadrant 3 in the Johari Window is hidden from our listeners. How far we disclose depends in part upon our values and the norms of the group. Some people value openness, others privacy. Self-disclosure reveals it. Over-disclosure occurs when the disclosure is inappropriate to the context.

The level of disclosure which is suitable to the context can be called 'appropriate self-disclosure'. 'Appropriate' is defined by:

- amount
- depth
- time
- the target, ie, the person(s) talked to
- the situation.

Our experience of action learning sets is that set members do engage in self-disclosure as the atmosphere of trust develops between members. We have seen earlier that the development of that trust depends on the set adhering to the ground rule of confidentiality. Knowing that what is said in the set will not be repeated by other set members outside the set is crucial. Action learning sets can provide the situation for a degree of self-disclosure that may not be available elsewhere.

Self-disclosure in a set means I am conveying something of myself and conveying the *willingness* to do so. This willingness can encourage others to take the risk of disclosure about themselves.

The facilitator can also model appropriate self-disclosure in the set even though she does not have set time for herself. Engaging in trauma, trivia and joy, for example, at the commencement of set meetings can help trust to develop (see Chapter 7).

Assertive behaviour

By assertive behaviour, we mean:

- Expressing my needs, wants, opinions, beliefs and feelings in direct, honest and appropriate ways.
- Conveying my own rights without violating the rights of others.
- Taking responsibility for myself and what I say, 'owning' my needs, feelings, etc. For example, if I say to someone, 'You've upset me', this is aggressive rather than assertive because I am placing responsibility for the anger on that person rather than owning my own feeling of being upset, in contrast to, 'I'm upset because . . .'.
- Owning my feelings means that I cannot be criticized for having them – they just are.
- That an empathic response is more likely than a 'should' response so that; 'I feel upset' is likely to be met by, 'I wonder if you feel upset because . . .', rather than, 'You should pull yourself together'.

Clearly assertive behaviour requires the skill of disclosure in order to express and own needs, opinions, feelings and emotions.

The action learning set is conducive to an assertive mode in that the process is designed to give the presenter the opportunity to express her needs, wants, opinions, beliefs and feelings in direct, honest and appropriate ways. Enabling the presenter in an action learning set to have that opportunity is achieved by other set members being aware of what is happening in the group, having the ability to communicate what they mean and the assertiveness to convey their message appropriately. Egan (1976) has stated; 'Assertiveness is the ability to take *reasonable* risks' (emphasis in the original). In the context of a set it enables the presenter to work on her issues effectively, supportively and without collusion. Set members are encouraged to acknowledge each other's rights as well as having equal time for expression of their own.

Chapter 9

Additional Skills

The additional interpersonal skills we have identified include the expression of emotion and empathy. Using these additional skills creates a rapport between set members which enables the giving and receiving of feedback. In terms of the action part of action learning, the presenter can then focus and specify action with the support of set members.

Management of emotion

With self-disclosure we can determine the extent to which we disclose ourselves. The disclosure by us is largely under our control and we have the right not to disclose. Emotions are not so easily controlled and may be released verbally and/or non-verbally. Yet we do seek to control the expression of our emotions even though we may feel them.

The purpose of this section is to suggest that a set can, with care and respect for each set member, enable the expression of emotions in a helpful way for each set member. A helpful way of expressing emotion is one that promotes congruent relationships, that is, appropriate emotional expression that underpins the relationships. Our emphasis in the previous chapter on telling our story as opposed to 'out there' history provided an example of an approach that encourages the expression of emotion.

In telling our story in a set when we disclose verbally we channel emotional expression through our words. However, emotions cannot always be channelled or controlled and may be expressed with other signs of emotion such as tears and laughter. Feelings about expressing emotions, particularly expressing negative emotions, will depend upon the values we hold as well as our self-awareness. However, one thing is paramount – the feeling itself is not at fault, it just exists. How we manage the expression of our emotions is partly dependent on the way we value our emotions, which in turn dictates a large part of our interpersonal style.

We manage our emotions from two points of view. We manage our own emotions and we manage our emotions in response to our relating with others. An example of the first would be if another person made me feel angry or hurt. An example of the second would be if another person made a hurtful remark and then realized it with some embarrassment. I might feel it was singularly inappropriate to have made the remark, but I do not have to compound his embarrassment with further comment.

In the last chapter we quoted Egan and Heron in asserting the tendency of British and American cultures not to have paid much attention, until recently, to the development of interpersonal skills. This is also true of the expression of emotion (Orbach, 1994). Whilst there are intra-cultural differences, we tend to be socialized not to express our emotions except in well-defined contexts. Some emotions are more 'acceptable' than others. Laughter is more acceptable than crying. Showing pleasure is more acceptable than anger. Emotion can be seen as being irrational, not quite in control and therefore an unacceptable obstacle to social interaction.

In fact feelings and emotions are basic human characteristics. They are neither good nor bad, right nor wrong. How we handle our emotions is a learned style of behaviour. We may be socialized not to show some of our emotions, such as crying, or anger. As a consequence we may also not be able to handle it in ourselves or in others. For example, many men feel that to cry is to show weakness which is linked to a recognition that women are traditionally able to work with emotions requiring caring and nurturing. This has resulted, amongst other things, in a channelling of women into (and men away from) work that is supposed to require these qualities. Apart from the gender stereotyping which this has created, with its consequential discrimina-tions, the bias has helped to diminish our attention to the expression of emotions.

Being socialized to discourage the expression of some of our emotions is useful. I may be angry with someone. That does not mean I can hit out physically or abuse them emotionally. However, some socialization may result in the inhibiting of the show of emotions so that we become fully 'locked-in' adults.

Jourard (1971) suggests that persons who are 'known' by others are healthier and happier than those who are not. The suppression of emotion in Jourard's view is a major component of stress in modern society. In our role as facilitators we have often heard a set member say that being able to give voice to and express their emotions has been a major breakthrough in tackling a major task in work or in life.

If a person does not express their emotions verbally there will be a tendency to 'leakage' – the non-verbal expression of the emotions. Both can of course be expressed together. Non-verbal expression will include tone of voice, gesture and body language. Verbally, emotions may also be expressed inadvertently when the words belie the intention, as in Freudian slips!

Positive or helpful expression of emotion

Emotion is present and normal and a part of all of us. How can we express or manage our emotions to good effect?

Emotions are OK

Emotions can get out of hand but that is about expression. Emotion in itself is a fact. We are living human beings for whom emotion is an integral part of ourselves. People who declare that they feel no emotion have just got the lid on tighter than the rest of us and will reveal 'leakages' in some way.

You may find that your interpersonal style is not characterized by the expression of feeling. Participation in an action learning set may give you the opportunity to explore your style in a safe environment.

Responsibility for emotion: owning it

We are each responsible for our emotions. If, say, someone lets me down I may feel angry. What do I do with my anger? I can respond with an accusation, 'You are making me feel angry', or 'I feel angry because . . .'.

With the latter I am taking responsibility for dealing with my own anger. This is important. If I make the former statement, the person to whom I am making it may feel accused, threatened and defensive.

Storing-up emotions

Saving or storing-up emotions is not helpful, for when they eventually emerge they may explode. It is better to express feelings as they arise even if they are negative. We may need a little time to identify what the emotion is and how we feel but that is different from putting the emotion into storage.

Assertiveness and expression of emotion

We have addressed assertiveness in Chapter 8. However, assertiveness has its place in emotional expression. If someone's behaviour is upsetting you then say so and why in terms of your own feelings, taking responsibility for your feelings as suggested above.

Knowing your own emotional states
Awareness of our emotional states enables us to express clearly in words what it is we are feeling and why. Set members may notice that they have difficulty expressing some emotions or express them indirectly.

Empathy

In action learning it is important for facilitators and set members to have and develop empathy. Empathy is one of the most valuable, if not the most valuable, relational skill we have. Empathy is used to enhance one-to-one relationships. We are using empathy here to add to the quality of set interactions.

By empathy we mean an ability to project oneself into another person's experience while remaining unconditionally oneself. Carl Rogers (1979) expresses it well; we have adapted the quote to action learning:

> Being empathic involves a choice on the part of the [facilitator] as to what she will pay attention to, namely the . . . world of the [set member] as that individual perceives it . . . it assists the [set member] in gaining a clearer understanding of, and hence a greater control over, her own world and her own behaviour.

In summary, empathy is an understanding of the world from the other's point of view, her feelings, experience and behaviour, and the communication of that understanding in full.

Egan (1976) built upon Rogers' ideas about empathy and developed a model of the skill which we adapt below.

Empathy is based on two pieces of information:

- what the speaker is feeling;
- the experience and/or behaviour which is the source of that feeling.

When these two pieces of information have been identified the next step is communication of the listener's awareness to the speaker. For example, I might say, 'John is really bugging me with the work overload'. The listener, if empathetic, will respond with something like, 'You feel upset because John is pressuring you'.

In starting to use empathy more explicitly the response is, 'You feel . . .

because . . .', or 'You feel . . . when . . . because . . .', which can be a useful way to get into using the skill. Once familiar with the approach, using the skill will be less mechanical.

Egan (1976) describes a number of ways in which listeners have problems in effectively engaging in accurate empathy. We will refer to his headings and adapt them to the action learning set context.

Let us take the following statement made by the presenter:

> I see myself as so ordinary. I'm not the person for this promotion. I don't relate well to others. I'm ordinary.

Her statement can be followed by a number of less than appropriate responses by set members.

The cliché – responses like:

> I hear what you say.
> I understand.

These are of no help to the presenter. Such statements or clichés do not convey to the presenter that she is understood; they are more likely to convey to the presenter that she is *not* understood and that the set member is responding in an automatic and unauthentic manner.

The question – a response to our presenter's statement might be:

> In what ways are you ordinary?

The question does not take account of the fact that our presenter has taken a risk in disclosing how she feels. The question does not convey empathic support about how and whether the set member is understanding her.

Interpretation – here the set member would respond by trying to adduce too early what is implied in the presenter's disclosure. An example might be:

> This ordinary thing is the outward problem. I bet there's something else behind it that's upsetting you.

Inaccuracy – here the set member may just be plainly inaccurate with a response to the presenter like:

> You're not very happy with the way the set is treating you

The presenter may be taken off-track or stop or hesitate because empathy, accurate empathy, has not happened and she may be blocked by what has been said. The set member may be listening to his own agenda about the presenter rather than attending to her.

Pretence – the presenter may have said the above at the end of a long and emotional description. The set member gets distracted by the length and possibly by the emotion but tries to convey that he understands, perhaps to avoid embarrassing the presenter by making it evident that she may not have been listened to accurately. However, such a pretence is not genuine and will only inhibit empathic support. It is quite appropriate for the set member to convey that he does not understand with phrases like:

I'm sorry, I was distracted for a moment. Could we start again please?
It seems to me that . . . but maybe I'm not getting it correctly.

The latter is tentative, suggesting to the presenter that maybe the set member has not understood her accurately. This leaves the presenter able to provide clarification and interaction with the set member until there is accurate understanding. It also indicates to the presenter that what she is saying is valued and important and encourages her to continue.

Responding too soon or too late – giving the presenter a chance to express herself gives the set member time to sort out feelings and content. However, spontaneity is valuable and 'interrupting' may be necessary if the presenter is beginning to ramble. Care needs to be taken here in order not to convey impatience.

Parroting – here the set member merely repeats back to the presenter what has been said. The set member needs to 'own' what has been said and then respond. This shows that the set member has got 'inside' the presenter in a way that conveys accurate empathy. Egan (1976) compares parroting with a tape recording where there is little mutuality or human contact. An effective response gets to the presenter in a way that parroting cannot.

Discrepancy – using language that is incongruent with the speaker's. Use similar language in response to that used by the speaker. This encourages rapport provided the language the responding set member uses is authentic to him. He then conveys that he is in tune with the presenter.

Longwindedness – rapport and understanding do depend on dialogue. If the presenter is conveying a story that is being attended to it may not be appropriate to intervene. Set meetings are more effective when set members realize that time has to be used with economy, that time is precious for each set member. A presenter conscious of her time, who nevertheless is able to convey her feelings with her content, will aim to be crisp with her description. Similarly, set members, when they intervene, will make their responses with precision to enable the dialogue to continue for the benefit of the presenter.

What empathy is not

Empathy is not:

- giving advice
- giving an evaluation
- making a judgement
- giving an interpretation
- making a challenge
- engaging the presenter in a re-orientation.

When a presenter shares a problem with the set, it is not necessary for set members to solve it for them, even though there might be the temptation! Your solution may not be appropriate anyway. Understanding of the presenter's problem or issue is much more useful – provided the set members communicate that understanding.

If set members are into solutions this could make for greater difficulty on the part of the presenter. Communication of understanding allows a presenter to move on to a discovery, in time, of her solutions and ways of handling them.

Empathy commits set members to the presenter and commits set members to stay with the presenter. That is a sign the presenter is valuable and worthwhile, to be respected.

The skill of empathy is rather rare in social interaction – few people experience it. When set members experience it they recognize the power of an understanding response that builds trust in a set. As facilitators of sets we have observed how set members acknowledge that they carry the skill discovered or enhanced in the set to other areas of their lives.

Giving and receiving feedback

The set may be able to give feedback to our presenter and she may wish to receive it. Here we are referring to the set members giving feedback that will be revelatory to the presenter. The Johari Window is again helpful here.

In window a we have the starting point, say in a new set. In window b the person began to disclose some of that which was hidden from the view of others from quadrant 3.

In giving feedback to the presenter other set members will enable our presenter to become aware of those behaviours, etc, of which she is unaware

	Known to Self	Not Known to Self
Known to Others	1	2
Not Known to Others	3	4

Window a: unchanged

1 <<<<<<<	2	
3	4	

Window b: disclosure and feedback

but which are evident to the set members. In Figure 9.1 the feedback is represented by the arrows from quadrant 2 to quadrant 1.

The result may be a new presentation to the group represented by window c in Figure 9.2. With growing trust in interaction with the others in the set, she will receive feedback about herself from window 2 which she is unable to know without the insight of others therefore enlarging quadrant 1 as in Figure 9.2.

What are the necessary conditions for set members to give and for our presenter to receive appropriate feedback following and in addition to the skills of effective listening and empathy? The necessary conditions are a set of behaviours which can be summarized as a climate of support.

Climate of support

A climate of support will exist in the set when its members are being genuine, ie spontaneous, open, role-free and not defensive. In addition, set members will offer respect to the presenter by giving their attention in a non-judgemental way and demonstrating a willingness to work with and for the presenter.

By 'genuine' we mean that the set members are being themselves rather than playing a role. An example of a set member in role could be where the

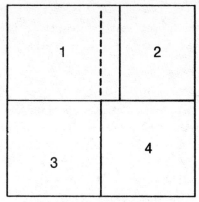

Window c: more open

Figure 9.2 *Effect of feedback*

member is, say, a manager at work, and he carries that role into the set, with the result that the presenter is unable to share her feelings for fear of a managerial response.

By 'defensive' we mean where any member of the set, including a presenter, is unable to accept feedback from colleagues, thereby isolating herself from the set. An example would be where the presenter exceeds her time and when this is called to her attention blames the set members rather than taking responsibility herself.

By 'non-judgemental respect' we mean behaviour which values the individual presenter as a unique person in her own right, suspends value judgements about her or her issue, accepting that she can determine her own course of action. It is useful to note here that these conditions coincide with the prerequisites for empathy addressed in the previous section.

If there is no trust and support in the set, feedback, however accurate, may not be heard, that is, it may not be received. In terms of the Johari Window for our presenter, quadrant 2 is inaccessible to her. Assuming a climate of support exists in the set, the giving and receiving of feedback is likely to occur.

How to give effective feedback

We can now consider how set members can give effective feedback. It may be useful to note that term 'feedback' comes from an engineering and systems model. The feedback loop is designed to inform the system about change. Positive feedback signals change, negative feedback no change.

Clarity
Be clear about what you want to say in advance. Think about what it is you wish to say and the way in which you want to say it.

Emphasize the positive
Our culture tends to emphasize the negative with a focus more on weaknesses than strengths. Most people need encouragement, to be told when they are doing something well, despite being in circumstances of difficulty. This does not mean being collusive with the presenter's circumstances. For example, a presenter was preparing to leave a full-time job to become independent. She conveyed that she feared being unemployed. A set member intervened to ask her whether she would be unemployed or self-employed. It was an insight offered that enabled the presenter to be positive about herself. The feedback was significant to her own self-image as well as being realistic.

Be specific
Avoid general comments which are not very useful to the presenter. If superlatives like, 'That was brilliant . . .', or 'That must have been hard . . .', are used, follow them up with specific statements about what was brilliant or hard, and why. We will consider statement-specific language later in the chapter.

Select the priorities
It is the presenter's time. Convey the feedback in precise form that gets to the core or essence for the presenter. One set member may convey broadly what another set member may have said. There is usually little virtue in repeating the same.

A set member may have an idea that takes the presenter forward; however, another set member intervenes with something else which the presenter picks up and 'runs with'. A memorable example of this was the occasion when a set member later in a review session said he had been itching to convey an idea but it was, 'An idea whose time was gone'. The set member lets it drop if he considers it of no use to the presenter. It is not to the presenter's benefit if the set member simply conveys the idea to get it off his chest.

Focus on behaviour rather than the person
The presenter may have disclosed her feelings about her work and what she felt has happened to her. It is more effective if set members respond with feedback that adduces specific behaviours she engaged in rather than broad statements like, 'You were ineffective with your manager'.

Refer to behaviour that can be changed
It is no use giving a presenter feedback on something in which they may have no choice, for example responding to a presenter who is committed to a job yet currently in a difficult predicament with a statement like 'Well, you could always leave'.

Be descriptive rather than evaluative
Rather than merely saying that something was good, be specific about what it was the presenter said that was good.

Own the feedback
Here we emphasize again the use of 'I' statements in preference to using words like 'one', 'you' or 'they', which convey a specious universality of agreed opinion. Using 'I' at the beginning of the feedback is important in showing that we are taking responsibility for that feedback.

What the feedback says about the set member
Feedback is likely to say as much about the set member giving it as the receiving presenter. The feedback will say a good deal about the set member's values and what he focuses on with others. Therefore the set member can learn about himself if he listens to the feedback he gives.

Receiving feedback

Listen to the feedback before responding
There is a tendency to respond to feedback immediately. Feedback can be uncomfortable to hear but we may be poorer without it. Feedback may give us insights which otherwise we may miss. The conditions in a set of genuineness and respect will underline the feedback given.

Be clear about what is being said
The presenter receiving feedback can check that what she has heard is accurate before responding to it. She may also wish to hear other set members and their feedback before responding.

Decide what to do as a result of the feedback
When our presenter receives feedback she can assess its value, the consequences of using it or ignoring it and then decide what she will do as a result of it. In the final analysis it is the presenter's choice what to do with the feedback.

In summary, the better presenters are at receiving feedback the more they encourage set members to give feedback. If a presenter demonstrates that she can receive it, she will help others to receive it. We can view the Johari

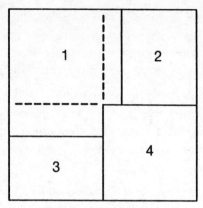

Window c: more open

Figure 9.3 *Effect of disclosure and feedback for the set*

Window c again in Figure 9.3 as a window for the whole set. As disclosure (quadrant 3) occurs and feedback becomes culturally acceptable in the set (quadrant 2 becomes more available for each set member) so the set attains a larger quadrant 1. From this more effective work can be done by each set member.

'Shoulds' and 'oughts'

When set members are conveying their story, they often use words like 'should', 'shouldn't', 'ought', 'oughtn't', 'must' and 'mustn't'.

Let us give an example. A set member has decided to bring the progressing of her postgraduate research as her task for the set. It is a doctoral thesis in its sixth year. She is burdened by the whole thing and wants it out of the way (as does her thesis supervisor) by completing it in the next year. Much has been done on it but the thesis has been in a state of lapse for a year. Life has taken new turns and the PhD is no longer top of the agenda.

She has been making superficial progress for the last month or so. As presenter, she is talking about her progress:

I have had another meeting with my supervisor. I didn't feel too good about the few pages I've done since I last saw her. She suggested I move to another chapter instead of being stuck with the current chapter. She asked me when I wanted to go for completion (of the thesis). I said that I should finish it by October next. . . .

There followed some clarification questions around the detail of the chapters she was moving from and to. After a few moments a set member asked her (in great contrast to the detail of the previous questions):

Are you doing this PhD because you ought to or because you want to?

The set member said it in a caring manner and toward the end of the presenter's time. She paused and did not answer. After some time she said that she needed to think that one through between now and the next set. The set left it at that. At the next meeting she said the question had stopped her in her tracks because she had not clarified that distinction even at the commencement of the research six years ago when she had finished her first degree.:

> The question faced me centrally about my commitment to the research. If it was a should or ought then there was a kind of rule that I was adhering to that did not necessarily have anything to do with me. If I want to do it, that is because of something in me that drives me – no one else. I have cleared in my mind that I want to do it, I want to complete it and have said that to my supervisor. Moreover, I have talked about it with my partner and at work and they acknowledge the pressure I will have for a few months and are with me. It helped enormously, once I was clear what I wanted, to talk through the implications with them.

We do not know, as she informs us, whether she started the research wanting to do it or because it had been an ought. She may have felt obliged to do it because it was:

- the 'done thing';
- some well-meaning 'others' wanting her to do it – colleague graduates, lecturers, parents, friends;
- it would be a good career marker.

However, she may also have started it because she actually wanted to (through interest in the discipline, area, etc), but it may have become an implicit 'ought' during the period.

She could well have decided between the set meetings that the thesis was an ought and given up or proceeded with the ought to a conclusion. The significance was that she recognized the reasons: what she actually wanted; what she was doing; and the desire to complete it – which enabled her to move the pace and progress to completion in the time agreed with her supervisor!

This story conveys the effect of these key words we often use. We may have oughts but we do have the choice as to whether we do them or not. The cost of not doing an ought may be high for the person – but that is their choice; the set has merely enabled her to make a clearer choice.

The other words we tend to use are 'must' or 'mustn't' or 'can't'. A set member may say, 'I must get this report in by the first'. This can be followed by the thought, 'Can you imagine what would happen if you didn't?' Similarly, 'I can't have three weeks for a holiday this year', followed by, 'I wonder what would happen if you did?'

These questions may be easier to ask ourselves. Asking them of other set members will require care. The framing of the question may be construed as implying that the set member should throw caution to the wind and be obtuse. Remember, it is the set member's life and responsibilities that are being addressed.

Generalizations

Another way in which we construct the world is to make generalizations that we apply to ourselves.

A presenter may tie himself up with statements like, 'I can't stand the managers at my company. They are all a bunch of autocrats'. He may have actually experienced three managers who are like that. However, he is making a generalization about all the other managers in the organization. Making that generalization may influence how he relates to other managers. No matter how approachable the other managers he comes across he is still influenced by that main thought.

A set member may have been given notice of termination of employment and is faced with the prospect of unemployment. Self-perception may be reinforced by statements like, 'No one will want to employ me. I am too old (too loud, too pushy, too young, a woman, black, past my sell-by date)'. Behind this statement (or its variations) may well be a wider macro-economic condition of widespread unemployment and organizations that are ageist, sexist or racist. Let that be acknowledged. But our set member is adding to the difficulty by excluding him- or herself by virtue of the generalization.

In a set it is useful for set members and the set adviser to keep an ear out for generalization, so that the presenter can be supported in examining a phrase that they may well have applied to himself in a way that acts as a block. In relation to the employment phrase above, a set member may say, simply, 'No one?', or 'No one will want to employ you?', with voice tone raised toward the end of the question, enabling the presenter to examine the meaning he has applied to himself.

Watch out for words like 'all', 'never', 'every(one)', 'always' and 'they', too. Putting a question mark after each of these words can help to expose them for what they may be - generalizations. Rarely are generalizations true *all* the time. By generalizing we stop ourselves from looking for exceptions to the rule. We also probably engage in more excluding of ourselves where we are involved. Recognize these words for what they often, but not always, are: limiting forms of behaviour.

Specifying actions

An important part of the action learning process is that point when a participant has reviewed their progress on an issue and after consideration and reflection on where he is now, has to decide upon the next step to take after the meeting and before the next meeting.

This usually follows a question from another set member or the facilitator like, 'So John, what's your next step?', or 'Where do you go from here, Mary?'. The action or actions the set member takes are important in enabling John or Mary to make things happen in relation to their issues rather than just reflecting upon the issues. Action learning is about providing the place for reflection on a set member's experience but also to learn from that reflection and move forward from what has been learned in order to make effective the action in future experience.

Before the presenter concludes his time, it is usual to determine the action(s) he wishes to take that he will aim to fulfil by the next set meeting. The words set presenters use to specify their intended actions are crucial. The words and sentences should be active and specific like:

- I will do X by the next set meeting.
- I will acquire Y by 3 November.
- I will practise giving myself one hour a week for planning the week ahead.
- I will write and complete chapter 10 by 4 July.
- I will tell J that I will make the deadline for the report on the 16th of this month rather than the 10th.

The presenter making these intentions could have questions as follow-ups to make even more specific and concrete his actions. Take the last example. Questions that make the action more specific and concrete for the set member could be:

When will you tell J? and/or
When is it most appropriate for you to tell J?
Where will you tell J?
How will you tell J your change of deadline?

and possibly, depending on the issues/relationship between the presenter and J:

What if J declines to accept the revised date?

The benefit to the presenter of these further questions is that they enable him to clarify and break down the detailed actions that may lie within a broadly stated action. In the example above, our presenter can think about the implications of 'telling J' and as a result be more prepared to ensure that the intention of a new deadline of the 16th of the month is attained.

Another benefit is that we all have different ways of seeing the world. Attaining a specific deadline in this example may appear, superficially, to be the same thing or have the same meaning to all in the set. Only by asking some of the more detailed questions will the set begin to approximate similar views and meanings of the set member's intention (reality). If the set had stopped at the first statement about the date of the revised deadline members may have made assumptions about the when, where, how and what ifs, which if ignored may have affected the success of our presenter in attaining his revised deadline.

These further questions may not always be necessary and set time may limit putting them. But supposing in the example above the presenter was informing his line manager of the revised deadline. Further questioning may well help the set member ensure the most appropriate context to secure his aim. Without these questions we may have assumed that 'telling' was sufficient! Placing the word 'telling' on its own conveys how unspecific the word can be.

Contrast the initial reasonably specific statements above with the following:

- I will look at . . .
- I will address the issue of . . .
- I will consider . . .
- I will bear in mind . . .
- I will think about . . .
- I will discuss . . .

The latter statements are loose in their application to specific and concrete actions to be taken by the set member. They may be considered concrete by the set member but we do not really know. The phrases can all be followed up with the question:

How will you consider . . .? or
What specifically will you do . . .?
What specifically are you trying to achieve?

These questions (or variations on them) will provide him with a closer focus on what he can actually do.

Remember that the set process is not an interrogation or a cross-examination. Use questioning with the set member's interests at the heart of the process, so that questions like those in the last paragraph might be softened and given a tentative flavour by:

I'm wondering what, specifically, you mean by . . . or
What, perhaps, could you do specifically to . . .?

Occasionally the reflection or story is so significant for the presenter that no action is required. He just needs to let the experience in his time in the set settle. For example, one of us was pursuing a project, preparing a postgraduate course for validation. Each set meeting would be used to consider problems to move the course toward successful validation. On one occasion, however, the feelings that I came to the set with had overwhelmed the task that I had brought to the set. Whilst I did not intend to, I found myself trusting the group to be able to disclose my feelings about a very important personal event that was overriding the task. I just let the feelings emerge and talked about what was happening at that point in my life. My colleagues in the set listened, empathized and gently pointed out the proximity of my time at the set meeting coming to an end and would I like an extension with the agreement of the set? I thanked them and declined. No action questions were posed. The set realized, as I had, that it was sufficient for me to have shared my feelings. After the set meeting I felt much lighter and regenerated and incidentally made ample progress on the task.

We would not wish to be rigid in asserting that every set member has to come up with action(s) every set meeting following their presentation and interaction with the set. Further, a presenter may on occasion tell her story, and the telling has an impact so powerful for her that her learning resides in the reflection. No specific action is required. We could say that the action is that no specific action is required!

PART III
THE USES OF ACTION LEARNING

Chapter 10

Learning and Development

We are committed to the action learning process because we believe that it is effective in supporting the learning and development of individuals and in the collaborative learning of groups and organizations. This chapter is intended to show how action learning contributes to learning and development.

We describe our view of learning and development in relation to the uses of action learning in the guide. We review relevant theories of learning which have informed our views in answering the question: how does this theory apply to action learning? We relate development to learning and wish to contribute to the view of learning and development being a social process. We also aim to make connections with you, the reader, in terms of your experiences of learning and development.

Learning

Learning is not neutral. We are bounded by our histories and upbringing. Brought up in a western, Anglo-Saxon culture, and asked what our notions of learning are, we tend to reply in terms of acquiring knowledge about things, events, concepts. That knowledge tends to be imparted to us in schools, colleges and universities where we are taught by 'expert' teachers. This kind of learning is usually top-down, authority driven and concerned with socialization. The learning is highly controlled and controlling. The syllabus is prescribed and general. The learning is individualized. At intervals we are assessed to find out the extent to which we have learnt something and this is a prerequisite to continuing on to the next stage.

The above is a caricature of the traditional elements of our education system. It does impart a view of learning as being associated with scholastic institutions. It suggests conditions of dependence rather than something happening in our lives where we can develop autonomy and be in control of our learning. An intention to extend our learning later in life usually means being encouraged to seek it off-site at the local college or university, separated from and unrelated or indirectly related to our lives and work. This approach has been challenged in the last few years.

The focus on the need for a flexible workforce and on 'transferable skills' has widened the educational net to include skills as well as knowledge. There is a new acceptance that educational institutions should work more collaboratively with the world of employment.

The term 'competence' is increasingly in use and attempts are being made to define those skills often previously left unmeasured. NVQs and GNVQs in the UK are influencing education and training in the workplace. In a real sense, skill is being more highly valued and brought more centrally into our view of learning. At the same time the development of skill in real situations is being emphasized. Although the highly specified nature of the NVQ may not accommodate complex skill development, the way it is assessed on the basis of real work experience is a step away from the fragmentation and separation of learning, development and work, which has prevailed in our educational system to date.

These assessment systems, essentially individual, mitigate against a collaborative view of learning and development. They prioritize the cognitive (knowing) and the conative (doing) over the affective (feeling) aspects of learning, whilst for the most part ignoring the relationship between the three.

The above is not to underestimate the attention given in formal education to structure the fulfilment of the whole person – the personal development of the learner. However, the emphasis is on the knowledge and skills acquired as measured by exams and competence-based assessment.

Essential in learning, we believe, are the following:

- *Learning as an intentional and conscious process* – the individual can set out to learn about themselves, their context, situation and working environment as opposed to simply living with and through events which might well impart learning but mainly unintended.
- *Learning as a process integrating the cognitive, conative and affective aspects of ourselves* – where learning and personal development meet is in the complex interrelationship of these three aspects of learning.
- *Learning as a reflective process* – reflecting on what we are doing and gaining insights and feedback through collaborative working enhances our

learning and encourages our development. Reflection becomes more than an individual process. Through the power of collaboration the quality of reflection is sustained. The key for us is that it is by the interaction with thought and action, action and reflection, that we are enabled with and through others to be aware of what we have learnt. Individual reflection is feasible but the insights gained by shared reflection are potentially richer and more challenging to the learner.

- *Learning about learning* – is a crucial element in the development of the individual. This meta-level awareness is an outcome of the collaborative and intentional reflective process.
- *Learning as a collaborative and social process* – where learning is not only individual but shared. The learning here is a product of the relationship and interaction between the individual and others in the set. The individual and others sharing and collaborating together create a learning that is common to all, greater than the sum of individual learning. This comes not only from the set's concentration on one individual's projects but also as an important benefit from working on the projects of other individuals. Thus the learning is about the things other than the issue brought to the set by the individual.

There is a second aspect to collaboration, namely the sharing of what is learnt with others in the wider environment. Learning is not simply individual gain but may lead to a sharing of the learning with the whole living and working context. The 'action' which results from the action learning process is a gift from the individual and the set to others in the working environment – some have called it free consultancy. 'You take your own project hoping to work on it and find that it is you and six others who are in fact working on it.'

Theories of learning

This is necessarily a brief account. We have attempted to explain the key ideas which have influenced and informed our own use of action learning and our current understanding of how this process contributes to learning and development.

Action learning

Revans (1983) describes learning in terms of the now famous formula:

$$L = P + Q$$

where L is learning, P is the acquisition of programmed knowledge and Q is questioning insight. P is, in Revans' phrase, 'the stuff of traditional instruction'. The skills and understandings represented by P are about the basis of training or of formal didactic instruction. Programmed knowledge is sufficient for coping with 'puzzles' – those things for which experts can help us find the answer – but it is insufficient in dealing with 'problems'. Problems have no right answers. Dealing with problems needs programmed knowledge but also questioning insight where the complexity of the context is taken into consideration in making decisions. This requires more than a trained and knowledgeable operator: it requires an holistic approach, an approach which is the essence of learning. Thus for Revans, 'There can be no learning without action and no (sober and deliberate) action without learning'.

Action learning is the approach to learning and development which links the world of action to the world of learning through a reflective process within action learning sets.

Conceptions of learning

People have different understandings about what learning actually is. In fact the question 'What do you mean by learning?' comes as a surprisingly difficult one to answer. Partly, this is because we tend to use the word learning for many very different activities and we use it as an active and a passive verb and occasionally as a noun – the result of learning is learning. One influential study has documented a typology of different answers to the question, 'What is learning?' The researcher suggests that individuals may use more than one conception in their descriptions of their learning at different times (Saljo, 1982). In brief the types are:

1. Gaining bits and pieces of knowledge
2. Memorizing
3. Applying knowledge (technically, as in figures into a formula)
4. Understanding
5. Understanding in relation to the real world.

The last two conceptions imply an interaction with learning and a personal interpretation while the first three imply a passive acceptance. Later a sixth conception was added, which is particularly interesting in relation to action learning as it is more personal in nature:

6. Developing as a person.

In this sixth conception, learning is seen as a change in self, so that real learning only happens when the world looks different as a result. 'I have changed and so the world looks different to me'. This seems to us to be the essence of development (Marton *et al*, 1993).

Action learning is clearly not about gaining bits and pieces of knowledge, nor about memorizing. It involves the person as a complex whole acting in the world. Action learning therefore supports the view of learning that is about development and understanding in relation to the world rather than separate from it. The learning in action learning is holistic and developmental. It integrates learning from experience with learning with ideas through the process of reflection.

Fear of failure

An aspect of research on student learning has been concerned with the anxiety that the assessment system brings to students and the problems that some students have with poor performance under pressure. Fear of failure is also a strong motivation and some people work hard due to this motivating force. Assessment anxiety is a feature of many work environments with performance indicators and related targeting playing the same role as examinations. Tests and targets can provide an incentive to work and act as a useful focus of attention. Where too strong an anxiety is provoked, however, the result can be debilitating.

Action learning is clearly of use here. Action learning sets work with the related feelings and emotions, not simply the content of a person's issue. The set can help to put a situation into perspective and relieve the anxiety of an individual working alone on a difficulty. Action learning sets can provide the support for coping with fear of failure. An effective set is supportive and yet challenging. At different times a set member will require more support and less challenge and different individuals have different tolerance of these. Fear of failure is not an equally distributed motivation. Some people suffer much more anxiety than others in testing situations, and this can vary over time (Entwistle and Wilson, 1977).

An action learning set is a good structure for coping with such individual differences. It works with *what is* by exploring the issue as it is presented and helps to move towards *what can be* through learning from the experience and planning the next action. The set members are not intimately connected to other presenters' issues and therefore are less likely to induce anxiety. Where the experience for an individual between set meetings has been negative or where the action plan has not been completed, the set member may fear failure. The reduction of the fear will depend on the appropriate balance between challenge and support in the set and on the set members' ability to empathize with the presenter's emotional state at the time. In particular, it is important that learning is the focus – we can learn from a failed action or even from an incomplete one. It is the learning outcome in relation to the presenter's issue which should be the focus of the set's attention. Often what is learned in action learning is not that which was anticipated. The value is in the development of the individual.

The learning cycle

In Chapter 2 we introduced the Kolb learning cycle, which underpins action learning. This cycle crucially links reflection with action in order to enhance learning from experience. Learning, however, occurs throughout the learning cycle and not just in the reflection stage. As I experience the world, I learn directly through feedback in context. I observe the effects of my actions and I may discover connections that help me to understand the consequences of my action. From this I go on to develop my understanding through reflection. I reform my ideas of the situation and of the effects of my action within it. In this second stage my learning consists of new ideas and new ways of viewing myself in the situation. This leads me into a planning phase where I hypothesize about how things could be different and my ability to produce a better outcome from acting differently. I am learning in this phase about my own motivations and re-evaluating my strengths and weaknesses in relation to the situation. I am learning also to evaluate one plan against alternatives. This leads me into the phase of next action where I test my hypotheses and learn how accurate my imagined outcomes are. This is an experimental phase where I learn about how rich or how incomplete was my picture of the context and how accurate was my assessment of my ability to affect it. This again leads to observations that begin the next phase of the cycle. Learning therefore is happening throughout the cycle of action and reflection. We consider reflection in greater detail later in the chapter.

Most of us find, however, that our opportunity to reflect on our experience is curtailed by the need to continue the action phases of the cycle. Action learning provides a formal mechanism to make the most out of the learning from each stage in the cycle.

Learning styles

Individuals vary in how naturally reflective they are. We also differ in our willingness to experiment and in how far we use our observations to inform our judgement. The idea behind action learning is to encourage individuals to move through all the stages of the cycle.

Honey and Mumford (1986) show how learning styles map on to the learning cycle. They identify four styles – Activist, Reflector, Theorist and Pragmatist. 'Activists' enjoy the experience itself; their tendency is to go from one action to another, circumventing the reflective, concluding and planning stages. 'Reflectors' spend a great deal of time and effort in reflecting; they may find it more difficult to move from the reflection into the conclusions required for taking the next steps. 'Theorists' are good at making connections and abstracting ideas from experience and reflection; their tendency is to stay close to the abstract and they are less good at moving from these ideas into plan and action. 'Pragmatists' enjoy the planning stage; they have a tendency to rush to this stage without much effort spent in the reflection and theorizing stage. Their plans will be weaker as a consequence. We can all recognize our own strengths and weaknesses in the descriptions of these styles.

The learning styles descriptions show how we all have a tendency towards a different balance in the time and effort we expend on different parts of the learning cycle. Some of us are keen on activity to the detriment of reflection, others prefer theory to experimentation, and so on. What action learning does is give equal weight to each of these aspects which build up towards learning. In using action learning sets some people find that they normally spend little time reflecting on past action and simply move from one action to another with little conscious thought. Others find that they are inclined to generalize from the past and move to action without careful planning informed by theorizing. Some people may find that although they feel comfortable inside the set meeting the action part of the cycle eludes them. The set can help by focusing on the learning about oneself which can be gained through exploring these patterns of our behaviour. Learning comes from the balance created by using all of these processes together. Through action learning we take a more conscious and deliberate attempt to integrate experience and reflection and learning about the world and oneself.

Reviewing our learning in the set we can see the effects of our preferences for some parts of the learning cycle rather than other parts. This is an important piece of self-knowledge which can be promoted through action learning. This knowledge can help us to develop the capacity (and the patience) to learn more effectively using the whole learning cycle.

An intrinsic orientation

Research undertaken by one of us at Surrey University documented changes over time in students' orientations to study (Beaty née Taylor, 1983). The research resulted in a typology of orientation types (ie, not types of students as each student demonstrated a dynamic mix of orientations). These were – vocational orientation, academic orientation, personal orientation and social orientation.

Orientation Type	Aims in Studying
Academic intrinsic	Intellectual interest
Academic extrinsic	Academic progression
Vocational intrinsic	Training for career
Vocational extrinsic	Qualification for job
Personal intrinsic	Self-development
Personal extrinsic	Proof of capability
Social extrinsic	To have a good time

The first three types were subdivided according to intrinsic or extrinsic interest in the content of the course. Where students have an intrinsic orientation, the content of the course is important to their aims, eg in the case of the intrinsic vocational orientation, as training for a job. Those with an extrinsic orientation were studying as a means to an end, eg for the vocational orientation, as a qualification.

The research found that when a student's orientation is known, their study patterns, including how much effort they put into the course and on what parts of the course, can be anticipated. In formal education it is possible for students to treat their study as a means towards an end, being fairly unconcerned about the difference to their own development except in the end product or a qualification. They react very differently to those students who want to learn out of an interest in the subjects themselves and in their wish to use their knowledge and skills.

Action learning stimulates an intrinsic orientation because it centres on the person and their own learning needs. This does not mean that they do not care about the results of their work outside the set; on the contrary, results in the real world are the test of a successful process. Action learning helps people to make a difference, both to themselves and to the world in which they live. It is not a process which encourages procrastination, or doing something simply for the sake of an external pressure.

It is likely that orientations are affected by the nature of structures which support learning. From our experience of action learning in higher education we see participants changing over time in the direction of more intrinsic interest and more personal connection with the process of learning. Within organizations, learners often find that action learning has more impact on them as people (intrinsic) than the narrower focus on a problem (extrinsic) with which they may have begun the process.

A deep approach

Research in Sweden and in Britain in the late 1970s and early 1980s looked at learning from the point of view of the learner. It described important differences in learning between those who took a deep approach and those who took a surface approach (Marton *et al*, 1984). The original research was in relation to reading tasks and the two approaches are described as the difference between concentrating on the 'signified' or the 'sign'. The distinction is about the intention of the learner. In the deep approach the learner is intent on understanding a message in a text or in making connections between experience and new ideas. In the surface approach the learner is simply trying to gather information one bit at a time. They are saying to themselves, 'Now I must remember this and now I must remember that'. In research undertaken since these first descriptions, surface and deep approaches have been described in various forms of studying and in different subjects. The approach taken by a learner affects the learning outcome so that although on memory tests immediately after the reading there is little difference, on comprehension tests those taking a deep approach do much better. After a time delay, those taking a deep approach also do better on memory tests. Not surprisingly, a surface approach to studying is found to be ineffective for learning.

The concept has found a wide acceptance in higher eduction and there are now many texts aimed at academic staff in universities (eg, Ramsden, 1992; Gibbs and Jenkins, 1992) that advocate teaching methods to support a deep approach. They describe ways in which a deep approach can be encouraged and ways that a surface approach can be easily induced through, for example, a too high workload and assessment of surface detail. If we turn to look at action learning as a process, how well does it encourage a deep approach? Action learning is essentially concentrating on the signified – it asks 'What did I learn from that experience?' 'How can I make use of that observation in what I decide to do next?' and so on. These questions are essentially about the meaning of an event. If a participant is taking a surface approach, intending to learn bits and pieces of knowledge without thinking about how they might be applied or how they relate to other things, then action learning would be an inefficient method. We suspect that such a participant might not see the point of a set meeting. A surface approach would tend to keep action and learning separate when the reflection process within a set is precisely to integrate the two. Action learning sets are fundamentally about supporting a deep approach to learning, looking for connections and personal implications of action. The learning comes from reflection on experience, from interrogating the difference between what was expected and what actually happened. The result of taking a surface approach in this environment would be a very curious collection of unrelated facts.

Action learning helps to induce a deep approach by providing the supporting structure for the part of learning and development which is often neglected, ie reflection on the implications of past action and planning next steps. This is one essence of a deep approach – the search for meaning. Action learning provides a structure in which set members can engage in that search.

Stages of development and ways of knowing

Perry's scheme of intellectual development in the college years describes nine stages of development which students moved through during their college years (Perry, 1970). They moved at different paces and there were sometimes blocks which held up the development. In the first stage students believe in right answers. They have a 'black and white' view of the world where there is little room for uncertainty. They believe that uncertainty is the result of a lack of knowledge. If students are at this stage of intellectual development they believe that the lecturer's job is to transmit the right answers into the head of the student. Perry's nine-point scheme shows movement towards the idea of relativism and then to a personal commitment within a relativist framework. The learner moves through a period of believing that any idea is as good as any other to a position of a personal commitment, to a set of ideas acknowledging that this exists within a multiplicity of possible committed stances.

This work has been reviewed by Belenky *et al* (1986), who endorsed the dualism found in men and women. However, Belenky *et al* 'focus on what women might have to say about the development of their minds and on alternative routes that are sketchy or missing in Perry's version'. They go on to build on the methodology for this research in looking at the experiences of women. From their interviews they describe five epistemological categories:

1. *Silence* – women experience themselves as having no voice and being subject to external authority.

2. *Received knowledge* – women believe that they are capable of receiving and reproducing knowledge but not creating it.
3. *Subjective knowledge* – knowledge is seen as personal, private and subjectively known.
4. *Procedural knowledge* – where women apply objective procedures for obtaining and communicating.
5. *Constructed knowledge* – women view knowledge as contextual and themselves as creators of knowledge valuing both subjective and objective strategies.

Does the structure of action learning help to move people through the stages of development described above, faster and in a more supportive way than other approaches?

Action learning is a process which encourages personal responsibility for learning and the development of skill in constructing personal knowledge. It supports the development from voicelessness to personal power in the construction of knowledge. This may depend on the facilitator and set members being aware of the different ways they can be viewed in the learning process (see later in the chapter – learning as a social process – and Chapter 14). From our experience, development through the stages can occur as participants take more responsibility for their own learning. There can also be rejection which comes from a misunderstanding by the participant of the role of the facilitator. In action learning sets the facilitator is not an expert in the traditional sense of provider of knowledge. If a participant believes that transmission from an expert is how one learns then the process will seem inefficient to them.

Levels of learning

In *Steps to an Ecology of Mind*, Bateson (1973) describes a number of levels of learning which capture distinctions which are important to us and yet are unlike other descriptions of learning. The levels capture not only what we learn but the mechanism of how learning is acquired. The levels of learning he describes include an acknowledgement of how new learning is united and assimilated with our current ways of seeing the world:

Level 0 – learning has been 'soldered' into our behaviour so that we react in specific ways to specific stimuli or situations. These responses do not easily respond to feedback; they are habitual.
Level 1 – this is a process of trial and error where we adapt to the environment,

finding ways to correct for wrong choices within a set of alternatives. Level I learning continues until it gradually tails off and learned responses become automatic and then result in Level 0 learning. In Level 1 learning, the context is construed as the same in each case, in order to transfer our learning from one situation to another.

Level II – because no two contexts are exactly the same, however, we are also learning to recognize and 'inhabit' a context. We are learning the significance of the context as well as the features of it. This learning, although a side effect of Level I learning, has a powerful effect in our world view and our associations about the objects and people that inhabit our world. Level II learning forms our character since it gives us the frames which we use to describe the world to ourselves. 'It is like a picture seen in an inkblot' (Bateson, op.cit.). This collection of associations, which in a composite way is our world view, can become a straitjacket without Level III learning.

Level III – this level of learning involves an ability to step outside of our world view and look at it from the outside. We become objective about our own subjectivity. This is more than merely labelling ourselves as having particular characteristics: it involves a recognition of our responsibility for our own way of being. Learning here is a process of gaining control over our habitual ways of seeing the world learnt in Level II.

In action learning we are attempting to learn to move through these different levels of learning. The use of the set challenges our own views of the world and helps us to move beyond our habitual responses. We actively encourage the individual to take responsibility not simply for furthering their aims in the project but for recognizing and taking responsibility for their own ability to do so. The action learning set's support for the project straddles the internal and external world of the learner. It may be that action learning is more powerful for those who are able to use all the levels of learning and that it will be less useful for those who remain at Level I. It would be possible to discuss the progression of a project simply through the process of trial and error. Bateson shows us how the higher levels are very challenging to the person. The challenge to action learning is to encourage learning at the deeper levels. The support and challenge within the set offer a potent tool for such progression. The process is one which demands courage of the set facilitator and the set members. Moving through the levels is a goal, not a requirement!

Freedom to learn

Carl Rogers' work has had a big impact on our view of learning and the facilitation of learning. His views on learning and teaching were formed over many years of being a counsellor and teaching in higher education. He begins from a belief developed from his own experiences of teaching and learning that 'anything that can be taught to another person is relatively inconsequential and has little or no significant influence on behaviour' and that 'the only learning which significantly influences behaviour is self-discovered and self-appropriated learning ... (this) cannot be directly communicated to another'. Learning that does affect behaviour requires a drop in personal defences and empathy with the other person. It also requires acknowledgement of uncertainties and attempting to 'clarify my puzzlements'. This allows me to get closer to the meaning of my experiences and to come to significant learning from them.

Rogers describes qualities and attitudes that facilitate learning:

Realness in the facilitator – a facilitator of learning must first be themself. Their feelings are accepted by them and are available to be communicated if appropriate. Their relationship with the learner is a real relationship, it is authentic.

Prizing, acceptance and trust – this is a non-possessive caring for the learner, an attitude which believes fundamentally that the other person is trustworthy and worth caring for. It accepts the feelings of the other person as relevant to their learning.

Empathic understanding – this is understanding the learner from their point of view and seeing the world through their eyes.

Trust in the human organism – this is a trust that the learner as a human has the internal capacity to develop their potential. The facilitator provides the opportunities but trusts the learner to choose their own direction.

Rogers' work focuses on the learning climate which can be fostered through facilitation rather than 'teaching'. These features of facilitation are very close to our description of the climate within an action learning set. The set members and the facilitator are supporting the learner by their attitudes towards her as a fellow human striving to learn.

Development

We have reviewed some theories of learning. In action learning we cannot separate learning from development. Learning and development are like overlapping circles. However, we would like to explore our meaning of development before integrating the two concepts. We will also be looking at development from the perspective of the individual and groups/organisations.

Boydell *et al* (1991) define development as:

> working with individuals or organisations to enable them to cross a threshold which has qualitative significance to them and their life.

Development is thus open-ended and holistic. By holistic in this context we mean that the person may be engaging in a multi-faceted task where the effect of the whole is greater than and more significant than the sum of the parts. This contrasts training with development.

Development and training

By training we envisage an emphasis upon the acquisition by individuals of specific, identifiable skills, adding to or extending existing skills. In training, the individual is likely to have training done for them or to them, typically where the person providing the training is 'up-front'. Alternatively, the individual may have some self-help manual to support them. Thus training is about:

> the transfer of knowledge or skills from one who knows or can to the one who does not or cannot . . . the trainer is the expert, the knowledgeable or skilled one; the learner is ignorant or unskilled (Boydell *et al*, 1991).

We emphasize the distinction between development and training because the words are often used loosely and interchangeably. Action learning is primarily a developmental activity.

For example, a personnel manager in a negotiation role will bring a whole variety of interpersonal skills and understanding to the role which, combined, will contribute to the overall negotiation context. Moving into that role can involve some initial training, say on negotiation and bargaining, but the whole of that role will involve development on the part of the personnel manager that is wider than those skills learned and applied in isolation.

Development as a conscious activity

Development can take place naturally in the course of maturity and experience. However, we are using the term in a conscious sense of people thinking about, actively reflecting on and learning from their experience. There is a sense of active responsibility on the part of the individual to take control of their development. Development is more open-ended than the more specific ends associated with training. In development there are no 'right answers', though there will be the exercise of judgement, wisdom and raising of more questions. This does not mean developing people to be less decisive or immobile either! Action without reflection may result in disaster. Reflection without action may be very useful provided the individual is aware of the repercussions of that stance. We are asserting that action with reflection will combine in development of the individual and, when with others, with their development as well.

Characteristics of development

There are other characteristics of development for individuals that can be identified. Boydell *et al* (op. cit.) use a universal example by tracing a child's development of mobility. A child moves through phases from being static, to rolling, crawling, walking and running. We will utilize these characteristics and draw upon the experience of becoming aware of and working with sexism as an example of personal development which had work and life implications for one of us. The characteristics of development are set out in numbered stages for analytical purposes. Obviously they are not so neat or necessarily sequential in reality.

1. The notion that development is both a continuous and discontinuous process.

   I became aware intellectually of the idea of sexism in my 30s. I incorporated the value of being non-sexist into my beliefs and vocabulary – what I espouse and what I say. There is discontinuity from the earlier stage when I was not aware of the idea and behaviour associated with sexism.

This phase ended in crisis.

2. Crisis is marked by discrepancy and incongruence which is experienced as shock and surprise and causes the disintegration of the previous phase of functioning and creates the condition for the discontinuous 'step-jump' to a new phase.

   The new shock or incident that made for discontinuity was a behaviour by me that was pointed out as very sexist (it was) which I had not been conscious of at the time I said it, yet was in contradiction with my espoused values. In other words my espoused values were in conflict with my values in use or what I *believed* differed from my *practice*!

In Handy's (1991) phrase it was the time when 'continuity ran out' and I had nothing to fall back on, faced with the fact of my incongruity of behaviour.

The shock, recognition and dramatic incongruity leads to a reframing and transforms my values of the earlier phase in 1.

3. There has to be a 'readiness' for that development to happen: we cannot be forced, only encouraged.

> I now realize that in the arena of dealing with my sexism what I do is even more important than what I believe. Despite the realization of my continued sexism in my behaviour I am ready to move on rather than not move on. If I am not ready I cannot move on.

4. Development takes place over time and over the life cycle. Some development occurs as a result of crucial phases in the life cycle, eg puberty, starting work or family, or retirement. Development is about the whole person, group or organization.

> In the example of my attendance to my sexism I am struck by how my behaviour had repercussions upon all my life, not just work. I began to integrate the values, behaviour and actions into my life and work.

5. Development is progressive, one way, towards growth, though occasionally we may regress, say, in times of crisis but we cannot revert to a position we have left forever. Normally we aspire to greater understanding, more effective behaviour, etc but occasionally things happen that remind us of having been here before. . .

> Like times when I still echo some old sexist traits but they are not usually as grotesque as the one that created the earlier crisis.

> Even if I 'reverted' to my old sexist ways and behaviours, I would be doing so knowing where I had been more recently and would have to live with that.

6. Development is not easy or inevitable. We may get stuck, cautious, very comfortable and defensive on occasion. In times of acute personal (and organizational) difficulty, survival and maintaining ourselves may be more important than developing. Wanting to develop may be desired but might just not 'happen'.

> Whilst I made for integration of anti-sexism in my personal relationships, there have been and are times when I have been hesitant and defensive about that integration.

7. Development is an upward spiral in which we may still meet old problems but at a more subtle level.

Now, working with equal opportunities in a developmental way with individuals and organizations, problems still emerge for me but at a different level. An example for me is, when is it appropriate to challenge a colleague engaged in an equal opportunities development programme?

Development and organizations

We can build on this personal example of development by relating it to manager and organization development in respect to the implementation of an organization's equal opportunities policies. For an organization to effectively implement such policies each manager may go through a similar complex process to that outlined above. Our view is that it is not simply a matter of personal change that a manager may experience (even though that is a necessary condition). A manager and the organization will, if the implementation and integration is to be successful, need to work with changes in practice and working relationships. For example managers will wish to model good practice in those relationships: be it, do it. They will need to be able to manage the changed expectations of staff and possible conflict arising between staff. The organization will wish to model good practice by removing institutional discrimination and creating the conditions for good practice.

A recent example where one of us was engaged in the implementation of equal opportunities policy in a public sector organization is useful here. All managers undertook internal workshop development. On completion of the workshops many of the managers recognized their own personal change and development. However, it would not be sufficient just to leave the personal development there. That alone would not bring about the necessary changes in working practices for effective implementation of the policy. Incorporated into the workshops and integrated into their work and that of the organization and its collective action were tasks, actions and processes that were to be built in to integrate the policy into the life of the organization and its members. Actions in relation to recruitment, selection and retention of staff as well as attention to the equalities issues relating to the quality of the service also had to be built in.

In summary, development is a complex activity that cannot be just acquired, or added on. Development is in the hands of every individual and collections of individuals as groups or organizations. As Boydell *et al* describe it: 'The impulse, ownership and evaluation belong to the developing being' (ibid).

The conditions for the effective development of each individual need to be created. How that development is encouraged, nurtured and enhanced is critical to the development of individuals and, by implication, organizations.

Learning, development and the individual

Action learning is developmental. It capitalizes on 'higher' levels of learning. Surface learning, extrinsic orientations, rote/Level I learning and received learning are unlikely to be enhanced by an action learning set. The set process is designed to promote deep learning, intrinsic learning, 'connected' Level II learning and, at its best, the personal development and commitment to Level III learning.

Clearly, set members may find themselves at any 'stage' or 'level' and an effective set will enable members to move, ie, grow, learn and develop. There is no prescribed or best point of arrival, as every set member pursues their own path to learning, their own personal journey.

We understand learning and development to be crucially linked within the essence of a person. If we ask the question, 'What does learning and development mean for the person?' the distinction between learning and development breaks down. In our view it is impossible to understand learning separate from its effects on the person; a person is their learning. Similarly it is impossible to talk about development without seeing this as an essential aspect of the person's being.

Learning and development are natural processes throughout life. After early childhood, however, the processes do not occur without effort. The intention to learn and to develop is an important prerequisite for effective learning. This is not to say that learning and development are not also a consequence of what life imposes on us. We learn very quickly in times of threat to our person or to those we love. We develop as a consequence of our experience and the more experiences challenge us the greater impetus to our development. We can also hold up our development and block our learning. By refusing to confront issues and by side-stepping experiences that challenge we can become stuck and intransigent.

Action learning can provide a vehicle for moving forward – to support and challenge the individual so that learning and development happen. This learning and development process can be fun. The action learning sets provide a group experience which is fulfilling through sharing.

Learning and development can also be painful. To learn and develop we may need to confront our self in a way which is outside of our established comfort zones. David Casey (in Pedler, 1992) describes this as breaking out of 'the shell of our understanding'. This shell is not ignorance. It cannot be broken by the addition of knowledge, ideas and perspectives from the outside, eg from other set members. Rather, it requires the pain. The pain comes from confronting the shell of understanding from the inside: 'Knowledge can be gained by breaking into shells from the outside, understanding can be gained only by breaking out from your own shell from the inside'.

A useful example is that given in the stages of development earlier in the chapter. Casey suggests that the set adviser's role is sometimes personal consultancy within the group setting, to ensure that the opportunity is provided for an individual to confront themselves 'from the inside'.

Learning as a social process

We have conveyed the significance of learning and development at the core of effective action learning. However, learning and development do not take place in a vacuum. Learning is not value-free or neutral. The review of some significant contributions to learning theory reflects a tendency we wish to counteract – of learning as merely an individualistic process. Jarvis (1987) stresses that:

> learning always takes place within a social context and that the learner is also to some extent a social construct, so that learning should be regarded as a social phenomenon as well as an individualistic one.

Salmon (1990) affirms this when she emphasizes the experience of learning situations as mediated through the learner's personal stance – by personal biography and social and economic forces. The learner's interaction with these 'gives rise to assumptions, beliefs, perceptions and ways of construing and acting upon experience' (Weil and McGill, 1990). Salmon adds to the learner's stance by emphasizing the supposed neutrality or objectivity of conventional understanding of learning or teaching where:

> *content* is viewed as essentially 'out there', independent of the persons of both learner and teacher ... there is typically quite a massive disregard of the inescapably personal meaning of every curriculum (Salmon, 1990, emphasis in the original)

That 'personal meaning' is deeply embedded in the way we see, interpret and grapple with change in our world. Belenky *et al* (1986) place personal stance in an educational context where a particular group may be a muted group in a dominant environment (see page 180 and Chapter 14). Salmon's reference to content being viewed as essentially 'out there' suggests an objectivity, which she challenges, about the content as well as the learner's (and teacher's) approach to it. Similarly, the process of learning is 'taken for granted'.

The individualistic emphasis of learning also rebounds against learning and development for individuals. As observed at the beginning of this chapter, the individualization of learning, the significance of 'competency', the trend to self-development if isolationist, suggests that the learner is on her own. This is not only a lonely experience but, as we shall see when we appraise the significance of reflection below, developmentally poor practice.

The other aspect we wish to emphasize about dialogue relates to the purpose of learning. We look to learning to be transformative and empowering (Chapter 14). Therefore the social conditions in which learning and development take place deeply influence the nature of that learning and development. We will now review aspects of the social conditions that prevail in action learning.

Emotional and political aspects of learning and development

We emphasize the emotional and social as well as the cognitive context in action learning. Set members can benefit from interaction with others through dialogue and the structured synergy that can be available to a set. This structured process is often conducive to enabling a set member to learn, develop and change. Vince and Martin (1993) capture this:

> One of the most powerful aspects of the Action Learning model is the clarity of roles, structure and timescales it provides. Its highly structured format often provides containment for the anxiety that is generated in the learning environment. The managers we work with appreciate the model because it is an approach that creates familiarity and trust while promoting practical reflection on management practice. The model therefore makes it possible for managers to stay with their uncertainty about taking risks, about their struggles.

Vince and Martin point out that traditional approaches to action learning emphasize the rational, task-orientated aspect of learning, in for example, the learning cycle. We have stressed the importance of process as well as content and the interaction of emotion and feelings in working with personal issues that enable learning and change. In Chapter 14, we stress the need to make explicit issues of power that exist in a set member's working context as well as being represented in sets themselves. We support the view of Vince and

Martin that the emotional and political (power) aspects of action learning need to be made explicit.

Emotions and feelings will surround the action learning process for a variety of reasons. A set member may be anxious about sharing an issue with the set; unused to taking responsibility for her learning; not being used to speaking out or challenging another set member. The anxiety created may be redressed by the trust and confidentiality within the set. In such a situation the set will be able to encourage the learning of the presenter or set member through the stages of a cycle of uncertainty – risk – struggle – to insight – a new way of seeing the(ir) world and empowerment. If the conditions are not appropriate, the anxiety may lead to flight or fight (Bion, 1961) ie, withdrawal or aggression expressed in some form, denial or avoidance, defensiveness or resistance, each of which or in combination 'creates the right conditions for his or her own willing ignorance' (Vince and Martin, 1993).

Recognizing and making explicit these two potential cycles, one which enables learning and empowerment, the other which inhibits learning and empowerment, is more likely to enable set members 'to make sense of processes of change, both personal and organisational' (op cit). If the set can make explicit the emotional aspects as well as the task-orientated aspects of work in the set, this is likely to encourage the set member to address the emotional aspects at work where previously these may have been ignored.

The political or power aspects of learning and development also need to be addressed. We have referred to this with the relationship between facilitator and set members in Chapter 5 and in relation to personal empowerment in Chapter 14. Action learning sets have a political dimension, in that they replicate interpersonally and in the set, the sense of power and powerlessness that is found in any other group or organization. Individuals can feel a sense of power or powerlessness *vis à vis* others. This is well illustrated by Marshall (1984) with her explanation of social power, where she introduces the notion of dominant and muted groups. This can be innocent in the sense that an individual may not be aware of their position or role but nevertheless live it (see Chapter 14). Issues of power can be implicit across the set as well. A set that is aware of power issues within the set and works explicitly with these politics will, as Vince and Martin express it, recognize that

> The political nature of action learning is expressed through the strategic choice available to learning groups to move in a direction that promotes learning, or a direction that discourages learning (1993).

Examples of power differences in a set could include: a white male set member unaware that the issue he brings to the set and his use of language inadvertently puts down women; a set member who dominates a set to the exclusion of others; a facilitator and/or set member who recognizes (or not) an example of racism by a set member but who does not challenge the set member (or is unaware of the racist nature of the statement).

The set may move to challenge the set member and (if necessary) the facilitator. If the conditions are appropriate the set can help the person and the set in a direction that promotes learning and empowerment for the set and the set member. We have again a potential condition of anxiety by the person wanting to take the risk to raise the issue and challenge the behaviour as well as possible anxiety on the part of the receiver of the challenge and other members of the set who hear the challenge and await a response. If the set is aware of the political aspect, the set will be able to encourage the learning of the set member or person being challenged through the stages of the cycle mentioned above.

Take the behaviour exhibited by the white male set member. Confronting, however appropriately, the behaviour means that the individual challenged and perhaps the person expressing the challenge may feel vulnerable and anxious. The set that is aware of these political dimensions is, despite the uncertainty felt and the risk taken, potentially more likely to move into the cycle leading to insight and new learning that is empowering for all. Working implicitly without recognizing this political dimension may mean that the set colludes with power relationships between set members that limit the effectiveness of the set. Furthermore, if sets implicitly replicate power relations elsewhere, the opportunity to work on the 'external' power relations will also be limited as the set will simply mirror that which is often implicit in organizations. Providing this political perspective in the action learning process gives set members the opportunity to reflect upon the:

> personal and institutional significance of different managerial (*or other set member*) experience (eg black/white, female/male, disabled/able-bodied, gay/straight) for the very practice of change within their work (Vince and Martin, 1993, emphasis added).

Thus the emotional and political aspects of learning and development in action learning sets have two potential perspectives and cycles that can be self-limiting or encouraging.

It is important to acknowledge the interrelationship between emotional feelings and political power in a set. Emotions promoting or discouraging learning are affected by the internal politics of the set. In our example above, if the set did not disturb the 'innocence' of the set member about his sexism, the set member(s) who wished to but did not confront him would be into avoidance with potential and consequential feelings of resentment and anger that remain silent or are expressed in another way. The set moves into the limiting mode of learning and the politics remain as they were.

The effectiveness of a set and its members is enhanced by the set's understanding of how it works – the process and the personal and interpersonal skills set members bring to the set. That effectiveness is further enhanced by the explicit recognition of the emotional and political aspects of learning and development. The wider significance is the ability of set members to apply such understandings and skills to other organizational contexts.

Facilitation, learning and development

Learning and development cannot be separated from the process in which it happens. We have made explicit throughout our guide the *process* of action learning and the role of facilitation (whether with a facilitator or self-facilitated).

The accustomed norms about the process in which learning takes place tend to be implicit, unexamined, taken as a given. We realize that the action learning process is unlike many other learning contexts, one which also places clear responsibility on the individual to learn within a collaborative context. We are working outside prevailing norms about the way to learn.

The 'novelty' of action learning raises this implicit norm as a tension between what the set member has been used to and the 'new' process in action learning. It is therefore important to make explicit these processes to enable set members to work with the tension and to help them recognize that much learning and development can occur through working on process.

If process is important for learning and development, then facilitation of that process is important too:

- Facilitation of process influences learning and development.
- By making the process explicit we provide the means for learners to empower themselves and each other.
- Facilitation of others' learning and development contributes toward that learning and development.
- By facilitating the review of process we become more conscious of process, the range of processes and the potential application elsewhere.

Facilitation in a set is thus functional and at the same time a social process. An example of the value of effective facilitation would be actively listening to a set member as part of the means by which she may be supported in her learning and development (Sue Knights in Boud *et al*, 1985) underpinned by the social interactions reviewed above which enable her to reflect – a key element in learning.

Learning and reflection

Reflection is an important part of learning and can be valuably adduced in action learning. In this section we uncover more meaning about reflection as well as underwriting what we have been saying above, that reflection is more significantly achieved in a social context.

Boud *et al* (1985) asked the question: what is it that turns experience into learning? They found that for reflection and therefore learning to occur the following need to be recognized:

- Learners can only learn themselves and only they can reflect on their experiences.
- Reflection is an intentional event.
- Reflection is a complex activity in which feelings and cognition are closely interrelated and interactive.
- That reflection is a part of cyclical process.

The last point here is a reference to Dewey (1933) and to Kolb (1984). Boud *et al* get into the detail about the relationship between learning experiences and reflection which we outline below.

How best can reflection be promoted? We will describe the kind of reflection that lends itself to the action learning process. Given an experience, there are three elements that are important in the reflective process.

1. Returning to the experience by replaying it by description of some kind, eg describing it to others.

This provides data and possible clarification for the learner and others and may provide insights not recognized during the experience, eg particular feelings of which the person was not conscious.

2. Attending to the feelings associated with the experience.

The learner's feelings may have at the time affected how she responded to the events. A negative feeling may have disabled the response to the event resulting in a less effective or inflexible response. Returning to the event enables an 'outside' view of what happened. Working on such experience in a set requires sensitivity which is underlined by our approach to skills in Chapters 8 and 9.

3. Re-evaluating the experience following attention to description and feelings.
This is undertaken via four aspects that are not necessarily stages but elements of a whole:

> first, *association*, that is, relating of new data to that which is already known; *integration*, which is seeking relationships among the data; *validation* to determine the authenticity of the ideas and feelings which have resulted; and *appropriation*, that is, making knowledge one's own . . . While reflection is itself an experience it is not, of course, an end in itself. It has the objective of making us ready for new experience . . . a new way of doing something, the clarification of an issue, the development of a skill or the resolution of a problem (Boud *et al*, 1985).

The summary above does not do justice to the writers. It does, however, exemplify the essence of reflection and what action learning sets can do for and with presenters by providing a process that enables reflection to happen.

Senge (1990), drawing upon the work of Argyris and Schon (1978) and Schon (1983), suggests some useful skills that enhance our skills of reflection. Skills of reflection:

> concern slowing down our own thinking processes so that we can become more aware of how we form our mental models and the ways they influence our actions (Senge, 1990).

Mental models represent images, assumptions, stories that we carry in our heads about people, families, organizations. 'Our mental models determine not only how we make sense of the world, but how we take action' (ibid).

Argyris (1982) distinguishes espoused theories and theories-in-use. The former represent what we say. The latter represent the implied theory in what we do. It is our theories-in-use that are our actual mental models (and we may not always be conscious of using them). A classic example of the gap between espoused theory and in-use action is to be found above in the section on development. In that example it was very hard to see my theory-in-use until it was pointed out by another person; in Senge's phrase, by someone who was 'ruthlessly compassionate'. 'In the quest to develop skills in reflection, we are each others' greatest assets' (ibid), is a useful reminder for set members.

Another skill to attend to in reflection is recognizing 'leaps of abstraction' (Senge, 1990). We tend to leap from a small piece of data to make a generalization about a situation without testing the data. From one or a few behaviours we tend to generalize a situation without asking deeper questions, eg, 'John is always late' after one or a few times when he was late. The generalization needs to be tested and John could be asked about his perception of the situation. We give more examples of how to use the skill to spot 'leaps of abstraction' in Chapter 9, where we discuss generalization. Being asked about our leaps by other set members helps us to spot them.

A further skill is the technique of drawing attention to what we really think but do not say, using what is known as the 'left-hand column' (Senge, 1990, drawing upon Argyris). The 'left-hand column' is about visualizing a sheet in two columns. On the right-hand column is what is said by the parties to a conversation. In the left-hand column is what I am thinking. In a set, members may be doing this mentally. This may be because we are sensitive, polite, or desire not to be critical. It is helpful, on occasion, for set members to convey their left-hand column to the presenter. An example would be where a set member is talking about a colleague at work who is getting on her nerves, is unable to complete work on time and is in a blaming mode. The set will endeavour to work with the issues she raises while the left-hand column is thinking: Is she aware of the strength of feelings toward her colleague? What is she contributing toward the relationship?

Senge (ibid) also emphasizes the skill of balancing inquiry and advocacy. When we are in harness at work we tend to be advocates of our positions and stances toward situations. Action learning sets provide a context for inquiring into a situation. This as part of the reflective process can provide a balance to the advocacy undertaken outside the set. Adversarial positions need not be taken in sets and may help provide enskilling outside in balancing inquiry with advocacy.

Finally, to return to our theme that the effective use of reflection is a social one. Without conversation and dialogue, reflection is limited to the insights of the individual (which are not to be underestimated). To borrow and adapt Habermas (1974) on this: personal reflection requires the detachment on the part of self to look at another part of self. In this Herculean task there is a danger of self-deception, and set members have an important role to play in the dialogue that promotes reflection.

As Boud *et al* (1985) state, unaided reflection misses a process that can be: 'considerably accelerated by appropriate support, encouragement and intervention by others'.

Reflection is about support for each other. But it is more than that:

Learning is not a desirable outcome or goal; it is the activity of making an interpretation that subsequently guides decision and action. Learning is grounded in the very nature of communication. Becoming reflective ... is central to cognition for survival in modern societies. It is the way we control our experiences rather than be controlled by them, and it is an indispensable prerequisite to individual, group and collective transformations. Mezirow (1990)

We endorse Mezirow who aptly captures our view of reflection and our stance on learning and development.

Chapter 11

Continuing Professional Development

In this chapter we explore the affinity between action learning and professional development and to show how action learning can support continuing professional development. The most well known use of action learning is in the management area but increasingly people are describing the enormous benefit action learning can have in other areas of professional development. We have designed programmes of action learning for professional groups, eg social services professionals, housing specialists, and health professionals. In higher education, action learning is being used in staff development programmes for managers, academic staff and administrators (see Chapter 13).

What are the generic features of professional development which make action learning such a useful process in these disparate areas?

What it is to be a professional

The term 'professional' is associated with work which is valued highly in society. The 'professions' – lawyers, doctors, social workers, accountants – are highly trained and often highly paid members of society. In this sense the term professional is a kitemark given to those who complete a rigorous and demanding training and then continue to develop their speciality within the profession through further formal training and experience. The professions are characterized by codes of conduct which they require of their members and also a degree of individual autonomy and responsibility for their working practice. Although professionals can belong to large organizations where their work is only one part of the whole, they tend to have a large amount of personal control and autonomy in their working practice. This brings with it a high level of responsibility and obligations for the maintenance of high standards and quality of work. The term professional is increasingly used to describe an attitude to work and not merely a type of work. We talk about a professional approach, meaning acting in a professional way: an approach to life and work which includes taking responsibility, being creative and not merely going through the motions and taking a questioning and critical look at our own individual practice. With this attitude individuals aim to use their knowledge and skill to develop working practice for themselves and for others. This professionalism can therefore be claimed by many more people than those in the traditional professions.

It is this second sense of professional which has a close affinity with action learning. Professionalism and action learning share the same values in taking individual responsibility for action and taking an active approach to development of the organization (where appropriate) and of oneself.

The nature of professional development

Professional development is the nurturing of an attitude to life and work which promotes a responsible, creative and proactive approach. The development of an individual with a professional approach goes beyond knowledge and skills to the core of personal growth and the ability to harness this growth into more effective action. It acknowledges that this development is never complete, there is always more one can learn about oneself and the complexity of the world in which we live.

Development of insight and wisdom

Whereas initial training can give us competence, professional practice requires the development of insight and wisdom in responding to the idiosyncrasies of the situations that face us. Professional development, therefore, crucially involves learning from experience. For a doctor, a lawyer, a teacher or a manager there is always a mixture of the expected and the novel in any situation. For a doctor, each patient has recognizable symptoms expressed through a unique individual context. In the classroom the teacher faces a blend of the known personalities and a unique interplay between them.

The challenge to the professional is to learn from experience in a way which does not cramp the fresh interest in each particular piece of work. Initial training can only provide the basic background for practice. Beyond this, a view of the unique circumstances must be involved in a judgement which becomes easier with experience and tacit knowledge built up over time. But as we build our experience, we may also become less attuned to the individual differences, become over-confident in our judgement and miss the signs of difference which are crucial to successful action.

Recognizing patterns in experience

We learn from experience through a process of observation, reflection and generalization and by recognizing patterns within the complexity of our experience. We also learn to tailor our actions by reference to our own internal store of experience which allows us to say, 'I have seen a situation similar to this before'. We learn to recognize emergent events so that they no longer take us by surprise. On the whole we do all of this naturally, without deliberate processes of record keeping.

We may also build up knowledge of our own individual habits, styles and tendencies. We learn to distinguish events that will challenge us from ones where we are comfortable and at ease. This store of self-knowledge is also fundamental to the development of professional practice.

Professional development and reflective practice

Although we all learn from experience, more and more experience does not guarantee more and more learning. Learning from experience tends to happen most effectively when the experiences are novel or where they are painful in some way. Our normal human reactions to events ensure that we think a great deal about things that have caused us pain: we search for a cause that will help us to act differently to the same stimuli in the future to avoid the pain. Over time, however, the same experience modified through the early learning will have less impact on us. For example, 20 years of teaching may not equate to 20 years of learning about teaching but only one year of learning repeated 20 times. Indeed, this repeated experience may have resulted in some inefficient or ineffective habits that may be very difficult to change.

Reflective practice, so important to professional development, is not an automatic result of experience. We need techniques and methods to encourage us to reflect and to enable us to learn from that reflection. Novel experience encourages reflection. Opportunity to experience novel situations may diminish with continued practice. We may need to seek the novel through deliberately exposing ourselves to new areas of work or different perspectives.

Painful experience can promote reflection. We think about what went wrong. Where the pain is great, however, this can lead to the opposite of reflection – a hiding from, or unconscious barrier to, thinking about it. In some circumstances then, we are likely to spend time reflecting whereas in others we may need help to face situations that we would rather not think about.

Most of our experience is neither particularly novel nor painful. There are, therefore, many times that our normal reactions to events are insufficient in themselves to encourage reflection. It is here that we need techniques and help from others.

The use of dialogue

There are things to be learnt from reflection with the aid of other people. For professionals the most immediate benefit can come from using various forms of feedback from customers and clients to encourage reflection. They are the other actors in the situation that we are reflecting about. Their perspectives, attitudes, responses and feelings provide rich data for our reflection on our professional practice. Moreover they focus our attention in a helpful way on the result of our work.

Peers can be very helpful in aiding our reflection. They are likely to be able to empathize, we may trust their professional ability to maintain confidentiality and so on. They aid our learning in that their own experience and knowledge adds insight into our reflections on our own practice. Unlike clients, they will notice our actions from the point of view of a professional. They will also be able to imagine clients' reactions to our suggested actions from this point of view.

A peer's view of the discipline can be an important focus for this reflection. On the other hand, a peer who is not in the same professional area could add a focus more on the process of professional action rather than on the content. The support of peers provides an opportunity for learning beyond that of private reflection by the individual.

While discussions do help us to reflect on our practice, rarely does a general discussion allow us to interrogate in a specific and deep way our own personal approach. It is easy to have a discussion about teaching and learning, for example, without feeling that there are any conclusions to be drawn about our own approach as a teacher. The concentrated and intentional process of deliberately reflecting with the aid of peers is altogether a more potent tool for professional development.

Developing appropriate links with others

A professional approach involves acknowledgement of our own limitations and a willingness to involve others or to take particular care with aspects of the work where we are less able. A newly trained professional will on the whole be more aware of the build-up of this experience than someone who is very experienced. After some time our ability to learn something new every day (or to believe that we can learn something new) tends to diminish. We may stop feeling like a learner and rely solely on our current skills and knowledge. It is at these times when the support and challenge of peers is crucial to our professional development.

Most of us experience a degree of isolation in our work. It is not so much that we work alone, more that we have few opportunities to reflect on our own practice. We can notice how other people work but we are unlikely to discuss differences unless they actively interfere with our own way of doing things. This can bring complacency and an increasing resistance to change. We may need to invest time in supporting our own development in a more formal way.

The need for emotional support

The professional's role is characterized by the responsibility that they have for their practice. This often means responsibility in relation to the welfare of other people, as most professional groups have clients who invest a degree of trust in their expertise. In doing these jobs there is an emotional content that is not so imperative in other work. We all have to relate to other people at work but the professional attitude requires the individual to take responsibility for the effects of their actions on other people. In some professional areas there are particular organizational strategies to cope with these pressures. Social workers, for example, have supervision on an individual basis, with a peer or more experienced member of the team, which provides a safe environment within which to discuss and to keep perspective on the emotional content of work. Most other professionals work without these formal processes.

The cycle of learning from action and reflection –
how development occurs

We have shown above how reflection does not automatically follow from experience and how learning does not automatically follow from reflection. We need to make a further link between learning from reflection and consequent development of professional practice. For example, it is possible to identify some behaviour of mine that is interfering in the effective learning of students. My ability to change will depend on developing this understanding through reflecting on practice and in deciding what I could do to make a difference. In some cases I may conclude that I need to use different techniques of teaching, implying a knowledge base in educational practice. In other cases the necessary change may be to do with my personal style of interactions with students. Of course, to change habits or personal traits is more difficult than changing techniques of teaching. In either case I must not only decide what to change but also how to learn about or develop the skills involved in this change.

The cycle of action and reflection must therefore be enriched through knowledge-based or skill-based development. It is not enough to experience and to reflect: we must make a conscious effort to develop our knowledge and skill and this may require further development.

Continuing professional development

Professions are now recognizing the need for continuing professional development (CPD). The Institute of Personnel and Development (IPD) is a leading advocate of CPD and has set out guiding principles:

- Development should be *continuous* in the sense that the professional should always be actively seeking improved performance.
- Development should be *owned and managed* by the individual learner.
- Development should *begin from the learner's current learning state* and, while fitting appropriate organisation or client needs, would not be over influenced by someone else's ideals. CPD is a personal matter, and the *effective learner knows best what he/she needs to learn.*
- *Learning objectives should be clear, though they may be complex,* and wherever possible should serve organisational as well as individual goals.
- *Investment of time in learning should be regarded as being as important as investment in any other activity.*
  (IPD, 1995, emphasis added)

The IPD has incorporated CPD into its professional standards because it ensures that professionals remain up to date, encourages their aspiration to improved performance, ensures commitment to learning as an integral part of work and helps to maintain the reputation of the profession. The IPD cites, as necessary, a minimum of five days or 35 hours CPD activity or the equivalent in learning outcomes per year.

The IPD professional draws up and implements a professional development plan (PDP) in order to structure their development. The PDP provides a focus and framework for identifying CPD needs, planning appropriate action, implementing learning activities, recording and reviewing progress. There is no uniform way to draw up a plan – each can be tailored to the individual. Support may also be sought from significant colleagues, mentors and managers. The PDP should take into account personal aspiration, professional development needs and an employer's requirements.

The IPD professional maintains a record of their CPD which lays emphasis on providing evidence of outcomes of the learning opportunities rather than just a list of inputs or activities. This requires analysing what was actually gained from having undertaken an activity. Reflection that enables a person to show what they have gained is essential to ensure that the process is really developmental.

Relevance of action learning

There are many means by which professionals can engage in their learning and development. The IPD cites professional work-based activities, courses, seminars and conferences, as well as self-directed and informal learning. The more formal elements include, for example, project management, secondment in and outside the professionals' organization, professional, graduate and flexible learning programmes. The informal can include reading and writing for professional journals, voluntary work, and observation/reflection on events in the course of work.

However, engaging in the opportunities may not necessarily encourage the reflection which is so important for development to take place. As the IPD maintains:

> The most important aspect of CPD is the learning outcome, not the precise amount of input. Experience alone does not create learning: reflection is needed to gain real benefits (IPD 1995).

The IPD therefore encourages their membership to engage in reflection by inviting them to consider their approaches to learning as well as considering their learning styles. The personal record is designed to help the individual elicit responses to the questions: What did you learn from it? How have/will you use this?

The professional can make much headway with this individually. The IPD also suggest the use of their branches and groups with a named CPD coordinator to support members in the development and implementation of their plans. The coordinator may, *inter alia*, enable linking 'together members to encourage learning through peer group support, mentoring, appropriate events and access to learning resources' (IPD, op cit.).

We would like to make more explicit the use of action learning which can provide a coherent structure that encourages specific and explicit use of the whole learning cycle including the key element of reflection.

Our concern in this area is that the individual may be left very much to their own devices to engage in reflection in a potentially isolated, solitary way. Continuous professional development is rightly *owned and managed* by the individual. This principle highlights the responsibility and control for development and learning in the professional. This does not mean that the developmental process need be an isolated one.

Indeed we would assert that the process can be enriched by sharing. Action learning provides a structure for learning and a *social* context for reflection (see Chapter 10). We believe this social aspect of learning is underrated. In a set each member is responsible for their own learning and responsible to other set members in supporting each other's learning. This is where dialogue, referred to earlier, is crucial. For set members to engage in a developmental dialogue, a balance of challenge and support behaviour is necessary. The skills to achieve such a balance are set out in Chapters 8 and 9. The process of dialogue creates the reflective conditions for learning. Focused development is provided by the professional's emergent plan for implementation.

We can now show how action learning meets the IPD's guiding principles, listed above.

Development should be *continuous* for the professional. That continuity can be maintained with the support of colleague professionals over time in a set described in Chapters 2, 3 and 4. We envisage that in the early years following acquisition of professional status, the support of a set would be particularly useful in order to attain an ease with the notion of reflection and learning how to learn.

In action learning the working assumption from which sets start is to *begin from the learner's current learning state*. As we state elsewhere, action learning works from where the set member is. No uniformity is imposed about where set members may be or ought to be. Linked to this principle is the clear recognition that *the effective learner knows best what he/she needs to learn.* The set member is encouraged to clarify what her learning needs are. An example of this approach in making CPD work for an individual is that drawn from self-managed learning (Cunningham, 1994). This is a rather more elaborate version of the approach of the IPD. The professional asks herself five key questions:

1. Where have I been?
   This is biographical in nature, drawing upon her background, previous experience, significant events in her learning about herself and the person she is.
2. Where am I now?
   This question invites her to articulate the skills and qualities that she possesses and what kind of person she is.
3. Where do I want to go to?
   This elicits important subsidiary questions: What do I want to do? What kind of person do I want to be? What skills and qualities do I need to gain to get/be there?
4. How do I get there?
   What learning programmes, opportunities and processes do I need?
5. How will I know that I have arrived?
   The questions that will provide evidence here include: How do I evaluate my learning? How will I assess myself so that I have the means to know that my learning goals are met? What measures do I need in order to assess myself?

Questions 1 and 2 enable our professional to clarify her learning needs. Question 3 is the basis for defining and setting her goals. Question 4, the *how* question, provides the means of attaining her goals. Question 5 provides the basis for her assessment of her learning achievements in the form of tangible evidence.

Returning to the IPD's principles, the approach, or variants of it, can help to ensure that our professional's *learning objectives should be clear, though they may be complex.*

Action learning reflects the last principle of CPD that *investment of time in learning should be regarded as being as important as investment in any other activity.* With, say, an annual cycle of CPD, the questions above could be spread over that period. Membership of an action learning set can provide the base for creating a personal contract that sets out what 'I' want to achieve with the agreement of significant others (such as colleagues in the set; line managers for project planning, implementation and review; joining a post-qualification programme). A contract and an agreement with others to go for it (even though it may be modified) helps to maintain momentum and tenacity. A planned intention to undertake something can remain at the planning stage for ever. With a challenging set the professional is encouraged to move from planning to implementation.

Having the continuing support and encouragement of an action learning set can provide the bridge over dips in motivation surrounding development. As we have shown earlier in the chapter, development can be painful and isolating as well as pleasurable and exhilarating.

Continuing professional development requires evidence for the person engaged in the process and, as in the example of the IPD, for the professional institute as well. The action learning set process creates the conditions and a framework for that evidence to be adduced. An action record of the set is itself evidence of the developmental process.

We endorse the approach being taken by the IPD and are aware of its application as a potential model for other professions. The formalization of continuing professional development in the IPD's approach has assisted us in conveying how action learning may be used by professionals to support and make effective their development.

Action learning and continuing professional development

As Pedler *et al* (1991) put it:

> Action learning involves reconstructive learning, or reframing, as well as simple additive learning or error-correction. We can only learn when we are ready to do so, and what we have learned in the past, including the 'professional deformation' which comes from long practice, can take a long time to loosen and transform.

Professional development demands a complex weave of reflective practice and opportunities for development of knowledge and skill. Reflection on practice is, however, the oil in the wheel of effective professional development. Action learning sets may ensure that development opportunities are better directed, ie, act as a diagnosis of the need for more formal learning on courses etc, as well as a bridge between experience and learning.

Action learning can provide an environment within which the professional can describe their own feelings about the emotional content of the work. The set provides an opportunity to take a risk by exposing our normal professional practice to supportive yet challenging scrutiny by others.

Professionals on action learning programmes frequently comment on how difficult it would be to gain, at work, the quality of attention that they have available within the set. While many of us rely on our friends and partners for the support to cope with these emotions, action learning sets can add a more formal environment which provides empathy rather than sympathy; a focus on learning and future action rather than on merely coping with the moment.

The set provides a rich environment to consider alternative approaches. The presenter's attitudes may be challenged but they are challenged in order to foster learning. There are no hidden agendas and no loss of regard from showing vulnerability. This may be a refreshing change within a normally competitive working life. It is this action learning environment which can be so supportive of our continuing professional development.

Chapter 12

Using Action Learning for Management Development

The purpose of this chapter is to show how action learning can contribute toward the development of managers and organizations. We initially consider some relevant contextual issues: what organizations need to encourage in their staff to cope in conditions of uncertainty; what we mean by management development; and the levels at which organizations may embrace development.

We will show how action learning can promote management development in three ways: through the development of the individual manager in the organization; via systems of management development to meet particular individual manager needs; and as a contribution to the development of the organization as a whole.

The changing nature of organizational life

The justification for using action learning as a significant process contributing to manager and organizational development is based upon the effectiveness of action learning as a developmental process. Action learning processes for individuals, groups of staff and organizations can contribute to their ability to work actively with uncertainty and continuous change.

The era of relatively predictable futures, linear development, rationality, formality, tight hierarchies and specialization is in decline, yet many organizations and the people who work within them still live the culture and expectations of that era. Many writers, organizational theorists and practitioners have witnessed the atrophy of organizations in this mode and the need for different mindsets or ways of seeing the world (Handy, 1991; Kanter, 1981, 1989; Morgan, 1986, 1988; Peters, 1987).

Peters (1987) describes how we live in a world of 'generic uncertainty' where technology, competition and ever-changing tastes require: market niche orientation with shorter production runs; international outlook and action; flatter, more responsive and stand-alone organizations within large organizations; a concern with quality and a closer customer orientation; participation adding value through people.

Handy (1991), in appraising the nature of change, conveys neatly what is happening: 'that the changes are different this time: they are discontinuous and not part of a pattern'. By the changes being different this time, Handy means that in the recent past, change did occur for us but it could be largely prefigured, like the anticipated stages of a professional career, where there might be some unanticipated events but they were usually 'more of the same only better' (*ibid*), incremental in nature. Embracing discontinuity in the nature of work would be where an individual can contemplate that 'work' may well take different forms, be on the periphery of an organization(s), change radically in its nature over the years, and live with the anticipation that it is likely to be very different in the future from what it is now.

The problem with change that is framed round more of the same and mere incremental change is that our thinking and learning is caught within that frame:

> In a world of incremental change it is sensible to ape your elders in order to take over where they leave off, in both knowledge and responsibility. But under conditions of discontinuity it is no longer obvious that their ways should continue to be your ways; we may need new rules for new ball games and will have to discover them for ourselves. Learning then becomes the voyage of exploration, questing and experimenting . . . (*ibid*)

One of the questions therefore is how organizations respond to create that reflective learning environment conducive to their maintenance, sustainability, survival, growth or transformation.[1]

Such reflective and questioning learning is potentially rebellious and an affront to those who control the way 'things are done around here'. But that is a reflection of the learning that is necessary – questioning that which is given. 'This is the way things are done around here' without questioning can

---

[1] Even here we are aware of not trying to forecast the future. We hesitate to use the term 'growth', the most recent positive word associated with firms, particularly in the private sector, without the other terms attached, like 'sustainability' which may also have greater plausibility for some organizational forms.

lead to catastrophe. Did there have to be a catastrophe like that at King's Cross for smoking to be banned entirely from London's underground rail system? Handy uses the example of the *Titanic* for another catastrophe having to happen before lifeboats were provided for all passengers. Whilst these may be extreme examples, more likely scenarios are a gradual demise of organizations whose purposes are fixed in the past and remain so.

For organizations to actively counter a fixed view means creating a working environment where its members individually and collectively can get into that learning, questioning mode to cope actively with discontinuous change. For Handy (1991), a significant arena will be in our work: 'that it is the changes in the way our *work* is organized which will make the biggest differences to the way we all *live*' (emphasis in original).

Thus the only consistent feature of organizational life is change. A key for us is how people respond to the effect of this truism. Given the lack of choice about change, our personal experience of working in organizations is that people are trying to cope with the change that is happening around the organization and with the consequences within the organization. The phrase 'trying to cope' is used intentionally. Many are aware of the rapidity of change. However a person may be aware of the change but be passive to or even a victim of that change. Or it can mean that a person is actively aware of the process of change as an agent and is actively working with the flow of that change for their benefit and for organizational benefits. This book is a contribution to enabling people more actively to live and work with the flow of discontinuous change.

Morgan (1988) is concerned with the demands that these changes will make on the competences required of managers and staff in the years ahead. In the light of the debate and activity around the idea of competences in the UK, we would concur with Morgan's definition:

Now more than ever, organisations and their members face the dual problem of how to do it right *and* how to do it well. In the process, the whole concept of competence is changing. Whereas, in the past managerial competence went hand in hand with the possession of specific skills and abilities, it now seems to involve much more. Increasingly, it rests in the development of attitudes, values, and 'mindsets' that allow managers to confront, understand, and deal with a wide range of forces within and outside their organisations, as well as in the development of operational skills. (Emphasis in original)

Whilst managers and staff still require specific skills and abilities they also require to enrich and sustain their mindsets to assess the relevance and implications of what they are doing so that they 'become competent at being competent' (ibid). It is in this framework that we can relate management development to action learning.

Manager and management development

We now define our view of who managers are; briefly distinguish training and development; distinguish manager development from management development; and define management development in two ways: as the systems required for manager development to occur and as organizational learning.

Managers: who is included?

We take a very broad definition of managers as people who *take* responsibility for their lives and work. In this sense 'everyone a manager' enables all staff to think and act managerially (Boydell *et al*, 1991). This also means that an organization can consider all staff in terms of their developmental needs.

We acknowledge that a narrower definition of manager can be made. Burgoyne (1988) when writing of the manager's development refers to managing that 'shapes' both itself and non-managerial work, which is 'what makes it [managing] different from other forms of work and what makes management development different from other areas of human resource development'. Thus some managers are also shapers.

We will maintain the two notions of 'everyone a manager' and some managers having an additional responsibility for the management of others.

Core activities?

Handy (1991) likens a person's work to the idea of a doughnut or, more appropriately, a bagel. The inner circle of the bagel represents the core of the person's or manager's work. For many in the past that represented the whole of their work. Beyond that was a clear boundary where someone else had a responsibility. That inner circle still exists for many but there is an outer circle of the bagel which is now a much more fluid, discretionary part of work which overlaps with the outer circle of others.

This trend is reflected in the traditional tendency for firm and clear divisions of responsibility for processes and tasks being replaced by an enhancement of many work roles in organizations, given technological advances and a move towards more integrated organizational design. The traditional mechanistic division often resulted in attitudes such as, 'Well, that's outside my brief, I can't help you', which is being replaced by 'How can we work through this task given our different starting points?'. Instead of emphasizing points of demarcation, we move to 'Where and how can we work on this problem?' This distinction highlights the contrast between the person who seeks to delimit her responsibility and the person who starts from a point of wishing to take responsibility for work for themselves, with colleagues and in the organization. This is not to be interpreted as a recipe for exploitation, more one of enabling individuals to meet their needs with others.

Thus managers are people who take responsibility for their lives and work, some shaping the work of others as well, who are increasingly working with others to achieve organizational and mutual ends. How do managers achieve these ends effectively through their training and development?

Training and development

We distinguished the terms training and development. In summary, training is about the transfer of, acquisition and addition or extension of specific, identifiable skills. Such skills are usually expert-led or have the support of a self-help manual. We saw in Chapter 10 that development is a complex activity and one which is complementary to training.

Development applied to managers involves the whole person in a continuous and conscious learning process that takes place progressively over time and the life cycle. Individuals and organizations may or may not be conscious of the need to actively engage in their development. Once conscious of the need and motivated to do so, then the best conditions for their effective development need to be created. How that development is encouraged, nurtured and enhanced is critical to the development of the organization.

We now make a distinction between manager development and management development.

The manager's development

By the manager's development we mean development that is consciously undertaken by the individual manager for her purposes. Her development is about 'the process of change, learning and development that affects how the person shapes and performs [their] tasks, roles and activities' (Burgoyne, 1988). The capacity of the organization to learn, survive and work with an ever-changing environment will depend upon the energy deriving from its staff and managers. That energy amongst managers will in turn partly depend upon the kind of developmental activities they engage in. The key questions that ensure energy is creatively harnessed will be:

● Does the developmental activity really *engage* the manager in her personal development in work and life?
● Does she have *ownership* of her development?
● Is the organization prepared to let the development of the managers happen in a way which engages their *energies* and *empowers* them?

Once these questions are recognized the organization supporting the manager's development can legitimately ask the following:

● What are the *benefits* to the organization of her development?
● What *value is added* to the organization by that development?

Note that there is a balance to be achieved here between meeting the legitimate needs of the individual and the consequential benefits for the organization.

Management development

By management development we refer to two distinct aspects:

(a) The totality of development that is undertaken by the organization for its staff – systems, structures and processes. We will call this the 'systems' of management development. These would include, for example, appraisal systems, career planning, planned and formal development on and off the job. Coaching, mentoring and action learning would be considered forms of planned development on the job.

(b) The effect of (a) on the organization as a whole – the synergy and learning that is achieved by the organization. We will call this the 'organizational learning'. This is now characterized by the term the 'learning company'.

Manager development and both aspects of management development interrelate. The systems of management development that are initiated by the organization will influence the quality of manager development – (a). The quality of manager development that is achieved will influence the extent and quality of organizational learning that is achieved – (b). This can be

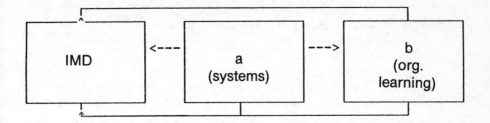

Figure 12.1 *The totality of development*

represented in Figure 12.1 where IMD is individual manager development and (a) and (b) are as defined above.

To use an old metaphor – the engine of development is in the people in the organization in terms of the energy they bring to their development. The systems of management development are the starter motor for individual development which in turn leads to group and organizational development. In effective individual manager development, rest the bases for that management development of the organization which is about the organization's learning and its capacity for learning.

Burgoyne (1988) writes of his concern for the emphasis:

> to focus too much on the individual manager (IMD) and the organisational systems (a) dedicated to his or occasionally her development, and too little on management development for the organisation as a whole.(b)

We have inserted in parentheses our notation from Figure 12.1 to link our distinctions about management development with Burgoyne's comment.

Burgoyne has provided a valuable model in which to place the contribution of the systems for development (a) and the development of the organization as a whole (b). Burgoyne considers there are six levels of maturity of organizational management development defined as 'the management of managerial careers in an organisational context', (a) above.

We shall briefly review the levels of maturity and then in the next sections consider how action learning can contribute to manager development and organizational management development (b).

Levels of management development policy
(adopted from Burgoyne, 1988)

Level 1
At this level there is no systematic or deliberate management development. What takes place is 'natural' management development where development for individuals happens as a result of people living and working. Development is intuitive, there is no conscious planning of development. This level is most likely to occur and be effective where the organization is new, relatively small and at an entrepreneurial stage.

Level 2
Here the organization responds to development through isolated and piecemeal activities resulting from imperatives facing the organization such as a felt or emulated need to engage in staff appraisal, quality or performance measurement.

Level 3
At this level there is a coherent link between the development needs of individuals identified at appraisals with career plans designed to realize that development. The only problem with this level is that a system of recording and notching-up of career progression may well be in place but the system and its results may well get out of synchrony with what is happening in and around the organization. In other words, changes will happen and the developmental framework is unable to respond to it.

Level 4
Management development policy and planning are closely linked to corporate planning. The organization actively clarifies its objectives and seeks to meet them through a management development policy which re-orients staff. For Burgoyne (*op cit*) this means 'it is possible for enough of the right people to be got into enough of the right roles with enough of the right skills quickly enough for the plan to work'.

The problem at this level is that the corporate plan may be non-implementable in management development terms. In other words, the people being developed are not 'malleable' to the demands of the corporate plan.

Level 5
At this level management development processes (a + IMD) relate closely

to the development of the organization (b) in that the former influences and inputs into the latter as well as being part of the implemented output of strategic planning. This is achieved through involvement of managers in their collective future as well as their individual development. Human resource vision configures with marketing, technical and financial considerations. Here the organization 'demarcate(s) the contours of managerial feasibility that must surround any new venture and change' (Burgoyne, *op cit*).

Level 6
An extension of Level 5 with management development processes used to enhance the nature and quality of corporate policy-forming processes, as well as informing them and implementing them. Organizational learning takes place at the corporate level. 'When the company takes a risk, it does everything it can to maximise the learning from that initiative, whatever the business outcome' (Pedler *et al*, 1991).

Our experience is that organizational life is more messy and less 'organized' than is suggested in some of the above levels. Burgoyne took the view at the time of writing (1988) that a large number of organizations, perhaps the majority, were at Levels 1 and 2. Levels 3 and 4 describe the limits of best practice achieved with any consistency. Levels 5 and 6 existed as occasional achievements, 'often precariously achieved and lost and often only occurring in some relatively autonomous part of larger organisations'.

Levels 5 and 6 are, in the view of Pedler *et al* (1991), the levels where the organization may be at the stages of functioning as a 'Learning Company'. A learning company can only happen as a result of learning at the whole organizational level: 'A Learning Company is an organisation that facilitates the learning of all its members *and* continuously transforms itself' (emphasis in original). 'Company' is used to convey the convivial rather than to denote applicability only to the private sector.[2]

---

[2] Pedler *et al* (1991) find the term 'organization' mechanical, abstract and lifeless. We would agree but there is a risk that because the term 'company' is used to mean private sector profit-oriented organizations, we may well implicitly exclude public sector, community and voluntary organizations. Therefore, despite the abstract nature of the term 'organization', we have used it in this book because of its universality. But we also use the term to include the people who make it up. The organization is greater than the sum of its parts. The organization will have its particular climate, culture, myths and values. However, these characteristics are only realized through its people.

We have considered management development in three ways: as the manager's development; the systems of management development designed to meet particular individual manager needs; and the contribution to the development of the organization as a whole. We now review how action learning contributes to these three forms of management development.

We will start with the development of the individual manager, using the term 'manager' in both the senses outlined earlier in this chapter: manager as 'everyone a manager' and managers with 'shaping' responsibilities for others.

Individual manager development

Our purpose is to convey how participation in action learning can make a particular and significant contribution to the development of managers – the IMD in Figure 12.1. We recognize and do not underestimate the fact that managers will learn and develop informally in their work and lives (Mumford, 1989). We also recognize that managers may (or may not) have planned career development programmes and forms of structured interventions such as appraisals, career planning, coaching, mentoring and secondments. We distinguish action learning as a form of at-work development where the manager is directly utilizing the experience of work, from off-the-job forms of development such as obtaining qualifications via courses, such as an MBA.

Self-development is another strategy which an individual manager may take up, possibly with the encouragement of the organization. Pedler *et al* (1986) define self-development as: 'personal development, with the manager taking primary responsibility for her or his own learning and for choosing the means to achieve this'. Their guide was in part a response to the movement that wished to counter the idea that a manager's development was something that was 'done to' a manager, with the idea that managers could take control over their own learning and development with a resulting increase in effectiveness.

In action learning the manager is taking responsibility for her learning within the supportive framework of sets underwritten by the organization as part of the organization's system of management development.[3]

What are the potential benefits contributing to a manager's capacity to

---

[3] However, in Chapter 6 we consider the use of self-facilitated sets which may be created by people without organizational support.

learn, develop and change by participating in a set? The significant benefits which we will consider below are: the development and enhancement of human relationships at work; effective approaches to learning and empowerment; ability to live with uncertainty and ambiguity; project management; and enhanced skills of facilitation.

Development and enhancement of human relationships at work

The relationships described below are developed through the deployment of a wide range of personal and interpersonal skills and abilities. Managers can enhance these through participation in action learning sets by working on relationships, working with others, reflecting on and moving to action outside the sets. Clarkson and Shaw (1992) clarify five aspects of relationships at work in organizations; they are set out in the box below.

Human relationships at work in organizations

- *The unfinished relationship* which carries the human need for dealing with the conflicts and hurts of the past, where the effects of past relationships are carried into the present, characterized by unrealistic fears and hopes which may or not correspond with the present.
- *The working alliance relationship* satisfies our need for 'doing' and competence where the relationship is between two or more people constructed round a shared task, which underpins much of what is done, 'aspired to in organisations and frequently least achieved' (ibid).
- *The developmental relationship* where the focus is on our growth and developing the adult professional where the individual is provided with information, support and challenge to meet their contemporary development needs.
- *The personal relationship* carries our self needs and our need for recognition as unique individuals, involving trust, authenticity and affirmation often gained through shared tasks, experiences and values in the workplace.
- *The transpersonal relationship* carries our need for being, meaning and connection, the latter between individuals or groups. It is deeper than the relationships above and importantly extends beyond the people that any one individual knows or works with, but may include at its best some form of shared values across an organization.

Clarkson and Shaw specify the key skills needed when people are involved in each type of relationship. Whilst their purpose is relationship training in organizations, we will convey how some of those relationship skills may exist and be enhanced in the action learning context. The enhancement of relationship skills is underpinned by the use of the basic interaction skills considered in Chapters 8 and 9.

An important qualification needs to be made here. It is not the function of an action learning set to provide for needs that should be met elsewhere. In particular, it is not the place to provide for unfinished relationship needs whilst, nevertheless, recognizing their existence. It is important that set members and facilitators respect the right of the individual to meet these needs in their own time in appropriate settings of counselling or therapy.

The unfinished relationship

- A person's capacity to 'recognise, minimise, neutralise, rechannel energy from unfinished relationships issues into the here and now task' (ibid). An example may be where a set member has low self-esteem which emanates from distant, past relationships and which affects his effectiveness in dealing with colleagues. The safety and support of the set may enable him to address the feelings and try out new patterns of behaviour.
- By working in a set the manager may, through being able to receive feedback as well as working on issues of significant personal relevance, develop self-awareness.

The working alliance relationship

- Team working skills are enhanced with the interpersonal and intra-personal skills and abilities that set members bring to the set. Managers, as set members, enhance and develop the key skills considered in Chapters 8 and 9 which are crucial to effective collaborative working outside the set. However, complementary to these skills are the skills of problem-solving, planning, goal setting, action and reflection which enable colleagues to effect tasks as well as get on with one another! Where organizations move toward less bureaucratic structures and control, to team- and project-based formats, these complementary skills become more important.
- Project team leading skills – frequently the core content work of set members is to progress projects. The project may be one where the set member is leading a team outside the set or one where the set itself is engaged in a project. The practice of sets engaging in reflection, planning,

action and moving forward, followed by further reflection, enables set members to be more effective through the articulation of the process.

The developmental relationship

- Counselling and enabling skills are enhanced in the set. Managers are increasingly expected to employ the skills associated with counselling without, of course, taking on the professional role of counsellors who may have a very distinctive role in the organization. Examples of a manager using some basic counselling and enabling skills are appraisal and career progression. In the set, the skills addressed earlier and the role of facilitation (Chapter 5) which set members model and then assume, are important here in enhancing managers' awareness and abilities to 'empower the individual to take appropriate levels of responsibility in discovering how to develop themselves' (*op cit*).
- Mentoring, where the manager is using a particular relationship skill, is also enhanced through set practice in that the set member models good mentoring practice in enabling the presenter to work through her issues. Likewise, as presenter the set member gains understanding of what it is like on the receiving end of mentoring.

The personal relationship

- Interpersonal skills have already been considered above in the set context and in Chapters 8 and 9. The effect of the particular style of set meetings where one set member as presenter has her time with support and challenge from others in the set, alongside review by the set, means that the set members can consciously reflect upon their own and others' impact interpersonally within the set meetings and in their work. In the set meeting, members can 'develop their ability to offer one another collegial authenticity, sharing without burdening, and listening without caretaking' (*ibid*).
- Set members may, in the supportive environment of the set, be able to practise their personal effectiveness, ie, their ability to work with their affective side, their feelings and emotions, in a way that may be culturally inappropriate in the wider organization, and in the process widen their repertoire of behaviours beyond the set in seeking with others to bring about cultural change.
- By its nature the set is a group activity enabling set members to work on their group process skills. The positive and empowering nature of the

action learning approach creates the climate for trying out, enhancing and developing interpersonal skills in the group setting.

- Set members may use some of their time in the set to work on and reflect upon the management of their personal boundaries, ie, the need to create personal relationships balanced with their role in the organization.

The transpersonal relationship

- A single action learning set cannot effect that connectedness between people across an organization. However, a set has the basis for linking the self with the whole represented by the set. When a set is effective each set member has a sense of the set being a whole of which they are an intrinsic part. That whole is also greater than the constituent members (and here we include the facilitator, if there is one). Set members, when sharing that feeling and value of a greater whole, tend to give a deeper worth to the meeting and working of the set and what they feel they gain from it.
- The connectedness *between* set members does not mean that there is necessarily a close personal relationship with set members outside the set meeting. It is simply that they share a feeling for the quality of connectedness that derives from the experience of the set. This is often in contrast to some of their other working relationships and their response to connectedness with others across the organization. We will refer to the issue of wholeness and the transpersonal in Chapter 14. Sets can thus give meaning to the transpersonal. The key which we will examine later in this chapter is how sets across an organization can contribute to the whole. Clarkson and Shaw capture our view: 'Organisations which pay no attention to the transpersonal are those without heart or spirit, that just 'go through the motions' (*ibid*).

  The action learning experience and process can provide a model of the transpersonal by enabling managers to recognize, understand and feel what it is like. Managers are then more likely to be instigators elsewhere in the organization in combining with others to create the conditions for effective transpersonal relationships.

Approaches to learning and empowerment

The action learning process enables managers to develop and effect personal change for themselves and with others. The process creates the conditions for learning and for empowering the manager, as learner, to act and engage with the complexities of their work and roles.

We have already reviewed the contribution to understanding of the learning cycle as developed by Kolb (1984) which occurs in the set process in Chapter 2. Revans (1983) placed firmly in action learning the idea that learning, to be really effective, has to be about real problems in real life with real people. Action learning is distinctive in that the process 'stresses that it is as important that knowledge be able *to help one to act in a situation,* as it is to just explain or understand that situation' (Morgan and Ramirez, 1984, emphasis in original).

Much of our tradition of learning is about knowledge and understanding. Though important, knowledge and understanding are only parts of the action learning process. On their own they may make little difference to how a person may act differently in the world. Action learning, by being problem-related, means that the set member is an actor who learns to understand her situation, gain knowledge *and* generate action in a real context.

Another key element in learning via action learning is its social element. Individuals are not learning on their own – they are with others. The social aspect of learning is missing in Kolb's explanation but not in Revans' work or that of others including, for example, Morgan and Ramirez (op cit) and Handy (1991). Weil and McGill (1990), in explaining the diversity of experiential learning, extend its meaning to take in the personal *and* the social so that experiential learning, of which action learning is a good example, means:

> the process whereby people, individually, and in association with others, engage in direct encounter and then *purposefully* reflect upon, validate, transform, give personal and social meaning to and seek to integrate the outcomes of these processes into new ways of knowing, being, acting and interacting in relation to their world' (Weil and McGill, 1990; emphasis in original).

Action learning promotes the above and encourages set members to take responsibility for their world which, with the social element of action learning, enables the set member as manager to empower herself. We all have a choice, even though we do not have full control over our lives, in how we respond to our world, passively or actively. Action learning enables people to consider that choice with a disposition toward actively interacting in the world. That stance can encourage and bring empowerment. That empowerment can be individual and social.

Another aspect of learning is the distinction between learning to solve a particular problem, referred to as single-loop learning, and learning that is learning about the way we learn to do such things, referred to as double-loop learning (Argyris and Schon, 1978). An example of single-loop learning would be where an organization's strategic plan reveals a potential increase in demand for a service which is responded to with a planned increase in trained staff, with consequential resources being committed to meet that demand. A double-loop approach to the revelation in the strategic plan would be to review different ways of responding to that demand other than the accepted response – in other words, to reframe the thinking beyond the 'more of', 'less of' approach. This means reframing the way in which we think about an issue by breaking out of existing norms. Given the need for organizations to be able to cope with uncertainty and inevitable change, the capacity of managers to think within single-loop learning may be an inappropriate response. Action learning sets can also provide the support of others who are 'outside' the problem to enable the set member to reframe the problem.

Action learning can provide the conditions for challenging the way we frame our understanding of problems. The enhanced ability to change our way of seeing the world means that we can have a wider appreciation of our world and with it greater possibilities as to how we choose to interact with that world. In that process is an empowering and active potential in contrast with taking our world as a fixed given, over which we have little or no room for manoeuvre.

Living with uncertainty and ambiguity

Linked to the need for the capacity to reframe our way of seeing the world is the loss of certainty. We now live in conditions of generic uncertainty. But growing up in a relatively certain world enables us to live and work in a mental frame that is similarly certain; thus our cognitive framework may be out of synchrony with the world around us.

The certainty framework may also inhibit learning because learning and change are inevitably about that which is unclear, uncertain, unsure. Handy (1991) refers to an attitude of mind that is a 'negative capability',

> which learners need to cultivate, to help them write off their mistakes as experience. . . . We change by exploration not by tracing well-known paths. . . . We start our learning with uncertainties and doubts, with questions to be resolved. We grow older wondering who we will be and what we will do. . . . If we cannot live with these uncertainties we will not learn and change will always be an unpleasant surprise.

An aspect of that certainty in the past in Western traditions has been the tendency to create separateness and dichotomize things which do not have to be separate. Thinking and feeling, knowing and doing, subject and object, order and change have been separated and treated as separate. These dichotomies are breaking down. The process of action learning encourages participants, in working with real, live issues and problems to rise above these separations.

Dichotomous thinking is also about either–or, this or that, hard–soft, win–lose, leading and following, task–process, creativity and discipline, static and dynamic. Managers working effectively in the uncertainty business operate above these apparent opposites by framing issues that enable their meeting and merger. Underlying either–or thinking and behaviour can be a competitive dogmatism based on a simplistic way of seeing a problem and a solution which may also create win–lose conflict between the people involved. The set process can uncover the dichotomous thinking for what it is, lead to a more creative handling of ideas and help the manager, as set member, to work beyond the dichotomous.

Project management

We have reviewed how managers as set members progress projects with sets in Chapters 2, 3 and 4. Projects undertaken via action learning sets can have the following range of characteristics:

- Operational through to developmental for the manager
  - an operational project would be one that may be to do with making more efficient and effective the way in which the manager currently undertakes her job. It should be noted that even here the project would have a conscious developmental impact on the manager because the set process builds in the articulation of the problem, planning, action, review and reflection, further planning and action in the cycle of learning as well as pursuit of the aims of the project.
  - a more explicit developmental project where the manager is working on an issue or problem beyond their operational responsibilities, above the 'parapet' of their own operational experience. Here the content of the project as well as the process is intended to be developmental for the manager.
- Manager-inspired through to organizationally inspired
  - we have already reviewed in Chapter 6 the different approaches to the use of sets by organizations. Where the organization wishes to use sets to enable managers to define the project issues, problems and opportunities

for manager development purposes, the manager is the determinant of the project, selected with some form of review required by the development manager responsible for creating the sets.

- more commonly, where the organization takes a responsibility for initiating the projects, the negotiation determining the parameters and boundaries of the project will be between the manager undertaking the project with the support of the set, an external client for whom the project results are required and the set with whom the manager will test the feasibility of the project.

- Projects are real, involving real issues and problems of relevance to the organization
  - for significant potential developmental and learning impact, the manager takes responsibility for implementation of the project. The manager can reflect on the actual effects of setting in motion the planned and intended effects of a project. This has a higher risk potential than simply taking a project to recommendation stage; implementation carries a greater responsibility for the manager. The learning may on occasion be about what went wrong, what can I (we) learn from the mistakes that happened?

Skills of facilitation

Using an action learning methodology to progress the project, Morgan (1988) was involved in a major Canadian scheme examining the skills and competences that would be needed by managers and senior executives if organizations were to be able to work with 'the turbulence of the modern world.' This required:

- viewing people as a key resource and valuing knowledge, information, creativity, interpersonal skills and entrepreneurship;
- replacing organizational hierarchies with flatter, decentralized, self-organizing structures, in which facilitation, networking and remote management are crucial;
- developing contextual competences that help actors from different organizations across the environment and cultures work on shared problems through networking and the creation of alliances.

Flatter, more fluid and self-organizing structures mean that managers will need to initiate meetings, project teams, working groups and networks. With traditional forms of hierarchical and mechanistic organizations, managers are able to exercise authority and control more unilaterally and directively. In organizations using networking, control is more consensual, requiring managers to manage their relations with others. Moving and nudging toward agreement, negotiation and orchestration require a wider range of skills. Such interactions also require attention to balancing action-oriented tasks and processes with creativity. Lessem (1991) anticipates facilitating skills 'becoming increasingly important in management' but feels they 'may only come into their own in the next century'. Facilitation skills developed by set members in sets can help underpin some of these ways of working.

Morgan used forums of participants to explore the issues of the project and recognized that participants could hit 'major roadblocks that can easily overwhelm and reduce the energy of the group'. Facilitators needed to be aware of that possibility and adopt a style that allowed them to intervene in an active rather than a passive manner.

We have already examined the skills needed by the facilitator of sets in set meetings. We emphasized the importance of modelling effective practice in order that set members acquire and enhance facilitation skills themselves. Morgan cites four facilitation functions, each requiring special skills. We draw upon them here to emphasize the importance of these to the manager in a wide range of contexts. Their significance is the extent to which these functions and skills are developed and enhanced in the action learning process.

Morgan's skills of active facilitation (adapted from Morgan, 1988)

1. The need to *manage group process*
   - understanding the dynamics within the group
   - sustaining a task-related focus
   - managing time
   - knowing when to encourage speculation and creativity or a more disciplined integration of ideas
   - knowing when and how to end a particular session so that participants have a sense of optimism and energy for the next step in the process.

2. The need to adopt *a reflective, synthesizing approach to group discussion* that summarizes and 'mirrors' issues back to the group, so that they are able to remember and integrate their ideas or deal with paradoxes that have been raised.

---

3. The need to make *interventions that 'frame' and 'reframe' the issues*, especially as a means of unblocking overheated or unproductive discussions or of energizing excessively myopic or 'groupthink' discussions.

4. The need to make an *unobtrusive record* of the group discussion.

(Emphasis in original).

The facilitative functions here are obviously more appropriate in a group discussion format. However, Functions 1, 2 and 3 are also intrinsic to effective set processes in relation to maintaining the process of the set as a whole whilst working on the presenter's issues. Function 4 is also maintained by the facilitator or one of the set. Set members, as they progress in a set, take on these functions and skills so that all share in the process of facilitation.

Action learning as part of the systems of management development

In this section we consider the systems of management development – the totality of development undertaken by the organization for its staff ((a) in Figure 12.1).

What contribution can action learning make to the provision of the systems of management development that should be designed to enhance managers' development?

Organizations survive, operate, and prosper in conditions of uncertainty and need to respond to that uncertainty. The quality of that response depends upon its managers, as important stakeholders. We have already defined managers very broadly. We contrasted their training and development and saw how their development, which belongs to them, is crucial to working with uncertainty. The development of groups of managers and the organization as a whole depended on that individual development.

To be effective, development undertaken for individual managers should *engage* them, give them *ownership*, *energize* and *empower* them in their development. For the supporting organization there should be *benefits* from and *value added* by that development, The developmental conditions should provide, 'the process of change, learning and development that affects how the person shapes and performs their tasks, roles and activities (Burgoyne, 1988).

Earlier in this chapter we used Burgoyne's (1988) model of levels of management development to convey, inter alia, the range and impact of the provision of type (a) management development. We recognize that organizations will be somewhere along that range. Any organization that wishes to use action learning as a part of its management development will want to ensure that other mechanisms are in place. Burgoyne (op cit) usefully defines the systems and processes which organizations can implement to move up the stepladder of management development incorporating that which occurs at lower levels:

1. Hard systems, ie those systems, procedures, rules and roles that are necessary to ensure that the organization contributes to the aspirations at each level. Examples include performance appraisal and review of career potential and development needs followed by an audit of the cumulative talent of the organization.
2. Soft systems involve the creation and maintenance of the attitude, culture, organizational and managerial style, ie the ethos and climate to make the aspirations at each level work and count. Without these the elements that make up 1 above will be aridly undertaken without commitment.
3. Collaborative career planning, ie a managed process of dialogue between every manager and the organization about career prospects and aspirations, skills and development needs.

Collaborative planning is a key for Burgoyne in making the aspirations in levels 3, 4, and 5 happen (see page 216). The planning creates good deals for both parties – the manager and the organization. What are the features of a good deal negotiated between both parties? They are the opportunity for the manager to take stock of themselves and their work:

- what they are good at, their potential, their tapped and untapped abilities;
- what they want to do now and in the future;
- their view of the organization and its policies;
- their contribution to the organization and their personal development.

The results are negotiated but informed decisions at personal and corporate levels (Germaine and Burgoyne, 1984).

Utilizing action learning

We have emphasized some of the key developmental benefits which contribute to a manager's capacity to learn, develop and change by participating in a set:

- enhanced effectiveness in working with the range of relationships at work, including team working, developmental roles such as mentoring, working with and encouraging cultural and trans-personal change;
- capacity to learn, reframe and empower self and others;
- ability to live with uncertainty and ambiguity;
- enhanced capacity to undertake project management;
- developing skills of active facilitation which can be utilized to manage group processes.

These skills and attributes are over and above the basic but important skills gained in and from working in sets that are addressed in earlier chapters.

The combination of these skills and attributes are important for managers (and organizations) in developing 'a capacity for self-diagnosis and self-development on an ongoing basis, so that they become competent at being competent' (Morgan, 1988). We would add that development is also a shared experience to avoid the notion of the self-development happening in isolation.

In Chapter 6 we reviewed how sets could be used by an organization in terms of whether set members worked from the personal development end of the continuum or the externally negotiated project end. In essence, does the organization sponsor managers to join sets where the set members engage in a project with a direct pay-off for the organization? Or do they create sets to enable managers to take their own issues to the set with perhaps a move toward a project at a later stage?

Whichever approach is used, the organization can still require the review of a manager's learning and reflection to be built into the career development planning cycle. The line manager and participant manager can negotiate and agree the developmental targets and aspirations the manager is to aim for, prior to set membership. Following a cycle of set meetings the manager can take into the next career-planning meeting a review of what she has gained from the set in terms of personal development, changes in the way in which she manages and pay-offs for the organization.

We would not mechanistically prescribe a structure for permeating the organization with sets (because we are addressing readers from a wide variety of organizations) except to say that they can be employed with variety. We have reviewed some possibilities in Chapter 6. Below are some possibilities which meet a variety of management development needs:

- Project development needs of the organization and/or the manager as set member.

- Personal/management development needs of the manager in their operational role.
- Group projects undertaken by the whole set for a project on behalf of the organization.
- Sets to meet specific developmental needs of managers. Examples include:
  - mentoring sets. Here managers new to mentoring join a set to deal with the issues deriving from their role as mentors. Apart from the support, learning and emulatory ideas that mentors may acquire, the existence of such a set may help create some consistency of practice across the organization (Cameron *et al*, 1992);
  - developmental sets. In some organizations managers may have a purely developmental role, working on 'frontier' issues for the organization. Managers working on a diversity of projects form a set and provide an engine for each other in progressing the projects;
  - increasingly managers are working on distance learning programmes to enhance their development as managers and/or their specialist function if they have one. Here managers use sets to work through the open or distance learning packages and practice, as opposed to working on their own.
- Set adviser sets. Organizations building-in action learning as a significant part of their management development processes will wish to build in the facilitation process to reduce costs of external facilitators. More important, developing internal facilitators entrenches the ethos inherent in action learning into the organization, with accompanying cultural benefits. In addition, it further enhances the facilitation skills necessary for managers (see the cascade effect in Chapter 6).

Manager-initiated sets

There are also organizations, or even parts of organizations at level 1 and beyond (Burgoyne, op cit), where manager development is natural and *laissez-faire*. Some organizations place importance on leaving managers to take responsibility for how they best use their time, part of which is for their development. This is true where the organization places significance upon the ethos of personal learning and development; higher education is a classic example. We would suggest that within such organizations, managers are able to create their own sets to foster their development either by creating self-facilitating sets or taking the initiative to persuade managers or staff developers to allocate resources to sponsor facilitated sets.

Action learning and the development of the organization

We have stressed that the development of the organization is dependent upon the development of the individual manager which in turn is dependent upon the conscious systems of management development that are created. Each is interdependent, with action learning providing:

- a process and a vehicle for manager learning and development;
- a part of the systems of development for manager development;
- a process and a vehicle by which managers utilize their development and learning individually and collectively to engage in organizational learning.

With Burgoyne's model noted earlier in the chapter, we are probably working beyond level 3 where management development systems exist but where they are out of synchrony with what is happening in and around the organization. Levels 4–6 increasingly link the systems of management development, and therefore manager development, to corporate strategies and development. At Burgoyne's most sophisticated levels the organization is learning and matching its development as a whole with that of its managers in tune with the directions of the organization, other stakeholders and what is happening within and around the areas of influence of the organization. The organization is developing as a learning company. As we have shown above, Burgoyne is aware that few organizations are beyond level 4, and levels 3 and 4 represent the limits of current best practice.

We think the model is useful as a mapping tool against which an organization and its key influencers can compare where they are with their possible aspirations. As a model it is difficult to take in the infinite variety of organizations. Despite the tendency to think of organizations as neat in form, structure and culture, they are more messy in reality. Given the trends outlined earlier, suggested by Handy, Morgan and others, organizations are going to become more diverse, decentralized and federal, with control more diffused.

If this is the case, then group and organizational learning may emerge from and within parts of the organization as well as the more coherent forms suggested by levels 4–6. Given this scenario, we can consider how action learning can influence group, sub-organizational and organizational learning.

We draw on Morgan and Ramirez (1984) and Morgan (1988) to underpin how action learning can support organizational learning by recourse to the law of requisite variety in cybernetics. For any system to adapt to its external environment, its internal controls and adaptive systems must incorporate the variety found in that environment. Reduce the variety inside and the system is unable to cope with variety outside. Therefore, project groups or planning teams should not filter out diversity. Select people to make for creativity for it thrives on the tension created by diversity, particularly where innovation and learning are required. Action learning processes and methods can provide the conditions for realizing innovation and learning through the diversity of its membership. Morgan and Ramirez (*op cit*) express the contribution of action learning succinctly:

> Whereas many decision-making procedures are variety-reducing in that they attempt to create a clear focus or decision domain by eliminating as much as possible, action learning seeks to create a situation that is variety-increasing. The outsider or non-expert who may only be tangentially linked to the way an issue is defined, may in the end have one of the most important ideas to contribute, by virtue of this distance and the fact that he or she is not immersed in taken-for-granted opinions.

Moreover, managers experienced in action learning who are able to embrace variety have the skills to deal with issues rather than take the first-sighted solution.

Organizational learning and cultural change

When action learning becomes an integrated management development activity across an organization and set member managers engage in 'reflective activism'[4] then at very straightforward levels the organization starts to engage in its own learning.

A simple example might be a manager who, on promotion, is expected to run meetings to effect some of the organization's business. The cultural 'code' here might be that those below a certain level of the organizational hierarchy do not run meetings; therefore our manager may be new to this role. He may well be unused to running meetings but will probably have been at meetings run by higher level managers. Easiest solution: emulate those who have done

---

[4] Morgan (1984) defines 'reflective activism' as the stance which encourages us (via action learning) to own the process by which we and others construct and sustain our worlds (Morgan uses the term 'reality' here), and by exploring those constructions we produce through reflection. 'Action learning encourages reflective activism that recognises that social change starts and ends with each and every one of us' (ibid).

it in the past. However, our manager has been a reflective learner via sets and is not satisfied with this approach. He may also be daunted by the prospect and take the issue to his set. A trivial issue to take to a set? It depends on who is asking that question as well as the significance of the meetings being effective. Our manager may take the following questions to the set (or they may emerge from his interactions there):

- What is the purpose of the meetings?
- What do we want to achieve?
- What is the relationship between the meetings, outcomes and action?
- What does it mean to run one of these meetings?
- What is an effective way of running the meetings? Are there other ways of achieving the purposes for which meetings are called?
- Are the meetings really necessary or are they simply a matter of history?
- Do I need to run them?
- Who is at the meetings; not at them; needs to be?
- Of those who come, who contributes; who is silent; who dominates?
- Where is the energy? Is there any? How can it be generated to good effect?

These are just starters. They are not intended to immobilize our curious and reflective manager but as means of learning how to run meetings. Learning how to run meetings as they have been run in the past by others is necessary – this could be said to be first-order learning. But this learning is within the confining limits of what has prevailed in the past. The manager acquires and learns the skills and knowledge necessary to do that which has been done before. Second-order learning (Bateson, 1973) means that our manager learns how to challenge existing assumptions and ways of doing things, so that some of the other questions above can be drawn across the mind in order to find ways of doing things which may be very different from those which prevailed prior to his promotion.

Moreover, second-order learning or thinking means that our manager engages in learning how to learn. The questioning, reflection, action and further questioning in collaboration with others in the set and outside is carried into all his work. The effect of this 'small' example is that the manager may bring about a significant change in the way that things are done – in effect be instrumental in bringing about a cultural change as well as achieving action via the changed ways of doing things.

Lift and translate one manager's ability to engage in second-order thinking across an organization and in the relation of the organization to its world, and we have the organization engaging in second-order thinking in relation to policy, operations, ideas and action – the components of a learning company (Pedler *et al*, 1991).

Our aim has been to convey, through very basic examples, how action learning can contribute to managers' development, be a part of the repertoire of the systems of management development and contribute to organizational learning. Action learning has been around for a long time. The process of action learning is in keeping with contemporary notions of development and learning and enables managers to work rigorously. Most important of all it is one of the ways in which managers can become conscious of the learning process which we believe is necessary for organizational learning.

Chapter 13

Action Learning in Higher Education

In this chapter we describe how action learning can be used in higher education. Action learning has become well known and widely used in management development; although it is less familiar in other areas. However we believe that the process of action learning can be applied in other professional areas. The growth of interest in independent, flexible and student centred learning provides a new impetus for teachers in higher education to look beyond their usual methods, to investigate new ones, especially those which have a good reputation in other areas. We are not, however, making the claim that action learning will be useful to all courses or to all students. The approach is clearly one which requires a motivation on the part of the learner to develop through reflection on action. Nor are we saying that action learning will suit all teachers. The skills of facilitation are not the same as the skills of lecturing or leading seminars. Action learning does, however, offer a powerful method to those who wish to bring together the world of theory and the world of practice. It offers a clear structure to those who see important links between education and the world within (personal development) and between learning and the world 'out there' (development of the material and interpersonal world). Therefore action learning is a process which can respond positively to the current trends in higher education.

Trends in higher education

Higher education in Britain is undergoing massive change. Growth has moved higher education from elitism towards a mass system with students and employers alike demanding easier access and more diverse outcomes. It is no longer enough to educate the mind: universities are expected to produce graduates who are also conversant with information technology, able to work effectively in teams and have good oral and written presentation skills – and all this on a diminishing resource in real terms. Flexibility, choice and movement around the system have also been a recent focus with the development of modularity and credit accumulation and transfer (CATS). Vocational routes into higher education have developed through GNVQs, which have had remarkable growth in the 16–19 age group in a very short time. National Vocational Qualifications are increasing the pressure on universities to change. The higher education system can no longer assume a monopoly of the initial training of future professionals.

Larger class size

Typical class sizes in many instiions of higher education today are likely to be 80 to 100, with small group work being defined as involving 16–20 students. One-to-one tutorials are rare and unlikely to be routinely available, with the possible exception of research students. This is familiar ground for other countries. The United States and many mainland European countries have had a mass higher education system for years. Such systems often involve a very different structuring of the relationship between students and teachers than that typical of the present British system. The danger of the speed of the increase in student numbers is that this system will not be able to adapt fast enough and universities may respond by modelling themselves uncritically on existing systems of mass higher education or by attempting to remain as they are and finding that resources are stretched beyond acceptable limits.

It has been argued (Gibbs, 1992) that we must make a basic strategic choice between a system which highly controls and structures the student experience, and a system which develops and relies on the independence of the student as a learner (see Table 13.1). Both control strategies and independence strategies can work well with larger classes but they require a different approach to teaching and learning and very different ways of investing in resources. Control strategies involve the teacher in predetermining the objectives of a course and structuring the course very tightly around these, perhaps with the use of set texts and multiple choice assignments. Independence strategies require the development of independence of the students through investment in skills development in the early part of the course and in methods such as student-led seminars and peer assessment.

Table 13.1 *Control and independence strategies* (Gibbs and Jenkins, 1992)

Problem areas resulting from large classes	Characteristic methods adopted	
	Control strategies	Independence strategies
1. Courses lack clear aims and objectives	Use of objectives	Use of learning contracts
	Highly structured courses	Problem-based learning
2. Students lack knowledge about their progress	Objective testing	Development of student judgement
	Programmed instruction and CAL	Self-assessment
3. Students lack advice on how to improve	Assignment attachment forms	Peer feedback and peer-assessment
	Automated tutorial feedback	
4. Library resources cannot support wide reading	Use of set books	Development of students' research skills
	Use of learning packages	More varied assignments
5. Tutors are unable to support independent study	Structured projects	Group work
	Lab guides	Learning teams
6. Students lack the opportunity for discussion	Structured lectures	Student-led seminars
	Structured seminars and workshops	Team assignments
7. Tutors are unable to cope with the variety of students	Pre-tests plus remedial material	Variety of support mechanisms
	Self-paced study	Negotiated goals
8. Tutors are unable to motivate students	Frequent testing	Learning contracts, problem-solving, group work
	High failure rates	

From the student's point of view, larger numbers can mean alienation, lack of personal attention and insecurity. Action learning lies clearly within the independence strategy, offering an individual focus within a group process which can help promote student learning and development.

Diversity in the student population

The student population now has a wider variety of age, previous experience, ethnicity and mode of study. Older and younger students, full- and part-time modes, and many other differences both complicate and enrich the higher education scene. Welcome changes to the structure of the system have encouraged the mature adult learner with more emphasis on part-time study. We are a long way from a total system of lifelong learning for all, supported by the formal higher and further education sector, but moves in this direction are being encouraged through various innovations such CATS points, APL (accreditation of prior learning) and APEL (accreditation of prior experiential learning) and a growing number of Access and 'return to learn' courses. Some implications of this diversity are:

- a need to negotiate the content of learning;
- a need to focus on the learners' context;
- the use of experiential methods of teaching and learning;
- the acknowledgement and use of the past experience of the learner;
- a need for flexible entry and exit points onto programmes of study.

Action learning is an approach which acknowledges and works with this diversity. Action learning cannot be imposed on the learner and will be worthless unless there is a large degree of independence for the learner to choose their goals and how they will meet them. The structure is particularly appropriate for part-time study which is related to the work of the learner and the process has the in-built ability to respond to changes in the cirumstances and interests of participants.

Student-centred approaches to learning

The diversity in the student population can be matched by a move towards more student-centred approaches to teaching, providing programmes to meet learners' needs. Teaching in higher education has involved a content of study, specified in advance by the teacher, who controls the pace and the method by which this content is learnt and assessed. As we move towards more student-centred learning, the control moves from the teacher to the student. In an action learning programme it is no longer possible for the teacher to control the content of the learning in terms of specifying in advance precisely what will be learnt and how that learning will take place. Instead processes such as learning contracts (described below) can help the teacher and the learner to guide action and learning through negotiating objectives and methods for meeting them.

Features of the formal education system such as pace, structure and content are already being negotiated between the teacher and the learner. The trend is towards approaches such as the use of open learning packages which, while controlling the content, allow flexibility in pace, place and timing of study. Independent study degrees maximize this flexibility and allow individuals to negotiate the content of their degree. The students define their own learning needs and a contract is drawn up by which they identify resources they need to support them in their learning, including the time of teaching staff.

The trend is also away from courses with a fixed cohort of students over fixed periods of time – modularity divides course content into smaller pieces allowing students more flexibility and choice in their study. It also allows increased efficiency in teaching basic material which can now be shared between different courses; for instance, basic statistics can be taught to accountant and engineering students at the same time.

'Roll on roll off' programmes of study allow students to begin a course at different times and, therefore, to finish at different times. This also allows greater scope for accreditation of prior learning, some of which will have been gained in the workplace through work-based training programmes or experiential learning. Here again, higher education institutions are moving towards the provision of programmes and awards and away from organizing and running set courses with predesigned syllabuses.

These new approaches to higher education provision are not without difficulties. Individualized programmes can be extremely costly to run. Without adequate support and opportunity for discussion with peers and tutors, the college/university is likely to become simply an award-conferring body other than a truly educational institution. Modularity, while increasing student choice, can damage the cohesion of a year group of students. Course membership becomes blurred with students less easily identifiable to their peers or to tutors, and a system which aims to maximize choice can result in isolation. Without group support, an individualized study plan, using open learning as a resource, may become nothing more than a correspondence course. While individual tutorials that support individualized programmes of study are very costly, action learning sets provide an individual focus with group support and therefore add value as well as being more cost-effective.

Action learning is a student-centred process which guides learning at an individual level. It is a process which can be built around other types of provision so that it serves an integrating function. Action learning sets can be formed where each participant is studying quite different modules but come together to provide stimulus, motivation, support and challenge to their peers.

Links between higher education and industry

A further trend is towards more explicit links between industry and education through the growth of sandwich courses, the new system of National Vocational Qualifications and various forms of 'in-company' accreditation. These innovations blur further the distinction between education, training and working life. Higher education is expected to provide graduates with transferable skill or capability of a general nature. Knowledge alongside skill will ensure capability and through experience this capability will produce competence. It is capability rather than subject knowledge that employers require of their staff (Stephenson and Weil, 1992).

Action learning has proved itself in helping the development of organizations and the staff within them. As a link between higher education and industry it holds great promise as being a process that would be recognizable and acceptable to both. It is powerful in legitimizing a functional link between study and work for the participants through their work on action learning projects.

Action learning also provides an ideal forum for facilitation of learning to be a shared activity and not simply the preserve of the tutor. Participants in action learning sets learn to take responsibility for their own learning and they develop skill in supporting their peers. These skills – of listening, questioning, observation, giving feedback, etc – are transferable to the world of work, where students will be required to work independently and in teams.

Nevertheless, the cultures of the educational establishment and the business world remain distinct and for the learner this can be a stumbling block. Students want their learning to be relevant to the world of work but will expect more of their higher education than a reductionist training for employment. They will seek realization of the learning process itself and 'personal development'.

> in the world of accelerating change (the knowledge explosion, the technological revolution, the information society that we are entering) learning must be a lifelong process if we are to avoid the catastrophe of human obsolescence. The single most important competence that people must possess to survive is the ability to learn – with or, more important, without a teacher. (Knowles, 1990).

The imperative for higher education is to facilitate the development of students' ability to learn about the process of learning itself so that they become competent to manage and fulfil their future learning needs.

Education, in the true sense of the word, is essentially about development of the person. Knowledge and skill are sterile without the discernment to use both wisely. Higher education is failing in its most important function if it does not provide opportunities for its students to develop wisdom as they learn: the world, more than ever, requires this outmoded virtue. Higher education must safeguard its capacity to develop the whole person through learning which requires ability and the environment which encourages and rewards reflection. It would be a travesty if the enlightened encouragement of access for more students and the links between industry and education merely served to narrow the focus of higher education to the production of trained graduates. The real purpose of higher education is the development of individuals who are able to serve the development of society. Higher education can develop both the pragmatic and philosophical, theory and practice; ensuring meanwhile that learners understand the process by which they may continue to learn. If it is to do this, approaches to learning and teaching must involve both the personal and intellectual development of the individual.

What is the difference between more traditional teaching and action learning?

If traditional teaching is characterized (acknowledging this as not always the case) as

- didactic,
- hierarchic/control located in teacher,
- dependent/passive student,
- lecture/tutorial based, and with
- cognitive bias,

what difference is there when action learning is used as a form of student learning?

Let us take an example where the tutor is introducing action learning to a group of students who will form action learning sets with the tutor as set adviser/facilitator, as a primary method of group learning on a course. Inevitably, the tutor will describe the approach, underlying values and procedures of action learning. Once that description is completed, the next stage is to *do it*, so that students can begin to appreciate this process and way of learning. The tutor as facilitator will model the process. Once the students pick up, use and adopt the process, the tutor facilitator can begin to relinquish the role of expert holding hierarchical control.

We examine how the tutor's role differs from her traditional role. Heron's (1989) three modes of facilitation are useful here (for more detail see Chapter 6). In the example above the tutor is initially in *hierarchical* mode as facilitator directing the process, exercising power over it and doing things *for* the group. She is even at this stage, however, modelling practice that will enable set members (students) to take on a more participatory, active role – ideally from the first set meeting. We then move on to Heron's second mode – the *cooperative* mode. Here the facilitator shares her power over the learning process and different dynamics of the group *with* the group. The group becomes more self-directive. The next mode beyond the cooperative is the *autonomous* mode. Here the facilitator respects the total autonomy of the set members. They are now in their *own way* using the set to meet their needs as defined by them. The set becomes self-facilitating.

Note the differences between traditional forms of teaching/learning. Traditional forms tend to stay hierarchical in mode (through lecture, seminar, tutorial) with the student in a dependent relationship until the completion of the course and the results of the examinations. At another level, because the student has been continuously at the receiving end of the hierarchical mode, she may continue to remain in that mode beyond the course, not having acquired the means and confidence to move to autonomy. Heron is suggesting that the hierarchical mode is appropriate at some times. In articulating the range of ways in which the facilitator or tutor may relate to a group of learners, Heron enables us to recognize the value base of our approaches to teaching and learning and that there are a range of ways of relating to learners. We can recognize the constraints with which we have worked in the past and realize the liberation of moving, for the benefit of learners, through the different modes to enable them to become autonomous learners.

How far learners move towards autonomy using action learning will depend upon the nature of its use. In this case also, the tutor is always likely to remain the one most versed and knowledgeable about the course requirements so that the set members are likely to want to use the set adviser as a source of information about the course. A set which is incorporated into a course with a tutor providing continuous support is unlikely to move into autonomous mode but can easily move into cooperative mode.

Another feature of traditional teaching/learning is the assumptions we make about the learner. Traditional forms of teaching/learning tend to treat the learners as uniform in terms of knowledge, understanding, motivation, commitment and background. As teachers we acknowledge these differences and that they affect the students' work on the course but we have little alternative but to teach 'as if' these differences did not exist. The tutor will unwittingly convey an assumptive model of the learner they are addressing. Yet the lecture theatre will be full of learners with a multiplicity of needs, concerns, dispositions and backgrounds, and for many of whom the delivered lecture may not be conducive to their learning.

Action learning starts from a different place. A key feature of action learning (as an example of learner-centred learning) is the personal stance and background of the learner. The process, modelled by the facilitator, takes learners from where they are *coming from*. What differences are there in the set? How can these be acknowledged and celebrated for their individual benefit and for the set? Who is motivated to learn? Who isn't? How can a learner be enabled to work with their lack of motivation? How is it for the returner who has had a 15-year gap since their last experience of formal education? How is it for the recent school leaver from a Catholic community in Northern Ireland? How is it for the women in a minority on this engineering course? How can this group meet the individual needs for each individual for their benefit, and that of all the set members?

The final contribution of action learning for learners is the idea of learning through 'dialogue'. In this chapter we have stressed the importance of enabling learners to become 'self-managed' and 'autonomous' learners. This may suggest that learning is something that occurs in isolation or in a vacuum. We do not intend to or recommend learning to be in a vacuum. Some learning is undertaken on our own but for us, learning means making sense of and changing personal meaning in a social context. For example, it is only by actually facilitating an action learning set that I can learn really how to do it, what it feels like and whether I like being a facilitator. For the learner as set member it is only by doing action learning that she really comes to 'know' action learning. Similarly, by communicating with others in the set, the set member is able to give real personal meaning to her thoughts, ideas, feelings and actions. Freire (1972) expresses what we consider is crucial about 'dialogue':

> only through communication can human life hold meaning. The teacher's thinking is authenticated only by the authenticity of the student's thinking. The teacher cannot think for (his) students, nor can he impose his thought on them.

> Authentic thinking, thinking that is concerned with reality, does not take place in ivory tower isolation, but only in communication.

Action learning can help realize learning as 'dialogue' (see also Chapter 10).

Structures for the use of action learning in higher education

The process and content of learning in sets

Where action learning is used as the basic teaching and learning process, other support resources will be needed. These resources act as stimulation, introduce content, provide opportunities for group discussion and so on. It is important for us that in advocating action learning we are not misconstrued. Facilitating action learning sets is not the only thing a teacher needs to be able to do; quite the contrary. Action learning sets provide a strong basis upon which to build a variety of teaching and learning experiences. Action learning sets support the link between ideas and action. The action, for the most part, takes place outside of the set and can be anything, including pursuing a particular content area through a specific mode of study. Ideas can be generated outside of the set as well as within it. The function of the set is to enable set members to learn from the link between ideas and experience; to generalize from the past and to plan for the future. The process of action learning is something that has often been unfacilitated in higher education – it is the part of learning that has been left to chance in traditional teaching and learning environments. But once it is discovered it has the power to clarify the remaining needs of the student.

In the examples of practice that follow, we have shown a number of different types of programmes using action learning. These demonstrate a variety of other processes which run alongside the action learning sets, such as workshops, to cover aspects of the course content.

When the basis of a learning programme is action learning sets, it is possible to 'deliver' the content in many different ways, from a formal lecture programme through workshops to open learning materials and independent study. The content of courses that use the action learning process does not necessarily have to change at all. What changes is the way it is learnt and the way that learning is used and becomes part of the person.

Assessing action learning programmes

Assessment is often the most intransigent part of the higher education system. While teachers will experiment with different forms of small group teaching and new ways of packaging materials, there is often a worry that changing the assessment will irrevocably damage the standards that are so jealously guarded. The move to independent learning modes puts assessment in the spotlight as the control of the teacher is no longer paramount. The logic of developing the learner as a learner, the reflective practitioner and the competent graduate conflicts in logic, and in spirit, with an assessment system which is controlled, implemented and validated separately from the learner. Self and peer assessment help to develop the ability of the learner, not only to learn, but to test and evaluate the results of that learning (Brown and Dove, 1991).

An unseen exam paper, where results are fed back baldly as a percentage, is obviously out of step with a learning philosophy built on reflection and feedback. Different mechanisms and procedures will judge the quality of learning in appropriate ways. Fortunately, as the examples below show, there is now an increasing range of precedents to show how action learning can be supported through an assessment process that is in line with its educational philosophy. It is important to note, however, that these assessment structures are built *on top of* action learning and are not essential to the 'correct' functioning of action learning. Rather, they are essential to the higher education system of conferring awards on graduates of courses and programmes of study. It would also be appropriate to have action learning as an unassessed part of a programme of study.

Learning contracts
Learning contracts are negotiated between the learner and the tutor or between peer learners to specify the outcomes in terms of learning that the student is aiming for. They usually take the form of a number of sections answering the following questions:

Where am I now (in relation to this subject)?

Where do I want to be?

How will I get there (including resources needed)?

How will I know when I have been successful?

These contracts can be highly specific or more general, and often pro formas are used to help the student in writing out the contract. Contracts (or learning agreements (see Race, 1992)) specify the resources a student needs in order to learn, as well as what they will do to learn, ie, they can specify work for tutors as well as work for students. Students are also likely to take some time to construct the contract and may need to renegotiate at times throughout the learning programme. This is particularly important when an area is very new for the student as they are unlikely to know, from the beginning, what they need to know.

A contract that is based on personal development will rely a great deal on reports from the individual. Self-assessment is obviously a crucial element in the judging of the success of the work done. The same format could be used, however, to specify learning of a particular concept or understanding a particular process and could be described in terms that would be easily judged by a tutor with expert knowledge. Thus, in specifying the objective, the appropriate form for the evidence becomes clear. There must be a logical match between the objective and the evidence used for judging the outcome. Similarly, some objectives lend themselves to a result, ie, successfully completed or not, while other objectives will result in development which is unlikely to be an end-point. Where the contract is used for assessment on a course it is important that those who will undertake the assessment are clear about the nature of the evidence they will receive and their criteria for judging it.

Portfolios
Portfolios can be a useful way of collecting evidence of learning to meet a learning contract. They are often a collection of materials and entries of diverse nature gathered over the course and put together in some structured way to provide evidence of learning and development.

Profiles
A profile specifies what has been learnt on a course. It can be a simple list of topics covered or a fuller description of learning outcomes. Profiles are particularly useful for courses of independent study where the syllabus is not specified in course documentation in any specific form. Profiles allow external people to see what was covered by the course of study undertaken by the student.

Journals
Journals or diaries capture the process of learning and the stages in a learner's

development over the time of the programme or course. They can be valuable as evidence to show learning and development at the end of the programme but they also act as a spur to regular reflection. A journal could form part of a portfolio.

Reflective document
This is a document written after the formal programme has ended which describes what has been learnt. It can be used in tandem with project reports where the latter only reports the method of working, results and recommendations, and does not adequately address what the learner has gained from doing the project.

Statements of relevance
These are written comments by the student on the relationship between input by the course tutors and their own learning with its practical application. They are reflective documents that draw out how the learner has made links between the general content of the workshop (or other input) and his or her own particular context.

Lessons Log
This is a tool for evaluation of the course or programme by the tutors rather than the learner. It has been used successfully on the Advanced Management Develoment Programme as a regular way of learning from the experience of running workshops which feed directly into future workshops and into the running of the same workshop next year. It is simply a record of the feelings and ideas of the course team immediately after every workshop (and usually at intervals during the workshop). It feeds very well into monitoring and review reports for the course and is invaluable in planning.

These descriptions show how the assessment of action learning becomes an integral and important part of the process of learning rather than a summative external snapshot of attainment.

Issues for the teacher wishing to develop action learning

Can any teacher be an action learning facilitator?

The answer to this question is yes, but the skills involved in action learning set facilitation are not the same as the skills of traditional teaching. Some teachers in higher education find that seminars turn into lectures because, they say, students won't discuss things or they haven't prepared adequately, etc. In order to be a set facilitator, I have to believe in the ability of the students to learn without my expert knowledge (they can get at that if they need to in another forum). Set facilitators are not teachers: they are facilitiating the process of action learning.

Tutors who wish to be facilitators may need to develop new skills. Sometimes the tutors specialize in the facilitation role and other teachers act as teachers of the content of the programme. This is a fairly new approach to higher education where speciality was seen formerly as between discipline areas. Now we have specialists in different teaching and learning methods and processes.

Is action learning expensive?

If a course is based on action learning it need not be more expensive to run. There will, however, be a need for different roles for academic tutors and a different use of space. Where action learning sets are grafted onto traditional programmes they do add a significant extra cost in staff time. Where action learning carries responsibility of important learning outcomes then its use is easily justified.

How can I introduce action learning to students?

As with all teaching and learning processes, the enthusiasm of the teacher will be an important factor. Chapter 7 describes a workshop that would be a useful induction programme for students new to action learning. As with all new methods of teaching and learning, it is usually easier to introduce at the beginning rather than half-way through a programme. Students who are used to group work will usually find the approach easy to adopt, but some may find reflection in a group difficult at first.

How easily can I get a course using action learning validated?

Validation is becoming easier since there are now many precedents for courses run along action learning lines, and documentation exists as well as external examiners who have a working knowledge of the action learning process. Students who have experience of action learning are the best ambassadors for such courses and evaluations of programmes using action learning help to demonstrate its effectiveness.

Models for the introduction of action learning into higher education

There are now quite a number of courses in higher education that use action learning as the main learning process. As one might expect, some of these are in the management development area. Indeed Pedler (1991) argues that, 'The six-month management development programme which has a "start up module", monthly learning sets, occasional workshops and a final workshop has almost reached the status of a new orthodoxy in some quarters'. Increasingly, other professional areas are using action learning as a development tool and undergraduate programmes are seeing the potential of action learning for supporting project work. Here, we give a few examples from our own experience at the University of Brighton where action learning has been put through its paces in a variety of courses.

Action learning to support research students

The Advanced Management Development Programme
The Advanced Management Development Programme (AMDP) provides a programme supporting research and development for experienced managers in private and public sector organizations.

The core philosophy of the AMDP can best be expressed in two premises:

1. Researching live business problems within organisations is a legitimate way of gaining a training in research.
2. A training in acquiring and analysing business information in managing real business problems is a vital form of management development at the end of the twentieth century. (Bourner, 1992)

This unique programme provides a structure of support to enable managers to gain a research degree and to become effective internal consultants for their firms. Action learning is at the heart of the programme. The managers form action learning sets of between five and seven set members early in their first year. They bring a work-based problem which forms the basis of their research project throughout the programme. The sets meet for a full day once a month throughout the three years of the programme. In addition to the sets, participants take compulsory workshops lasting between two and five days and choose optional weekend workshops on different research methods during their first year.

Research degrees are inevitably individualistic, as the learner is not on a course about what is already known so much as on a search for new knowledge. Management research, however, is usually applied and of immediate importance to the organization as well as the individual. Action learning is most appropriate for this type of course since it provides support for individuals in their research and yet the responsibility for development lies with the individual participant. It can support the individual in making their research link to their management practice (Bourner, Frost and Beaty, 1992).

There are programmes elsewhere which aim to develop the manager whilst producing tangible results on real projects but this programme also develops the manager as researcher. A recent revalidation of the programme concluded that the programme was going beyond other similar courses by using research to develop the manager at the same time as the organization to which the manager belongs. Examples of projects include:

- developing a new marketing strategy for a medium-sized printing firm
- investigating of the match between espoused values of a large company and management actions as perceived by staff
- development of a strategy for European links for a large educational institution.

Action learning to support undergraduate project work

Action learning sets in BA Business Studies
In this course the action learning set is designed to cope with the larger intake of students and the consequent feelings of anonymity in students. The sets support the students in their project work by working on the issues that each individual student is currently facing with their projects. The course is taught in a traditional way with lectures and small group work. The sets are designed to support students in the process of working independently on their projects. The sets have facilitators for some meetings and are self-facilitated at other times. Assessment of the project remains with the course tutors, who are not facilitators of the sets, and this helps the set to be separate from the course as a whole. Students are encouraged to use the set for their own issues and this changes the nature of the set process from the remainder of the course.

On the sandwich degree, sets are also used to support the placement year when students are out in industry for part of their studies. Here the sets meet to share experiences and to reflect on their learning. The set members' action plans help to formulate actions to enhance their learning from the experience of the placement in order to write a report in diary form used to assess their learning from the experience.

Action learning as support for continued professional development

The certificate in teaching and learning in Higher Education

This is a course for teachers in higher education aimed mainly at an in-house group of new academic staff. The programme runs weekly for three hours over one year. It consists of workshops on aspects of teaching and learning in higher education interspersed with fortnightly action learning sets. The participants draw up a learning contract to describe what skills they wish to develop over the year and they then keep a reflective diary or learning log which includes evidence of work done against their contract. The sets agree these contracts and act as peer assessors of the learning log at the end of the year. Learning contracts are usually made up of three or four areas and the following examples show the type of objectives which have been included:

- To develop my ability to work with large lecture groups through learning how to use IT to produce handouts and overhead transparencies.
- To write a learning package to support a particular area of mechanical engineering.
- To develop my confidence so that I can increase the variety of small-group teaching methods that will work with my students.
- To produce documentation for a new module on the combined sciences course.
- To develop a system of filing for student and course records that helps me manage my administration.
- To improve my relationships with colleagues so that I become integrated into the team and am able to champion the importance of my discipline area.

The rationale for the programme is that of developing the reflective practitioner (Schon, 1983). By this we mean that the teacher learns to question and evaluate his own practice and by reading about teaching and learning and through observation of his peers, develops his own practice. This is a process which becomes habit and remains part of the art of the teacher – as reflective practitioner. The sets enable each individual to draw together the theory and ideas from the workshops and the issues and problems of their own particular environment through an action-focused discussion of the teacher's individual situation. This action-based approach constantly reforms the view of learning that the teacher holds and over time builds his confidence in using a variety of methods and in adding his own innovations.

The results are often of much deeper significance than first anticipated by the participants. The action sets motivate and energize as well as solve problems and generate good ideas. Some have said that they do not think they would have survived their first year in teaching without their set. The stress and pressure of the first year of teaching can be mitigated through the understanding of peers and the safety of an objective group to which the teachers can bring their problems and generate action plans. Senior staff, who have found that their new colleagues become active and innovative teachers earlier in their careers, and the course has now become mandatory for new staff who have no previous teaching experience.

This course above is an example of action learning used explicitly for staff development. There are many, less formal ways that action learning can contribute to the development of staff in higher education. There are a number of reasons why we advocate the use of action learning by staff. Most obviously, in order to enable student learners to acquire the skills to be set members and in time self-facilitate, staff need to enhance their understanding of the set process. By doing it we learn about it. This is particularly true of action learning where the process is so critical to its successful use. By forming sets for their own developmental purposes, staff will also enhance their skills as set advisers. It is possible also that their understanding of learning and teaching will be enhanced through using action learning to support their own development (Beaty, 1995; Gibbs, 1995).

As teaching and administrative staff in higher education take on managerial responsibilities (eg, course leader, admissions tutor, placement adviser, faculty officer, head of department) action learning sets can be used as an in-house form of continuous development.

Independent sets in the University of Brighton

Since 1987 there have been voluntary staff sets meeting in the business school at Brighton. The first set worked over 12 months and when it came to a natural end the individuals decided to begin other sets to cascade their experience to others. This has worked well and almost half of the staff in the business school have been or are currently part of an action learning set. Some sets have gone beyond the business school to include other staff and some sets are now working on particular topics (eg, research), thus combining the power of individual issues with a specific focus. This has provided individuals with support for their work, has increased the level of knowledge staff have of each other and the general issues in the school, and has enhanced the general level of empathy in the school (Chapter 6 discusses the uses and issues of self-facilitated sets).

Chapter 14

Action Learning: A Contribution to Individual, Organizational and Social Change

Reflections

We have aimed to demystify action learning and make it more accessible to potential users. We are conscious that in writing a *how to* book on action learning we are in danger of being prescriptive in suggesting that this is *the* way. That is not our intention. By making explicit how action learning may work effectively, we may contribute to practitioners moving into experimentation and further questioning insight. Our intention is to provide some insights into how action learning can be 'in balance' so that set members have the conditions for reflection, insight and action.

When we started to use the approach in our work and for our development there was little guidance that went beyond a rational, structured, task-orientated and cognitive model of action learning. We do not underrate these aspects – we have endeavoured to enlarge on them where necessary. We have also emphasized the need to get into doing what is an experiential form of learning (Weil and McGill, 1990) rather than contemplating it!

Our purpose has been to complement and balance the above by stressing attention to the process – by getting into the detail about how action learning can be effective for practitioners (see below). We also highlight the affective aspects of working in sets. A presenter does not only bring a task or issue – content, to a set but also feelings and emotions – the affective. The quality of work undertaken by a presenter can be deepened by the recognition that we all bring our feelings to the complex activities in which we are engaged. A set attending with care to process ensures that risks taken by a presenter will be handled in a way that is more likely to be effective than a set that pays little regard to how it works.

The highly structured nature of action learning creates the conditions for potentially effective group working with a set member's concerns. Like any other group, there are social power relations within it, eg facilitator, set members, black, white, women, men, this means that people will experience different senses of power and powerlessness in a group. So also in action learning sets. There is an equality of working together that is evident. However, as in any group, sets are not neutral places. Recognition of this and aiming to work with difference will also help for greater effectiveness in the set as well as enable set members to recognize this political aspect elsewhere in their lives.

We act as facilitators and designers of action learning in professional, management development and higher education contexts. One significant feature is the contrast noted by set members, between this method of learning and working, and their previous experience. The term action learning does have some disadvantage in that outside the education sector (and even here) the word 'learning' is not commonly used. The word is associated with particular experiences in earlier school, further/higher education and professional lives (wherever they stepped off this path). Past association and earlier models of teaching and learning can influence the early stages of sets.

Working in sets provides another contrast. Practitioners soon find differences between the way a set works and the way they may work with others in organizational and other group contexts. Experiencing and articulating the differences can help the set be effective and lead to a carrying over into the organization and other groups.

Another intention in writing the guide has been to develop some aspects which may have previously been understated or undeveloped, which take action learning forward. These are:

- giving emphasis to process skills used in sets;
- focusing on personal and relationships development within and outside the action learning process;
- broadening action learning to include independent and self-facilitated sets;
- using action learning to support continuing professional development (Chapter 11);
- deepening the potential for action learning to be used for manager and organizational learning (Chapter 12);
- bringing and extending action learning into the learning process in higher education (Chapter 13);

- action learning as a sustainable and 'green' way of working, which we introduce in this final chapter.

We will develop some of the themes not considered earlier in the guide.

Process skills

Detailed consideration of the processes which make for effective action learning, that is, how a set works best for the set as a whole and for each set member, have tended to be understated in the literature, and possibly the practice, partly because of the attention given to project and task orientations. We endorse Mumford (1991):

> The task is a constantly seductive feature of the total process. Learning about the process by which the task is achieved has been given a derisory amount of emphasis.

This led us to give attention to the skills required to enhance the process within the action learning set by considering the skills used by set members and facilitators (Chapters 3–6, 8 and 9). The use of skills, their enhancement and reflection upon their use in the set, represent an opportunity for set members to utilize them with more 'intention' in the set as well as in other contexts. Working with these skills in the set process deepens set members' use of these skills outside the set. The result is, ideally, to enhance their process skills and problem-solving effectiveness outside the set. As Morgan (1988) suggests:

> The special character of this approach [action learning] is that it generates knowledge through the design of a learning process that itself proves to be a means for approaching and 'solving' problems being addressed . . .

Instead of 'knowledge' we could insert 'skills'. Morgan borrows and adapts the famous phrase from Marshall McLuhan and concludes: 'In other words, the medium . . . is part of the message'. The medium of the action learning process is part of the message for learning and tackling problems elsewhere.

Personal relationships development and empowerment

We have a threefold purpose in giving emphasis to the personal and relationships. First, the understatement of process means there is a tendency to omit the significance of the personal interactions that will inevitably be a part of how a project or task is achieved and whether and how significant learning takes place.

Moreover, in Chapter 6 we show a continuum along which set members concentrate on projects at one end, and personally-oriented development in organizations at the other. The emphasis to date has been on the sponsored project end of the continuum. At the personal end, a set member may choose to concentrate upon their development and/or work on their relationships with people in their working lives. We have aimed to add legitimacy to the ability of set members to work with their issues and problems. In organizational settings, working on these can have as much significance as projects.

Second, there is a recognition that personal and relationship skills and development have been understated in the management development and higher education fields. In the management development and organizational area, many problems faced by managers have two aspects: the technical, involving content, sometimes specialist knowledge – the cognitive element; and the social and emotional, requiring intra-personal and interpersonal skills – the affective element. Garratt (1987) stresses the need for an integration of the technical with the people side of learning in organizations, particularly organizations in the Western tradition. Writing of directors (but applying to managers) he asserts:

> An important part of developing the thinking processes of competent directors is getting them to handle the 'soft' areas of people and emotions as well as the 'hard' areas of analysis and judgement, and to believe that both are necessary to be effective.

For Garratt the need is to strike a balance between the two and that successful directing (and managing) and thinking are a key to organizational learning. Further, a low emphasis on the people and emotional side leads to poor problem-solving. Garratt's quotes around 'soft' and 'hard' we take to be ironic as they should probably be reversed!

In higher education there has been a similar picture with the emphasis upon knowledge, content and the cognitive as opposed to the conative (doing) and affective sides of learners. We have already reviewed this in the previous chapter.

We believe the use of action learning, and with it, attention to the whole person, including the personal and emotional, can extend the learning and effectiveness of managers in organizations and teachers and student learners in higher education.

Third, there is a need to recognize difference and diversity among people.

There is a positive benefit to individuals, groups and organizations in acknowledging people in terms of 'where they are coming from' and their wide-ranging life-cycle differences.

Until fairly recently, there has been a tendency to make assumptions in organizations about 'the way things are done around here'. Managers and staff have had to fit into implicit norms of behaviour that actually represented and reflected the power of those who ran organizations. Our society is still in transition in this respect – some organizations are endeavouring to acknowledge and work with difference, whilst other organizations are still living innocently with the assumptions of the past. This has recently been referred to as 'the power of innocence' (Baddeley and James, 1991):

> People's personal positions are arrived at and sustained by being in a group of people whose understanding of the world is similar to their own. Thus their position is both sustained by other group members ('That's the way the world is') or even attributed to the group ('If you're a manager this is what you think'). The last thing the fish discovers is water. Innocence derives its power through being comfortably and unreflectively surrounded by others of like mind. From this stance individuals cannot see themselves colluding with the larger flow of institutional direction and its consequences.

'This is the way things are done around here' is being replaced by the acknowledgement that those who created the world in which such a condition could prevail are having to reflect upon those norms and share power with those who previously did not share power with them. An obvious example is where women are increasingly finding but challenging the 'glass ceiling' above them and white men are discovering that the 'innocent' power they have held is untenable. That ceiling is, for some men, unwittingly applied at the personal level but is also institutionally discriminatory. A similar position applies in respect of race, disability, age and sexual orientation.

The key is to overcome the discriminatory practices without resorting to scapegoating or blaming those who have traditionally held power, as well as enabling opportunity for those who have not shared power. For both groups the result can be empowering and create a necessary pluralism.

> As the cloak of hegemony is discarded the individual can re-centre, . . . rediscover themselves and build their own connections, relationships and identity. This may

involve a personal crisis but losing one's innocence need not entail an enduring loss of personal power (Baddeley and James, 1991).[1]

Let us not attribute the change necessary here to the use of action learning! What we can say is that action learning provides a process for managers in organizations to address and act on their personal position in work and with other people in relationships. The nature of action learning encourages the idea that what we learn (particularly at the fundamental level of how we see the world) does not have to be fixed and rigid. Rather it encourages us and gives us the skills to view uncertainty as something to be worked on and with rather than resisted – that we can each have a say in how we construct our realities.

Action learning also 'strives to be proactive and empowering' (Morgan and Ramirez, 1984). People have a choice as to whether they engage with the world and realize that reality in an active or passive manner. If they consciously choose to be active, by reflecting upon their experience and then acting so that they influence the nature of that experience, they can influence their reality. If they choose to be passive or fit in, then they are 'reacting to the construction of others' (ibid). Action learning encourages people to take responsibility for the way they relate to the world.

People may have the theoretical choice as to whether they enter actively into responding to their world and take some control over their lives. Whether and how people interact with their environments will depend on factors like their socio-economic position. But that interaction in the environment will also move forwards and backwards in terms of the person's personal sense of power in their environments. A significant contribution to our understanding has been the research undertaken by Belenky and colleagues (1986) researching the learning experiences of black and white women from different social and economic backgrounds embarking on higher education in colleges in the USA. They found that women moved forwards or backwards along a spiral referred to as 'ways of knowing'. These were influenced by their interactions with others in particular learning environments, and the ways in which they made sense of their experiences as learners (we are all learners in a variety of organizations – not just at college).

---

[1] The term 'hegemony' is for some a bit like 'culture' – 'When I hear the word "culture", I reach for my gun'! It can put people off. We simply take it to mean the prevailing plateau of power or ways of doing things with which most people live.

Belenky *et al* identified five categories of ways of knowing in relation to the spiral which also reflects a spiral of personal power in relation to learning: silence; received knowledge; subjective knowledge; procedural knowledge; and constructed knowledge. We refer to these in detail in Chapter 10.

Silence could be said to represent one end of the spiral where the effect of the learning environment is one of lack of power; at the other end there is constructed knowledge where women not only have their voice but are able to live, work and learn as constructors of knowledge – reality.

The most significant change we have seen as facilitators in action learning sets is when set members (women and men) have found their voice and realize that they can influence and transform the circumstances of their lives.

Independent and self-facilitated sets

Our intention has been to broaden the use of action learning beyond organizational confines. By 'independent' we mean that action learning sets are not sponsored by an organization as, say, part of the management development systems of the organization, or as part of a course in higher education. By 'self-facilitation' we mean that a set works without a set adviser. We have explored both forms in this guide, in Chapter 6.

It is possible for independent sets to have set advisers who may act in a voluntary or consultancy/paid capacity. Given our approach to facilitation we have argued that it is to the benefit of sets to move toward autonomy for two reasons: to prevent dependency and for set members to take on facilitation skills as they model those skills of the set adviser. Some independent sets may go straight into self-facilitation where there are, amongst the set, members with the skills to ensure the set works effectively. This guide is intended to be useful to support the initial stages of the set's life.

Put independent and self-facilitation skills together and we have a means of people coming together to work on their life issues as they each determine. Underlined by the value of voluntary commitment to a set, we have the ingredients for an empowering group of people.

It is a model that can be applied where people come together in voluntary organizations where the 'workers' are unpaid. It can also be applied to people in paid employment where the organization places a high value on self-organization, like higher education institutions and research bodies. In Chapter 6 we explored the ways in which this can work. The organization gets indirect or even direct pay-offs by encouraging such association to happen.

Action learning as a transformational and sustainable way of working and learning

So far in this chapter we have concentrated, in the main, on the empowerment of the individual. However, we cannot separate the individual from the social – the group, the organization, the community. Social change and development without individual transformation is ultimately totalitarian. Individual change without social change is difficult for the individual to maintain. Action learning is a form of cooperative and collaborative enquiry that links individuals to the group (the action learning set), to a range of groups outside the set and to organizations and the community. Morgan and Ramirez (1984) link action learning with individual and social transformation in an essentially democratic way:

> Action learning stresses that it is necessary to appreciate that human beings and their wider society are in one another in the most basic sense, and that effective social transformations must involve both. Action learning recognizes that effective change must start with the individual, but reverberate in its effects throughout a social system.

Action learning sets provide the milieu for personal transformation within a small group – social unit – an action learning set. If sets reflect in a small group, the whole of a social system, then action learning can spread its nature and effects throughout the social system as a whole.

Another related but unusual way of looking at action learning is the idea that it is a sustainable, 'green' or ecological form of learning and action. One of our sets included Shirley Ali Khan who was undertaking a major national project on 'The Greening of Polytechnics', using her action learning set at the University of Hertfordshire (formerly Hatfield Polytechnic) to support the progress of her project. Shirley found the action learning approach very relevant to the theme of her project and had this to say about action learning:

Shirley Ali Khan: Action learning is 'green'

My perception of action learning is that it is a process that enables individuals to make connections – connections within themselves; connections between themselves and their groups; connections between themselves and their homes and working communities; connections between themselves and the world.

Because the connections are personal, learning is always personally relevant as opposed to didactic learning, which is often personally irrelevant. Relevant learning is quality learning.

An understanding of the interconnectedness and interrelatedness of all things is associated with the holistic way of viewing the world. The holistic view is an ecological view that leads to an understanding of people as a part of (as opposed to apart from) the environment. This view encourages the re-evaluation of the environment, since with it comes the realization that to abuse the environment is to abuse oneself. New personal values mean new personal responsibilities, including environmental responsibility.

Making connections is only part of the process – the understanding and knowledge part of learning – the subject being life. This life literacy includes environmental literacy. The number of connections made determines the level of life literacy and, in turn, the level of environmental literacy achieved.

The other parts of the process can be summarized in terms of developing life skills/competency and the translation of life and literacy and competency into action. In other words the process goes beyond holistic viewing to enabling people to be whole. Being whole would include being environmentally responsible. Wholeness can be both freeing and frightening.

We can consider action learning as an evolving eco-system. Mature eco-systems in nature are massively decentralized and based upon the principle of unity-in-diversity – the rain forests are a classic example. Immature eco-systems are massively centralized and compartmentalized and based upon the principle of unity-in-uniformity. Bureaucratic organizations are examples of immature eco-systems (Southgate, 1985). Action learning is a decentralized form of group consisting of persons across an organization or between organizations or a community. Action learning promotes unity-in-diversity because it is more likely to reflect the diversity of its 'community'. Instead of being variety-reducing in seeking solutions to problems, sets 'seek to create a situation that is variety-increasing'

Bureaucratic and hierarchical organizations tend to be alienating and energy-reducing. An example would be an organization in which what vision there is will be manifested from above in a hierarchical form to be imbibed by a docile work force who are supposed to harness their energies to that vision. Action learning sets are energy-creating and uniting. Organizations which engage in action learning mature and lose their dependency on traditional ways of organizing. Action learning is one of the processes that enable people to develop ownership for and invest energy in what they are doing.

Conclusion

In this guide one of our main endeavours has been to enhance the importance of the subject, the person and the personal in action learning. The purpose has been to redress the imbalance that has resulted in organizations giving priority to the objective, the detached 'out there' knowledge which became associated with management and with higher education. We have sought, as others are doing, (Weil and McGill, 1990) to (re)integrate subject and object, personal and 'out there', the thinking with the doing and the feelings, emotions and values. We have also endeavoured to relate working in action learning sets to the attention people give to what they implement between set meetings in order to be more effective and enterprising. To echo a recent view,

> The idea of an enterprise culture has been captured by certain politicians. However it is possible to liberate this concept from its selfish, self-centred overtones. It is possible to see the notion of being enterprising as synthesizing active, outgoing entrepreneurship with caring, supportive collaboration. . . . We need to value the bottom line . . . *and* a concern for the human condition (Cunningham, 1990). (Emphasis in original.)

The integration of the subject – people – into the bottom line is not a soft option. Combined with reflective learning it is a tough option but one that we believe can challenge and change us and the organizations in which we may work.

Bibliography

Ali Khan, S (1991) 'Action learning is green', a statement written for the authors.

Argyris, C (1982) *Reasoning, Learning and Action: Individual and organzational*, San Francisco, CA: Jossey-Bass.

Argyris, C and Schon, D (1978). *Organizational Learning: A theory of action perspective*, Reading, Mass: Addison-Wesley.

Baddeley, J and James, K (1991) 'The power of innocence: from politeness to politics', *Management Education and Development*, **22**, 2, 106–18.

Bateson, G (1973) *Steps Towards an Ecology of Mind*, London: Paladin.

Beaty, E (1995) 'Staff Development Across the Hierarchy', in Brew, A (ed.) *Directions in Staff Development*, SRHE/OUP.

Belenky, M F, Clinchy, B M, Goldberger, N R and Tarule, J M (1986) *Women's Ways of Knowing: The development of self, voice and mind*, New York: Basic Books.

Bion, W (1961) *Experiences in Groups*, 2nd edn, New York: Basic Books.

Bliss, E C (1976) *Getting Things Done: the ABCs of Time Management*, London: Futura.

Boud, D, Keogh, R and Walker, D (1985) *Reflection: Turning experience into learning*, London: Kogan Page.

Bourner, T (1992) *The Advanced Management Development Programme*. Definitive Course Document, University of Brighton.

Bourner, T, Frost, P, and Beaty, E (1992) 'Management Development by Research', *Personal Review* Vol. 21 No. 2.

Boydell, T, Leary, M, Megginson, D and Pedler, M (1991) *Developing the Developers*, London: Association of Management Education and Development.

Brown, S and Dove, P (1991) *Self and Peer Assessment*, SCED Booklet No. 67, Standing Conference on Educational Development.

Burgoyne, J (1988) 'Management development for the individual *and* the Organisation', *Personnel Management*, June, 40–44.

Cameron, L, Jesser, P and Harvey, D (1992) 'Formal Mentoring/Action Learning: Transforming tomorrow today', conference paper to 2nd Action Learning Congress on Action Learning, University of Queensland, Australia.

Carr, W and Kemmis, S (1986) *Becoming Critical: Knowing through action research*, Victoria: Deakin University.

Clarkson, P and Shaw, P (1992) 'Human relationships at work in organisations', *Management Education and Development*, **23**, 1, 18–29.

Casey, D (1991) 'The Shell of your understanding', in Pedler, M *Action Learning in Practice*, Aldershot, Gower.

Cunningham, I (1990) 'Beyond modernity – is post-modernism relevant to management development?', *Management Education and Development*, **21**, 3, 207–18.

Cunningham, I (1994) *The Wisdom of Strategic Learning*, Maidenhead: McGraw-Hill.

Dewey, J (1933) *How we Think*, Boston, Mass: D C Heath.

Egan, G (1973) *Face to Face, The small group experience and interpersonal growth*, Monterey, CA: Brooks/Cole.

Egan, G (1976) *Interpersonal Living, A skills/contract approach to human relations training in groups*, Monterey, CA: Brooks/Cole.

Egan, G (1990) *The Skilled Helper: A systematic approach to effective helping*, Pacific Grove, CA: Brooks/Cole.

Entwistle, N and Wilson, J D (1977) *Degrees of Excellence: The academic achievement game*, London: Hodder and Stoughton.

Freire, P (1972) *Pedagogy of the Oppressed*, Harmondsworth: Penguin.

Garratt, B (1987) *The Learning Organisation*, London: Fontana.

Germaine, C and Burgoyne, J (1984) 'Self-development and career planning: An exercise in mutual benefit', *Personnel Management*, April.

Gibbs, G (1992) *Improving the Quality of Student Learning*, Bristol: Technical and Educational Services.

Gibbs, G (1995) 'Changing Lecturers' Conceptions of Teaching and Learning Through Action Research', in Brew, A (ed.) *Directions in Staff Development*, Buckingham: Society for Research into Health Education (SRHE) and Open University Press.

Gibbs, G and Jenkins, A (eds) (1992) *Teaching Large Classes in Higher Education: How to maintain quality with reduced resources*. London: Kogan Page.

Habermas, J (1974) *Knowledge and Human Interest*, London: Heinemann.

Handy, C (1991) *The Age of Unreason*, 2nd edn, London: Business Books.

Hargie, O, Saunders, C and Dickson, D (1987) *Social Skills in Interpersonal Communication*, 2nd end, Beckenham: Croom Helm.

Hawkins, P and Shohet, R (1989) *Supervision in the Helping Professions*, Buckingham: Open University Press.

Heron, J (1989) *The Facilitator's Handbook*, London: Kogan Page.

Honey, P and Mumford A (1986) *Using Your Learning Style*, Maidenhead: Honey.

Institute of Personnel and Development (IPD) (1995) *A Vehicle for Learning*, London: IPD.

Jarvis, P (1987) *Adult Learning in the Social Context*, Beckenham: Croom Helm.

Jourard, S M (1971). *The Transparent Self*, New York: Van Nostrand Reinhold.

Kanter, R M (1981) *The Change Masters: Corporate entrepreneurs at work*, London: Allen & Unwin.

Kanter, R M (1989) *When Giants Learn to Dance*, London: Simon and Schuster.

Knowles, M (1990) 'Fostering Competence in Self-directed Learning', in Smith, R M (ed.) *Learning to Learn Across the Lifespan*, Oxford: Jossey-Bass.

Kolb, D (1984) *Experiential Learning: Experience as the source of learning and development*, Englewood Cliffs, NJ: Prentice-Hall.

Lessem, R (1991) *Total Quality Learning: Building a learning organisation*, Oxford: Blackwell.

Luft, J (1984) *Group Processes, An introduction to group dynamics*, Mountain View, CA: Mayfield.

McGill, I, Segal-Horn, S, Bourner, T and Frost, P (1990) 'Action learning: a vehicle for personal and group experiential learning', in Weil, S W and McGill, I J (eds) *Making Sense of Experiential Learning*, Buckingham: Open University Press/SRHE.

McLean, A and Marshall, J (1983) 'Intervening in cultures', working paper, University of Bath.

McLean, A and Marshall, J (1988) *Cultures at Work*, Luton: Local Government Training Board.

Marshall, J (1984) *Women Managers: Travellers in a male world*, Chichester: John Wiley.

Marton, F, Beaty E and Dall' Alba, G (1993) 'Conceptions of Learning'. *International Journal of Education Research*, **19**, 277–300.

Marton F, Entwistle, N and Hounsell, D (1984) *The Experience of Learning*, Edinburgh: Scottish Academic Press.

Morgan, G (1986) *Images of Organization*, Newbury Park, CA: Sage.

Morgan, G (1988) *Riding the Waves of Change*, San Francisco, CA: Jossey-Bass.

Morgan, G and Ramirez, R (1984) 'Action learning: A holographic metaphor for guiding social change', *Human Relations*, **37**, 1–28.

Mumford, A (1989) *Management Development: Strategies for action*, London: Institute of Personnel Management.

Mumford, A (1991) 'Learning in action', *Personnel Management*, July, 34–7.

Orbach, S (1994) *What's Really Going On Here?* London: Virago.

Ouchi, W G and Johnson, J B (1978) 'Types of organizational control and their relationship to emotional well-being', *Administrative Science Quarterly*, **23**, 292–317.

Pedler, M (1992) *Action Learning in Practice*, 2nd ed., Aldershot: Gower.

Pedler, M, Burgoyne, J and Boydell, T (1986) *A Manager's Guide To Self-development*, 2nd ed., Maidenhead: McGraw-Hill.

Pedler, M, Burgoyne, J and Boydell, T. (1991) *The Learning Company*, Maidenhead: McGraw-Hill.

Perry, W G (1970) *Forms of Intellectual and Ethical Development in the College Years: A Scheme*, New York: Holt, Rinehart and Winston.

Peters, T (1987) *Thriving on Chaos*, 3rd ed., London: Pan Books.

Race, P (1992) 'Not a Learning Contract', in Baume, D and Brown, S (eds) *Learning Contracts: Vol I: Theoretical Perspectives*, Birmingham: SCED.

Ramsden, P (1992) *Learning to Teach in Higher Education*, London: Routledge.

Randall, R and Southgate, J (1980) *Cooperative and Community Group Dynamics*, London: Barefoot Books.

Revans, R (1980) *Action Learning: New techniques for action learning*, London: Blond and Briggs.

Revans, R (1983) *The ABC of Action Learning*, Bromley: Chartwell-Bratt.

Rogers, C R (1969) *Freedom to learn*, Columbus, Ohio: Merrill.

Rogers, C R (1979) *Carl Rogers on Personal Power*, London: Constable.

Rogers, C R (1982) *On Becoming a Person*, London: Constable.

Saljo, R (1982) *Learning and Understanding: A study of differences in constructing meaning from a text*. Gothenburg: Acta Universitatis Gothenburgensis.

Salmon, P (1990) 'Personal stances in learning', in Weil, S and McGill, I J, op cit.

Schon, D A (1983) *The Reflective Practitioner: How professionals think in action*, New York: Basic Books.

Senge, P (1990) *The Fifth Discipline: The art and practice of the learning organization*. London: Century Business.

Southgate, J (1985) *Community Counselling Circles*, London: Institute for Social Inventions.

Stephenson, J and Weil, S (eds) (1992) *Quality in Learning: a Capability Approach in Higher Education*, London: Kogan Page.

Taylor, E (1983) *Orientation to Study*, Surrey, unpublished PhD thesis.

Vince, R and Martin, L (1993) 'Inside action learning: an exploration of the psychology and politics of the action learning model', *Management Education and Development*, **24**, 3, 205–15.

Weil, S W and McGill, I J (1990) *Making Sense of Experiential Learning*, Buckingham: Open University Press/SRHE.

Wilkins, A L (1983) 'Organizational stories as symbols which control the organization', in Pondy, L *et al* (eds) *Organizational Symbolism*, Greenwich, CT: JAI Press.

Zuber-Skerritt, O (1992) *Action Research in Higher Education – Examples and reflections*, London: Kogan Page.

Glossary

Facilitator
The person who guides the processes by which the set operates.
Presenter
The set member who is presenting their issues, problems and opportunities to the set.
Self-facilitated set
A set that operates without a facilitator where the set members assume the skills of the facilitator.
Set
The name given to a group that forms an action learning set. A set usually consists of four to seven people plus a facilitator.
Set adviser
Another name for a facilitator.

Addresses

Ian McGill can be contacted at:
9 Nelson Terrace
London N1 8DG
Tel: 0171 250 3108

Liz Beaty can be contacted at:
Teaching and Learning Unit
University of Brighton
Brighton BN1 9PH
Tel: 01273 642977

International Foundation for Action Learning is a charitable organization and an invaluable resource for the background to action learning and its continued development; useful for building up a network of contacts in the field. The contact is the Secretary, Krystyna Weinstein:
46 Carlton Road
London SW14 7RJ
Tel: 0181 878 7358

Index

accelerated learning 38
acceptance 81-2, 183
accreditation 241
action learning
  and fear of failure 175-6
  and organizational learning 232-3
  as evolving eco-system 262
  as transformational and sustainable way of
    working and learning 261-3
  definition 21, 173-5
  development pathways 108
  focus of 27
  for trainers and developers 14
  future directions 255
  'green' 262
  holistic approach 38-9, 257
  in companies 12
  in higher education 13
  in industrial and service organizations
    (private, public and voluntary 12
  individuals 24-5, 27
  introducing to students 249
  nature of 62, 114, 121, 259
  'one at a time' convention 60-61
  organization sponsoring 83
  potential value 113
  projects 23-4
  specifying actions 165-7
  taking initiative and gaining commitment
    for 95
  types of 94-109
  underpinning 30-32
  use of term 22-3, 255
  values underpinning 33-4
  versus traditional teaching 242-5
  views of participants 28
action planning 54-5, 64-5
  feasibility of 72
  suggestions for 72
action points 54-5, 62, 64
  from previous set meeting 72
  recording 55-6
action research 32
active listening 68, 134-7
activists 177

Advanced Management Development
  Programme (AMDP) 248, 250
adversarial positions 196
advice 61
affective element 257
ambiguity 224-5
anxiety 69, 71, 77, 175, 192
assertive behaviour 149-50, 153-4
assessment systems 172, 175, 246-8
attention 37, 133-4, 158

BA Business Studies 251
body language 68, 134
brainstorming 48, 64
Brighton experience 106-9
  independent sets 253
  self-facilitated sets 102-3, 105

caring 81-2
catastrophe 211
Certificate in Teaching and Learning in Higher
  Education 251-3
challenges 36, 38, 62, 68-9, 192
change
  in organizational life 209-12
  incremental 210
  nature of 210
  problem with 210
client, role of 97
climate of support 158-9
cognitive element 257
collaborative career planning 229
collaborative planning 229
collective reflection 90
commitment 33, 37, 45, 77, 104-5, 134
communication 59
competence 172, 211
confidence 38
confidentiality 37-8, 60, 66-7, 77
constructed knowledge 181, 259, 260
consultants 14
continuing professional development 12-13,
  198-208, 251-3
  and reflective practice 200-201
  developing appropriate links with others 202

research students 250–51
review 73, 85–93
  individual set members' achievements 93
  set norms 91–2
right-hand column 196

Salami Technique 55
sandwich courses 241, 251
scepticism 33
second-order thinking 234
self-assessment 246–7
self-awareness 151
self-development 230
  individual managers 218
self-diagnosis 230
self-disclosure 146–9, 151
  appropriateness of 148–9
  cultural bias against 147
  'I' statements 146
  story versus history 146–8
self-facilitated sets 57–8, 94, 101–3, 105, 243, 260–61
  application 106
  benefits of 103–4
  Brighton experience 106–9
  effectiveness of 104–6
  extending 106–9
self-screening 115
set adviser 57, 109
  role of 97
  see also facilitator
set adviser sets 231
set culture 83–5
set cycle end point of 58
set facilitator see facilitor
set meetings
  appropriate settings 45
  beginning 47–50
  climate 82–5
  comfort and energy levels 46
  creating 106–9
  duration of 105
  end of set review 106
  ending 54–6
  environment 43, 45–6
  facilitating 76–8
  feelings at 40–1
  freedom from interruptions 45–6
  frequency of 105
  future 77
  ground rules 46–8, 66, 76
  'I' statements 77–8
  member participation 41–2
  note-taking 105–6
  overrunning 43
  planning of 44–5

preparation for 72–3
proforma approach 49–50
reviews 56, 73, 86–7
rounds 49
setting the tone 45–6
space and comfort 45
starting 49
time allocation 42–3, 51–2, 105
time impingement on 41–5
time-keeping 43, 105–6
time negotiation 49–50
time schedule 44
timing issue 42, 77
types of process 52–4
use of individual time 52–4
venues for 45
warm up 76–7
see also facilitor; presenters; projects
set members 26–7, 59–73
  achievements review 93
  as expert 65
  as friends 59
  facilitator relationship to 78–81
  function of 60–61
  learning to receive 62–3
  leaving and joining 56–8
  main function of 35
  number of 105
  personality of 41
  potential 104–5
  problems/issues of 28–9
  relation to world outside 77
set norms, review 91–2
set progress 56–8
set reviews, process skills and reflection 89
sets
  as groups 75–6
  basic structure 58
  choices along continuum 99–100
  closure 58
  definition 21
  determining issues brought to 95–6
  effectiveness of 193, 255
  effectiveness review 106
  essence of 60
  evolution 56–8
  facilitated 94
  focus of 38
  functions of 25–6
  impact of 87–8
  improving 90
  independent 13–14, 260–61
  independent action learning 94, 100–101
  independent continuum 100–101
  learning in 245
  life cycle 76